Anatomy of Disaster Relief

To Valerie and our sons
Toby and Timothy

Anatomy of
Disaster Relief
The International Network in Action

Randolph C. Kent

Pinter Publishers London and New York

© Randolph C. Kent, 1987

First published in Great Britain in 1987 by
Pinter Publishers Limited
25 Floral Street, London WC2E 9DS

British Library Cataloguing in Publication Data

Kent, Randolph C.
    Anatomy of disaster relief.
    1. Disaster relief
    I. Title
    363.3'48   HV553

    ISBN 0-86187-294-0

Library of Congress Cataloging-in-Publication Data

Kent, R. C.
    Anatomy of disaster relief.
    Bibliography: p.
    Includes index.
    1. Disaster relief.   2. International relief.
    I. Title.
    HV553.K44   1987   363.3'4526   87-18531
    ISBN 0-86187-294-0

Typeset by Comersgate Art Studios, Oxford
Printed by Biddles of Guildford Ltd

Contents

Foreword

Over the past few years many books have been written about disaster relief. It is a subject of enormous but sometimes morbid interest, particularly in view of the increasing number of disasters during the present decade. The culmination has been the tragedy of Ethiopia. For months Ethiopia dominated our television screens and this was followed by Sudan and now Mozambique. Because of the magnitude of the disasters and the extent of media coverage the emotional response by the public has been almost universal and the generosity astonishing. Hundreds of millions of pounds and dollars have been raised from unofficial sources over the past three years, far greater amounts than ever before.

This compassion has resulted in great public interest and involvement by ordinary people and their wish to know more about the whole story and background to the contentious subject of aid, and this includes relief, welfare and development. Why do these disasters occur? Are they all the result of natural happenings or are some the consequence of man's failures and mistakes? Could they be prevented and what is now being done to avoid future tragedies? What do the governments of the rich world do to help the poor of the so-called Third World? Is the aid that is given the most suitable? What is the role of the United Nations agencies? How do the non-governmental agencies (NGOs) fit in and should the charities involve themselves in such vast undertakings of relief? Ethiopia suffered a famine situation in 1974 when 200,000 people died. How was it possible for an even worse situation to occur just ten years later, when possibly up to one million people died though the exact number can never be known?

To answer some of these questions this book has been written; few are better equipped than Randolph Kent. His experience both in research and work in the field has given him unique insight into the whole subject. The result tells a sad and sometimes depressing story of muddle and inexplicable failure to learn from past mistakes. At the same time, however, there is much optimism. The courage and commitment of those working in the field and the bravery and determination of the victims themselves prove beyond doubt that man's love for his neighbour and his capability of adjustment to the rapidly changing scene of the present day is beyond reproach.

Dr Kent has been able to untangle the multitude of skeins of the whole spectrum of disaster relief and, what is even more important, he remains objective, which must often have been a difficult task. His story, as I have said, is a sad one. Yet the donor governments, UN agencies, including the UN itself, and the NGOs have in so many ways, almost entirely through the dedication and character of many of their officials, done tremendous work in bringing relief and understanding to situations of human suffering; this must always be the aim and objective of disaster relief. Looking back over twenty-five years of close involvement with the whole field of disaster response and operation, the names of many such people come to my mind, many I have been fortunate enough to have as friends.

In covering both good and bad in a constructive way the author lays blame where blame is due but is also generous in his praise when this is demanded. A book that only told of the negative would have been worthless and used as a tool by those who are always ready to condemn overseas aid to those less well off then themselves. The replies to those who condemn and those who work for improvement are all in this book and it is invaluable for those concerned with the situations of the sudden and sadly increasing number of disasters throughout the world.

The chapter dealing with this vulnerability is perhaps the most important; the book deals mostly with natural disasters but many, if not the majority, are man-made. In his book *Africa in Crisis* (Earthscan, 1985) Lloyd Timberlake states very firmly that although the recent disaster situation in the Sahel countries of Africa (including the recent drought in Ethiopia) may have been an act of God, the famines were the direct result of unsound economies, and bad agricultural and environmental strategies. Particular emphasis must be placed on the present scale of environmental destruction. In Uganda, where the recent military and civil disturbances caused an unknown number of deaths, the situation of disaster in the infamous area known as the Liweru Triangle was entirely political in origin. Again, the present famine in Mozambique, whilst certainly worsened by drought, is almost impossible to assist because of the military operations instigated and supported by a neighbouring country. With this vulnerability for disaster always present the likelihood of increasing disaster situations makes continuous study essential. Some form of early warning system must be the answer.

In the end, of course, the basis of disaster is poverty but until this is recognized and accepted within the corridors of power, whether governmental or United Nations, the need to face increasing situations of disaster must continue. It is here that development is involved; this is the subject for another book but it does mean that disaster cannot be divorced from development—there is no fixed dividing line as many would wish us to believe.

No book on disasters can ignore the media and the powers of the press, and the chapter dealing with this is one of the most fascinating. What makes news at the time of emergency? Is it just the pictures of dead bodies? Is it the opportunity to preach political morality? Does media muck-raking influence relief to the extent of causing yet more deaths? On the other hand, it was not until Michael Buerk of the BBC made his film of the actual disaster in Ethiopia in October 1984 and brought the full horror to the sitting rooms of the world that there was a real response to a situation that had been growing unheeded for three years and ignored by those who should have known better. Without such shock tactics public response could not have forced official action and the NGOs would not have been able to raise the record amounts of money that made possible the work they did. Despite the distaste caused by some aspects of press coverage, media involvement cannot and must not be ignored. It is to be hoped that more responsible and understanding attitudes can be encouraged by governmental agencies and NGOs alike. One problem is that without adequate exchange of information at field level, different agencies give different stories to the press and this causes confusion. It is, however, a problem that must be faced and the media representatives and the agencies will both gain if they can work out more methodical ways of approach.

One result of a disaster situation is that the country concerned is faced with an influx of relief workers from a large number of agencies; many are ill-trained, they do not speak the local language and their educational standards are very different from those of the host country. This causes little or no attention to be paid to the culture, traditions or behavioural patterns of the victims they have come to help. The relief personnel may have great commitment and dedication to the work in hand but a failure to understand and accept local conditions and ways of life can negate so much of what they have to offer. Dr Kent's comments on the political influences that dictate the aid policies of donor governments step on many toes but his outspoken comments destroy many sacred cows.

But what is the answer to the many questions raised by Dr Kent and what is the future for disaster aid? The agencies themselves agree that much could and should be done to improve their operations and it is sometimes difficult to understand why there is reluctance to implement necessary changes. Solutions are suggested but without strong backing and perseverance by all concerned to bring about innovations and new approaches and correct mistakes, little can be done. This demands determination by the NGOs, the many research bodies and institutions concerned with disaster relief, the governments that support the UN and the European Community, the governments that themselves give large amounts of bilateral aid and, of course, the UN itself. But the UN can do nothing without the instigation of member governments. The UN and its agencies are but the servants of these governments and they should always remember this. Dr Kent's proposals for the reorganization of the UN Disaster Relief Organization (UNDRO) are very relevant. Above all, however, there is the great need for all agencies, official and otherwise, to improve their collaboration one with another and the exchange of information. Dr Kent recommends cooperation; however necessary this may be, it would be unrealistic to believe that this would be possible. But to co-ordinate planning and operations, to institute standard procedures of function and above all to inform each other of what is proposed and what can be implemented costs nothing, except perhaps a certain sacrifice of independence. It may be that this is what all agencies fear most of all. But all concerned agree that a sharing of information would be ideal though at the same time problems are put forward as to why it might after all not be very easy. There is a strong feeling of *laissez faire* whenever the subject of co-ordination is brought up. Dr Kent demands that more priority must be given to the subject as without it necessary improvements cannot be made. The reasons and his suggestions for improvement make the study of this book essential for all concerned with the anatomy of disaster relief.

Michael Harris
Oxford
June, 1987

Introduction

Anatomy of Disaster Relief seeks to investigate the structure of the international disaster relief process. In attempting to explain the process, I found myself spanning a variety of disciplines. No single discipline seemed in and of itself sufficient to deal with the complexities faced by the international relief network. One has to have an appreciation of the complexity of disasters themselves, and this immediately forces one into realms of development, psychology, sociology, nutrition, anthropology and logistics. Similarly, disaster responses include all these disciplines as well as an appreciation of organizational behaviour, political and international relations. Hence, given that this work is offered to a wide range of readers—academics from a variety of disciplines as well as practitioners—I know all too well that I have risked repeating what for some may be conventional wisdom or, even worse, I may have oversimplified issues in which I have no formal qualifications. Be that as it may, I hope the effort as a whole will lend all who read it some insights into the dynamics of disaster relief.

The investigation begins with disasters. They are complex phenomena, while at the same time open to very common-sense solutions. However, until one sees the complexity of the phenomena, there is the ever-present hazard that one person's commonsense can compound the disaster for another. The complexities of disasters and disaster relief are the themes of Chapter 1.

International disaster relief, depending upon how one defines each of those three words, is either as old as civilization itself or a development essentially of the last century. I have opted for the latter. To understand both the strengths and weaknesses of the present 'international relief network' one ought to see it in perspective. Chapter 2 traces the evolution of the international relief network from the mid-nineteenth century to the present, with predominant emphasis upon developments since 1945.

Why those who provide relief can at best be described as part of a 'network' rather than a 'system' is an important starting point for Chapter 3. If one takes a look at individual types of relief actors—governmental, intergovernmental and non-governmental organizations—one begins to see the justification and, perhaps more importantly, the implications of the semantic tussle between a 'system' and a 'network'.

While each type of actor in the international relief network has its own particular characteristics and idiosyncrasies, all are influenced by a set of factors that determine the dynamics of the relief process as a whole. In Chapters 4 and 5, four such factors are considered: the priority formulation process; perceptual variables and persuasive communications; organizational behaviour; and interorganizational relations. All four are inter-related and all are fundamental to an understanding of the international relief network in action.

Finally, given the inherent characteristics of individual types of relief actors and the dynamics of the relief process as a whole, are there practical recommendations that one might proffer to improve present approaches to the plight of disaster victims? Chapter 6 borrows Stephen Green's title, 'Towards a More Responsive System', as a first step towards an answer. Ten years ago, Green offered many valuable suggestions to improve international responses; but for me these suggestions did not adequately address the very constraints imposed by the factors explored in this book. Because of these constraints, the recommendations arrived at here at best only gnaw at the periphery of very basic problems. My own interpretation of the factors that hamper effective international relief suggests that realistic improvements can only stem from incremental adjustments to the present process.

As I review the gaps between what I had initially set out to do in my research and what I think I might have achieved, there are two issues which became of growing personal importance that I feel I have only partially answered. The first concerns the criticisms so persistently levelled at the administration of international relief. These criticisms seem to belie the commitment and dedication of the vast majority of those 286 officials from governmental, intergovernmental and non-governmental organizations whom I interviewed for this book. Given their often extraordinary efforts that I had witnessed in the field and at headquarters levels for almost five years, I wonder if I have adequately explained the gulf that too often appears between their commitment and the inadequacies of international assistance?

Secondly, I really never fully addressed an issue that bothered me throughout my involvement in disasters and disaster relief, namely, what prompts individuals to assist their fellow human beings? There seems something perverse in the trigger mechanisms. The vulnerabilities that create disasters are so often predictable well before disaster events actually occur; nevertheless human beings generally must be on the verge of death, at the end of their tethers, before their plights elicit assistance. Donors, though probably well intentioned for the most part, seem to need the images of utter helplessness before they can summon up the commitment to care. Why, I wonder, does compassion only seem to begin when human vulnerabilities are exposed in their last desperate form?

That these and many other such gaps might well exist in this book are due to my own failings. However, the opportunities to explore these and other problems were provided in so many instances by others. The Economic and Social Research Council of Great Britain provided me with generous funding to undertake extensive research on three continents from 1982 to 1985. When further funds were required, the ESRC did not hesitate to supplement my original grant (HR 8640). In 1986, the Nuffield Foundation provided me with funds to study emergency assistance to refugees in Africa and the UN Office for Emergency Operations in Africa. Some of the findings derived from the Nuffield-funded project have been incorporated into this work.

Of course a debt of no less equal proportions must be acknowledged to the many individuals who helped me in my research. Given the delicate nature of some aspects of disaster relief, I am extremely grateful for the frankness of so many of those whom I interviewed. There were some instances where I had been asked not to make direct attributions. I have respected such requests, and citations in these instances indicate the country, date and institution as a source, but not individuals.

As I reflect upon the numbers of people who contributed to this work, I realize that there are just too many to give each individual mention. They range from senior UN officials to farmers in the delta of Bangladesh, from government officials to drivers in Ethiopia. It is because of the kindness, cooperation and assistance which so many have shown that I am resisting the temptation to single out particular individuals. And yet I feel compelled to give way to temptation in a few instances.

This work has been dedicated in part to my wife, Valerie, not only for reasons of affection but also because she symbolizes the values that demonstrate true understanding and concern. Besides her constant support, she also played an active role in the preparation of this manuscript by reading and correcting chapter after chapter. I would also like to thank my mother and father for their consistent enthusiasm and moral support. Charles Kent performed an invaluable role in gathering information, arranging appointments and handling all those tedious bits and pieces that only a devoted father would be willing to do.

If it were not for Mokammel Haque and Abdul Qayum the number of doors that were opened to me in Bangladesh and Pakistan would have been far fewer. If it were not for Sylvia Leone and Ann Wells, all too many administrative and secretarial matters would have remained undone. If it were not for Dr Barbara Harrell-Bond and Michael Harris, this effort would have seemed a lonelier intellectual exercise. And, of course, if it were not for Heather Bliss of Frances Pinter Publishers, this work might have been significantly slower in coming together. However, already I see the problem emerging that I originally feared. There is insufficient space in this brief introduction to thank all those to whom I am so indebted. Perhaps they will recognize that, though they are not mentioned, they are gratefully remembered.

Randolph C. Kent
Robertsbridge
June 1987

1 Disaster Dilemmas

The face below the shaven head was young, but the body seemed very old. Her back was stooped, as if bearing a tremendous burden across the parched, ungiving ground. Yet, the young girl from Tigre bore no burden, other than the loss of her third child that week to the ravages of famine. The desolate relief camp in Korem, tucked between the rugged hills of Ethiopia's Wollo province, was the site of eighty-one similar deaths on that October day in 1984.

Several hundred miles north-west of Korem, along the Ethiopian border with Sudan, an Eritrean paramedic tried to stem the flow of blood from a shrapnel victim who had been caught in an air-raid outside a food distribution centre in the village of Orota. The paramedic was a member of the Eritrean People's Liberation Front, which had been fighting the government of Ethiopia for over twelve years. The shrapnel victim was a nomad. He had come to Orota because he had heard that a new shipment of relief grain had recently been delivered. The futility of his eventual death was compounded by the fact that, even had he lived, he would never have been able to carry the few kilograms of grain to his own hungry family eighteen miles away. Relief supplies had run out the previous day.

Only a few miles from Orota, a group of five emaciated figures stood around the wood and straw *tukol* that had been the site of the family's home and farm for almost sixty years. The young skeletal figure of a man was taking leave of his mother. He, his wife and family were going to make the seventy-mile trek to the Sudanese border, where rumour had it that refugees were being fed. They all knew that his 58-year-old mother was too old to risk the journey; they all knew that they would never see her alive again.

A month later, he recalled, he still had the scars from the sharp prickles of the palm tree to which he and his family had clung during the six-hour cyclone. As winds of more than 150 miles an hour pounded the flat coastline of what was then East Pakistan, his wife lost her grip and plunged into the raging waters which were coursing through their village from the Bay of Bengal. His wife drowned, and so did the baby which she had tied to her.

The tall American priest looked down at his large, folded hands. He just didn't know. Perhaps one million, maybe two. It was difficult to calculate the number of victims caught up in the violence of the civil war throughout East Pakistan in 1971. He reflected on the irony of seeing Pakistan relief camps established by the Army outside a village that the soldiers had burnt down only a day before.

The thing she remembered most vividly was the mud. The shabby tents which housed over 100,000 refugees in Salt Lake Camp, just on the fringe of Calcutta, seemed to float in urine and faeces. She was only 7 at the time but she still remembers several of her friends who had fallen victim to cholera. She survived, however, as did the vast majority of the ten million East Pakistanis who fled the civil war to the relative safety of India's border provinces.

Categorizing Disaster

The faces of disaster are many. Indeed, between 1970 and the end of 1985 an estimated 2,730,199 human lives were lost to natural or man-made disasters, and a further 811,287,091 human beings suffered the agonies of starvation, loss of homes and extensive dislocation. To assist the plight of the afflicted, during this fifteen-year period, the international donor community provided over $8,629,276,576 worth of emergency assistance.[1] Yet, even with such demonstrations of goodwill, one nevertheless needs to ask whether such assistance contributed—within the bounds of a realistic criterion—to relieving the suffering of such vast numbers. This question and concern lies at the root of this book.

The answer must begin with an understanding not only of disaster phenomena but also of the nature of disaster relief. Both terms pose difficult conceptual problems, and both have undergone significant transformations in the eyes of analysts in less than two decades.

Conventional Categories

Disasters are about vulnerability—the susceptibility of a potential victim to the life-threatening impact of a 'disaster agent'. A disaster agent, *per se*, is not life-threatening. For example, a drought or an earthquake in uninhabited land will not necessarily cause a disaster. It is only when an agent exposes the vulnerability of people that the disaster agent can lead to a disaster. Traditionally, disaster agents have been divided into two categories: natural and manmade. The former encompasses three broad types. There are those of the 'sudden onset' variety, like earthquakes, cyclones and floods. They are characterized by a rapid build-up, and are assumed to offer relatively little warning before they strike.

A second type are those subsumed under the heading 'creeping disasters'. Insect infestation and drought are two examples. In theory, indicators of such disaster agents are more readily predictable than those of the sudden onset variety. Closely related to this second type is a third, namely, 'chronic disasters'. Chronic disaster agents are those that appear to have no specific time limit. They are 'ongoing', usually accepted as emanating from irreversible structural deterioration. These kind of agents arise from such factors as soil erosion and deforestation.

The second category, that of man-made disasters, is equally as broad as the first. Man-made disaster agents arise out of conflict, conflict within communities and states, conflict across state boundaries. Such conflict might result in people seeking refuge in other countries or in moving to other areas within their own countries. The man-made disaster begins when such victims of violence are no longer able to assume that they will be able to ensure not only their livelihood but their very survival.

The conventional division between natural and man-made disasters, however, does not incorporate the entire spectrum of disaster agents. The former normally assumes that there are factors over which human beings have little control. The latter is underpinned by an assumption of calculated or perceived acts of physical violence. If one holds to these conventional demarcations, then two further categories should be included: technological and ecological disaster agents.

Additional Categories

Technological disaster agents are phenomena increasingly arising from the breakdown of modern industrial and technological systems. In November 1984, a huge industrial suburb in Mexico was destroyed after a single bottle of butane gas started a series of explosions that ended in catastrophe. Only a few days later, in Bhopal, India, 200,000 people were severely affected after gas leaked from the local Union Carbide factory. In March 1979, a series of breakdowns in the cooling system of the Three Mile Island nuclear reactor in Pennsylvania could easily have led to a 'core meltdown, a catastrophic event that could involve major loss of life.' [2] None of these can be classified as either 'natural' or 'man-made', as conventionally defined, but all reflect a dimension of disaster agents which expose a wide range of vulnerabilities. In the words of the French Commissioner for the Study and Prevention of Disasters, 'As our society becomes more sophisticated and mechanised, our vulnerability to catastrophes increases.' [3]

Ecological disaster agents, though very often related to technological agents, might nevertheless be regarded as a separate and fourth category. Their impacts —for example, acid rain—are generally more cumulative than those normally considered as technological agents. They also take longer to expose the vulnerabilities of potential victims than their technological counterparts.

Good examples of ecological disaster agents often emerge, with no little degree of irony, out of well-intentioned development programmes in Third World countries. The creation of the Akosombo dam in Ghana is a case in point. Designed with the intention of developing new fishing industries above the dam in artificial inland seas, the dam has done nothing but create an ecological disaster. The portion of the Volta valley now underwater is clogged with petrified trees, not only making fishing impossible but also depriving local people of access to forest materials needed for fuel and houses.[4]

However, as the developed world is increasingly aware, the hazards caused by disrupting the balance of ecological systems are not threats specific only to the developing world. The ecological disaster agents created by modern farming techniques, by reversing the flow of rivers and by the release of a wide variety of chemical wastes into the atmosphere, seas and rivers are all kept at bay in the developed world by resource margins not enjoyed by the vast majority of the globe. Only these margins of accumulated wealth and resource reserves have prevented such agents from unleashing, to date, major disasters in the developed countries.

Vulnerability: Is There a Difference?

The conventional categories of disaster agents offer useful if not only too obvious distinctions. Clearly, there are differences between an earthquake and a civil war. The analysis required to predict and prepare for the consequences of one differs from that required for the other. However, despite the ostensibly practical reasons for such distinctions, these separate categories hide a very fundamental conceptual problem which lies at the core of all disasters. In the final analysis, while disaster agents may differ, do not disasters have one common source —mankind? Although the agents of disasters may differ, do the causes of disasters differ?

In and of themselves, disaster agents need not necessarily lead to disasters. The critical variable between an agent and a disaster, as mentioned earlier, is the vulnerability of the exposed group. Cuny makes this point well when he compares the results of two serious earthquakes that occurred in the early 1970s. One quake, measuring 6.4 on the Richter scale, took place in 1971 in San Fernando, California, with a population of over seven million. According to Cuny, San Fernando suffered only minor damage and fifty-eight deaths. The second took place two years later in Managua, Nicaragua. Despite a slightly less

severe magnitude of 6.2 the Managua earthquake 'reduced the center of the city
to rubble, killing an estimated six thousand people.'[5]

The difference between the two incidents lies to a very significant extent in the
resources and structures of the two societies. In the words of Wijkman &
Timberlake, 'A mild earthquake in a shanty town of heavy mud-brick houses on
the side of a steep ravine may well prove a disaster in terms of human deaths and
suffering. But is the disaster more the result of earthshocks or of the fact that
people are living in such dangerous houses or on such dangerous ground?'[6]

The point can be put in another way. Out of 825 major disasters that had
occurred from 1970 to the end of 1985 in a total of 119 countries, only
twenty-four occurred in the developed world. These twenty-four took place in
seven developed countries and resulted in the deaths of 6,588 and the disruption
of lives—in terms of relocation, lost possessions and homes—of approximately
2,534,000. In other words, over that fifteen-year period, countries distinguished
by highly developed systems and infrastructures suffered 3 per cent of the
world's major disasters, accounted for less than 1 per cent of all disaster-related
deaths (0.05 per cent) and severe social disruptions (0.0469 per cent) due to
major disasters.[7]

Conceptually, the distinction between types of disaster agents has too often
hidden the real underlying causes of disasters. These causes are found in the
interconnected ways in which mankind deals with its environment and structures
its social systems.

A Disaster Defined

The relationship between disaster agents and vulnerability leads one to a basic
definition of disaster, for a disaster occurs when a disaster agent exposes the
vulnerability of a group or groups in such a way that their lives are directly
threatened or sufficient harm has been done to economic and social structures,
inevitably undermining their ability to survive. At the heart of most definitions
of disasters also lies the assumption that the survival of directly affected groups
will normally require assistance from outside that group—be it from neighbouring villages, central governments or from distant countries.[8]

Most conventional definitions of disaster view the 'event', the 'hazard' or the
'emergency' as an aberrant phenomenon, one which is unique and distinct from
'normal' life. 'In hazards work', writes Hewitt, 'one can see how language is used
to maintain a sense of discontinuity or otherness, which severs these problems
from the rest of man–environment relations and social life . . . What emerges is
that "hazards" are not viewed as integral parts of the spectrum of man–
environment relations or as directly dependent upon those.'[9]

The propensity to separate disaster phenomena from normal life distorts some
of the most fundamental aspects of disasters. By regarding disasters as discrete
occurrences, the observer evades basic causation. One ignores the fact that
disasters are an integral part of environmental abuse and economic and social
exploitation, and instead hides in the assumption that disasters, 'by definition',
are 'separate', 'uncertain' and 'unprecedented'. The truth more often than not is
the opposite. Disasters are the consequence of the way humanity lives its 'normal
life'. Disaster agents do not foster vulnerability, but the ways in which human
beings organize their social and economic lives do.

One six-inch nail that joins a beam to the vertical joist of a house in a Jamaican
village means that the probability that that house will be destroyed in a hurricane

is significantly lessened. However, the ability to afford that nail means that the home-owner's economic and social situation become critical factors. His place in society, his ability to influence the structure of that society, to partake of its resources, all play a part in owning a six-inch nail.

Separating disasters from normal existence is a convenience. By treating them as discontinuous and unpredictable, the solutions which could abate them are given a relatively low priority in governmental and inter-governmental decision-making units. Those governments of resource-poor countries often regard pre-disaster planning and prevention measures as luxuries that they can ill afford, given other seemingly more pressing and predictable priorities. The natural link between development and disaster mitigation is lost in the assumption that the former is a pressing need but the latter is more often than not an uncontrollable 'act of God'.

Similarly, those governments and inter-governmental institutions that have adequate resources also conveniently separate out disaster mitigation from other kinds of activities conducted between themselves and disaster-prone states. As will be discussed in the following chapter, disaster relief cells have grown in a variety of forms as adjuncts to many donor institutions, but rarely does appropriate disaster mitigation find its way into financial and development considerations between developed and disaster-prone nations.

The belief that disasters are discontinuous events, separated from normal life, also provides opportunities for donors to demonstrate humanitarian concern without becoming embroiled in prolonged commitments. Time and again, officials from various relief agencies will draw arbitrary lines between relief and development in order not to become 'mousetrapped in some larger programme'.[10] Such distinctions reflect a certain political reality which in turn suggests why such distinctions are convenient to maintain.

In an age in which the media have made everyone a participant in the plight of severely afflicted peoples, disasters have also been over-simplified. Disaster agents are shown as readily apparent, and so, too, are their consequences. However, the reality is that disasters—in terms of causation, impact and appropriate response—are by no means as obvious as is so often portrayed. Returning to the definition of disasters suggested above, the effect of a disaster agent is very much a matter of perception and understanding of the society of the afflicted. What an outside observer may understand to be a disaster may be differently interpreted by someone in the disaster-affected community.

In 1972 there was a prolonged drought in much of New Guinea, occasioned by severe frost. According to Waddell: 'The immediate reaction of local expatriate observers was to interpret this "extreme geophysical event" as being of disaster proportions.' Following representations to the central government, a massive famine relief operation was mounted. The only group that did not regard the ground frost as a disaster was that for whom the operation was initiated. 'All the available evidence indicates', concluded Waddell, 'that they knew quite well how to deal with a familiar hazard.'[11]

However, in Ethiopia, twelve years later, the perceptual dynamics were reversed. Despite clear indications from local farmers as well as the Ethiopian government that continued crop failures would lead to a major famine, outside observers regarded the same famine indicators as too ambiguous to launch a major relief effort.[12]

Even when disaster agents may be relatively apparent, their impacts—disasters—very often are not. Perceptions, knowledge about the social, economic and survival structures of the afflicted are all crucial to a clear understanding of 'what is a disaster' in any particular situation. They, in turn, are fundamental in what we shall later term the 'relief process'.

Complex Disasters

Although the relationship between man and his environment has always been a fundamental—though only recently recognized—factor in disaster phenomena, what is becoming more evident is the intensity of that complex relationship in particularly vulnerable societies. With increasing frequency, natural disasters lead on to man-made disasters or man-made disasters trigger natural disasters. And clearly the cycle of despair intensifies and vulnerabilities become more enduring.

A 'complex disaster' is one where one disaster agent exposes vulnerabilities which open the way for the impact of other disaster agents. Based on the kind of disasters that have affected many parts of the resource-poor world of the 1970s and 1980s, let us construct a brief example of the evolution of a 'complex disaster'.

Imagine a country which has recently become independent, a country comprising an amalgam of geographically-based ethnic groupings. It is essentially an agrarian society, with a relatively limited amount of export earnings based upon two cash crops. The inability of previous governments to feed the burgeoning population in the capital and the discontent amongst various ethnic groups who had felt excluded from political and economic participation have led to a military coup.

The new military government, whose senior officers mainly represent members of a small but 'traditionally military' minority, must face, as did their predecessors, what one analyst has called 'the gap between promise and reality'.[13] A weak administrative structure and limited revenue increase that gap. Nevertheless, there is no doubt in the leadership's minds that the urban population of the country must be given priority attention. This priority is reflected in the introduction of subsidized food to urban areas. However, despite this priority, land reform for the present population represents a close second.

Although the coup has been greeted with mixed reactions by the outside world, few are willing to condemn it outright. In part this muted response is due to the fact that the coup appears to offer a modicum of stability to the region, and in part because there are still repayments due on loans for industrial development projects that had been undertaken over the past ten years. These loans and interest payments, it is hoped, will be covered by income generated from export crops.

To maintain subsidized food prices, the government decides that the only alternative is to pay below-market prices for farmers' produce. The farmers, faced with declining incomes, find that the purchase of seed and fuel has become very much more expensive. They cut back on production, and, although land reform has provided them with small plots of their own, the need for fuel forces them to cut down the few trees they have available.

Reduced production obviously limits the amount of food available not only for rural but for urban populations also. It also means that agriculture offers fewer and fewer opportunities, and many farmers and their families abandon their plots and move to the capital city. There, with no employment prospects and little, if any, money, they join the growing numbers of slum-dwellers inhabiting the steep slopes of the hills which surround the capital.

The increasingly deforested lands of those farmers who remain on the land are now more and more subject to erosion. Much of the rainwater, instead of sinking into the soil, runs off the land and escapes into rivulets winding down barren, rocky hills. There are insufficient resources to dig new wells and water catchment projects have been delayed because of other national priorities.

The fourth anniversary of the coup has ominously coincided with the second year of rain failure. Very few crops have grown, and the rural population hoards a considerable portion of its meagre harvest. The government all the while is obsessed with the need to maintain sufficient and subsidized food for the capital. However, the reality is that there is increasingly less food to subsidize. Black market prices quadruple within three months, leaving the vast majority of the urban poor with little access to food. Discontent within the city increases and, at the same time, famine in the countryside is signalled by large groups of peasants journeying to the capital in search of assistance.

With few resources to stem rising discontent, the government resorts to force in order to quell the growing number of disturbances. Ethnic solidarity creates divisions within the ranks of the army and the police force, and soon these divisions are reflected in a general breakdown of authority not only in the city but in rural areas as well. In the wake of mounting disorder, security can no longer be assured. Various factions of the army turn against those who do not belong to their own ethnic communities. Villages are looted and burnt, and many of the inhabitants are killed. The only recourse for those who remain is to flee to the security of neighbouring states. As refugees pour across the border, the problem of famine is further compounded, for many of those who could have prepared the next season's growth are now refugees or else dislocated within their own country.

This hypothetical case reflects three aspects of a complex disaster. The first is the direct involvement of man in the creation of both aspects of the series of disasters which struck this hypothetical country. On a macro level, the dependence upon cash crops and the very international economic system which constrained allocation of resources within the country were directly involved in exposing vulnerabilities within the society. The priorities that were established by the military government—the way in which food was subsidized, the attention to one section of society only, i.e. urban populations, the structure of the military government—all were direct influences in the creation of the disaster. On a more micro level, if resources could have been more adequately directed towards wells, water catchment systems and indeed 'dry farming' methods, the disaster could clearly have been mitigated. For that matter, had cash-crop farming been reduced and had the government been able to build up local food reserves, once again the impact of rain failures might easily have been avoided.

Secondly, the plight of that country reflects the fragility of so many social structures around the world. The decisions taken by the military government were perhaps not necessarily good, but, given the pressures it faced on assuming office—both national and international—they were at least understandable.

The developed world can still protect itself from the consequence of inconsistent decisions by the continued margin of its resources. Whether you call them the Common Agricultural Policy, regional employment premiums, unemployment benefits, soil banks or Federal insurance guarantees, governments' miscalculations or disaster agents can be tolerated to a degree by resource margins.

However, in resource-poor countries, this too often cannot be the case. Vulnerabilities are poised very near the brink of disaster. It takes relatively little to expose them.

Finally, this hypothetical case emphasizes the inter-relationship, if not the perverse logic, of a complex disaster. A natural disaster agent exposes the weaknesses of a particular section of a society, and ultimately the very capability of that society to exist comes into question. Given the government's loss of legitimacy as seen by many within the society, the return to some form of normality becomes increasingly more difficult. The society itself becomes more and more prone to the ravages of conventionally defined 'natural' and 'man-made' disaster agents.

While this hypothetical country may seem geographically specific or its particular disaster limited in terms of general relevance, it is in fact not. Floods in Bangladesh, earthquakes in Mexico or Guatemala, 'El Nino' in Bolivia and Peru, refugees from Kampuchea in Thailand all reflect the dynamics of the complex disaster. Where resource margins are slim and where priorities cannot accommodate contending interests, the most vulnerable are the first to suffer the impact of a disaster agent. As a disaster exposes the vulnerabilities of an ever-widening band of potential victims, the very structure of society finds itself threatened. New disaster agents, for example civil unrest, become embroiled in the initial one, and the cycle of despair becomes increasingly irreversible. In the final analysis, however, complex disasters merely demonstrate that disasters themselves are fundamentally about the nature of man's interactions with his environment, a point sustained by the trend towards 'mega-disasters'.

Mega-disasters

Increased complexity goes a long way to explaining why the very size of disasters—measured in terms of numbers of those affected—is also on the increase. The sheer scale of human suffering occasioned by any single major disaster reveals its 'mega' proportions. Stephen Green wrote several years ago that 'though disaster-related natural phenomena do not appear to be increasing in frequency, there is evidence that the human cost of disasters worldwide is steadily mounting.'[14] Green's prediction is correct on one level, for what one has been witnessing throughout the 1970s and 1980s is the accumulative and geometric impact of disaster agents bearing down on societies that are increasingly resource-poor and increasingly unable to cope with intensifying social and political pressures.

Regrettably, however, Green's assumption that disaster-related natural phenomena 'do not appear to be increasing' is wrong in one very important respect, namely, that there has been a significant increase in such phenomena. The increase, however, is not necessarily due to any fundamental change in global climatic conditions. It is due to the fact that man's interactions with his environment have created the conditions which not only leave him more exposed to disaster agents but which also engender disaster agents themselves. Disasters arising out of floods is but one example. According to an UNDRO analysis of 'hydrological aspects of disasters', on many occasions other factors operate either to exacerbate an already occurring flood problem or to create a flood problem entirely of their own manufacture.

'These factors are associated most often with the promotion of a hydraulic surcharge in water levels. They include the presence of natural or man-made obstructions in the flood's way such as ice jams, bridge piers, floating debris, weirs, etc. . . . Also included are the generally unforeseen river surge events caused by sudden dam failure, land slip or mud flow.'[15]

Thus, we are left with the possibility that both the scale of any single disaster and the overall number of disasters are increasing. Chambers, in discussing one type of disaster—that arising out of 'mass distressed migration'—forecasts a growing mega-phenomenon: 'There are indications that the scale and frequency of MDMs will increase. Those reasons are a continuing combination of economic crisis, including low and unstable food production, ecological deterioration, population and other pressures on resources and political instability.'[16]

If one analyses Figures 1.1 and 1.2 and Table 1.1, the evidence would suggest that not only has there been a steady increase in the numbers of afflicted since the 1960s (Figure 1.1), but also that disaster agents—both natural and man-made—have increased as well (Figure 1.2). While the Soviet Union's famine of 1932–4 (official deaths 1.5 million, estimated deaths 5 to 6 million), or the 1939 north China flood (estimated 800,000 drowned) stand out as examples of how devastating disasters can be, the world has seen over the past two decades an increasing number of disasters which engulf large sections of vulnerable societies (Table 1.1).

Table 1.1 *Disasters affecting more than 100,000/500,000 people per event*

Year	No. of disaster events	Affecting 100,000 people/event	% of total events	Affecting 500,000 people/event	% of total events
1965	46	7	15	1	2
1966	46	9	20	0	0
1967	57	20	35	2	4
1968	48	14	29	2	4
1969	36	11	31	4	11
1970	50	11	22	3	6
1971	51	10	20	5	10
1972	29	9	31	6	12
1973	30	10	33	7	23
1974	20	6	30	4	20
1975	25	10	40	8	32
1976	24	11	46	7	29
1977	25	12	48	6	24
1978	33	14	42	6	24
1979	41	18	44	7	17
1980	33	11	33	5	15
1981	22	10	45	2	6
1982	35	9	26	3	9
1983	43	21	49	4	9
1984	41	17	41	13	32
1985	38	18	47	13	34

Source: based on statistics compiled by the US Office of Foreign Disaster Assistance

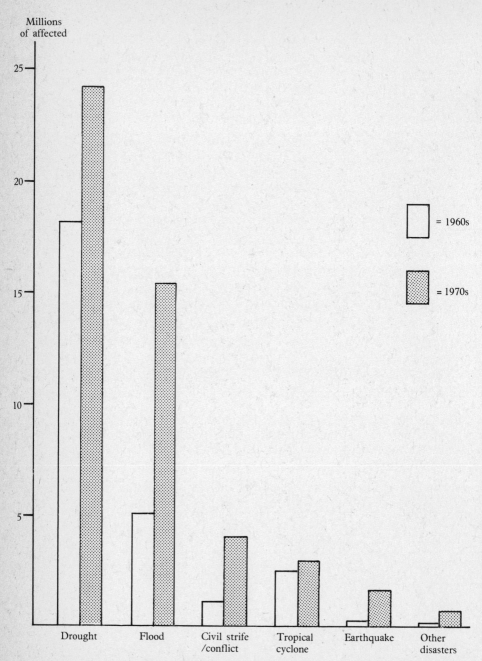

Figure 1.1 Average number of people affected per year by disasters
Source: This table comes from the Swedish Red Cross, *Prevention Better than Cure*, Stockholm, 1984, p.39.

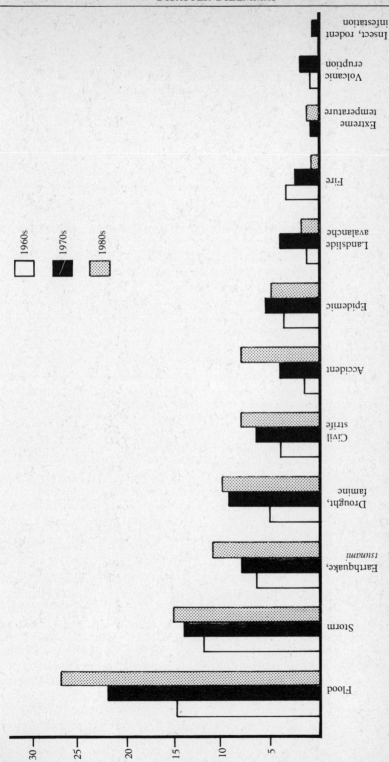

Figure 1.2 Average recorded annual disaster events in the world
Source: This table comes from the Swedish Red Cross, *Prevention Better than Cure*, Stockholm, 1984, p.35.

* *Tsunami* are large sea waves caused by an earthquake abruptly moving the ocean floor. By the time a *tsunami* reaches a shore line, it can be at least 30 metres high and be moving at at least 50 m.p.h.

One cannot ignore the fact that modern methods of assessment and data-gathering have improved over the past three decades. Even with this qualification, the figures above give some credence to the prospect that the world may be on the threshold of an era in which the sheer volume of intensive human suffering arising from disasters could well be one of its hallmarks.

Disaster Relief

Disaster relief poses dilemmas for relief workers and the afflicted which are every bit as complex as disasters themselves. In its most basic sense, disaster relief is divided into three stages. The first, the emergency phase, entails measures to ensure the immediate survival of victims. During this phase, relief is principally concerned with temporary shelters, medical treatment, food and clothing. The underlying assumption is that, without this kind of assistance, the conditions of the victims will deteriorate to such an extent that their very lives will be in immediate jeopardy.

The second phase is normally regarded as the rehabilitation phase. Having dealt with the immediate threat to life, relief becomes directed towards restoring a degree of 'normality' to the afflicted community. This phase involves such assistance as materials to rebuild housing, provision of seeds and equipment to produce crops, to dig wells, etc. In other words, rehabilitation is concerned with those basic steps required to restore the community to a point where it can stand on its own feet again.

Post-rehabilitation, or the third phase of disaster relief, overlaps with general approaches to development. In theory, post-rehabilitation is undertaken to reduce the vulnerabilities which a disaster agent may have exposed. Its scope is potentially limitless. It may involve the creation of new and more resilient forms of housing; it might lead to the creation of barriers against flood-prone rivers; it might even involve establishing local community organizations to seek ways to promote pre-disaster planning.[17]

Ostensibly, these three phases of disaster relief are quite straightforward and, as described, provide a logical sequence for addressing the problems presented by a disaster. Yet, lurking behind each of these seemingly clear objectives lie three areas of ambiguity: what kind of relief is appropriate? who is to decide? and towards what end?

Appropriate Relief

Relief assistance is frequently provided in conditions redolent with ambiguity, misconceived assumptions and sheer operational difficulties. In each phase of a relief operation, uncertainties reign. In the emergency phase, both the numbers of afflicted and the appropriate responses are rarely easy to determine. When to turn off assistance once one has arrived at the rehabilitation phase is, again, often a difficult calculation to make. Finally, the consequences of intervention in the post-rehabilitation phase may well have serious and by no means always positive consequences for the long-term economic and social structures of the afflicted community. Here, too, appropriate long-term calculations are not easy to make.

On 12 May 1985, one day after a fire destroyed the wooden stands at Bradford Stadium in England, police were still unable to say categorically how many football fans remained unaccounted for. Yet, the press and the concerned public of many donor countries nevertheless appear incredulous that governments in less developed countries—in Colombia or Mexico after an earthquake or in Ethiopia during a famine—are unable to be precise about the numbers of afflicted following a major disaster.[18] Nor, for that matter, can specialized organizations such as the United Nations High Commission for Refugees always be sure of the numbers of dislocated people over whom they have nominal responsibility.[19]

Determining the number of people who might require assistance after a disaster is fraught with difficulty. Often, in developing countries, there are few accurate population censuses. Populations may migrate seasonally from one area to another. Families may not be sure where a head of household or children might be after a disaster impact has subsided. Some disasters may occur in areas that are virtually inaccessible, and that, too, makes accurate head-counts an added complication.

Even the most basic information required for a relief operation, namely, how many are in need, escapes easy analysis. Furthermore, what those needs might be is equally difficult to determine. In many disaster relief operations, as one experienced Oxfam official observed, there is normally a dispute between those agencies that feel that medical treatment should have priority and those agencies that see food as a priority.[20] Obviously, both may often be needed, but the point is that, in organizing a large-scale relief effort, it is the matter of priority which becomes the operative issue.

In countries with few trained relief workers, with limited air- and sea-port facilities and with poor transport capabilities, the issue of priority matters very much. However, the problem is that needs do not lend themselves to easy analysis. Where food might be required, should attention be given to the normally most vulnerable groups, i.e. children, by providing high-protein supplements, or should the emphasis be placed on mass feeding of the adult population? The former might save the children, but without the latter, those children may soon be orphans.

These kinds of dilemmas carry on into the rehabilitation phase of relief. For example, when is it appropriate to turn off the emergency aid tap? If relief assistance, such as food aid, is prolonged beyond the time when it is most urgently required, it can undermine basic steps towards rehabilitation. Cuny emphasizes this inherent danger when he discusses the plight of 'marginal farmers' who depend upon one single crop in Guatemala. Food aid that continues to be given for too long can affect the whole supply chain. Because of free food, farmers' crops lose value; farmers receive less for their produce, and, rather than being rehabilitated, they either 'sell out and leave the land or the next year they are forced to plant less than in the previous year due to lack of capital to purchase seeds and fertiliser.'[21]

While donors are increasingly agreed that emergency food aid should be provided speedily but for a relatively short period of time, it is not necessarily easy to determine when that time has arrived. One section of the afflicted community may have recovered sufficiently well to re-enter the normal food-purchasing cycle, but another section may not. Uncertainty, once again, may pervade the relief process. So, too, is it difficult to anticipate the consequences of assistance arising in the post-rehabilitation phase of disaster relief operations. In more than one country, post-rehabilitation efforts have created temporary boom economies fuelled by the financial and resource inputs of relief workers. Whole service and construction industries have blossomed in the wake of short-term post-rehabilitation projects—for example housing—only to collapse once the projects are completed and relief officials move away.[22] It can be difficult to foresee, particularly in light of the enthusiasm generated so often by such projects, the dangers that may lie ahead.

Not only are disaster relief operations complicated by the ambiguity generated by disaster events, but they are also fuelled by a variety of misconceptions. Perhaps one of the more obvious is that which assumes, 'If you're hungry, you'll eat anything'. Time and time again, disaster relief prompts responses that are based on the assumption that the surplus of one society and culture will be adequate to satisfy the needs of disaster-afflicted peoples from other societies and cultures. Tinned pork is sent to Muslim countries, stilletto-heeled shoes find their way to mud-caked villages in south Asia, the Ethiopian child is provided with a detested product called Horlicks and his parent is given a tasteless substance called rice.

Relief, to be effective, must be sensitive to local conditions and values. Children will often refuse to eat, no matter how hungry, rather than eat something unpalatable. Similarly, adults will not transgress fundamental norms merely in order to eat.[23] However, these very obvious misconceptions are increasingly understood. Nevertheless, more 'sophisticated' misconceptions still infuse the relief efforts of even the professionals. Medical intervention in the aftermath of disasters is but one area.

Despite an increased understanding of relief requirements in the first phase of assistance, there continues to be a tendency to assume that certain kinds of disasters—for example arising out of floods, earthquakes—will necessitate mass inoculation programmes. This instinctive response stems from a very fundamental dilemma. Often areas that are severely affected by such disasters, for example Bangladesh and India, always have sporadic outbreaks of diseases such as cholera. In the rural regions of Bangladesh, for example, cholera 'usually occurs in small sporadic village outbreaks, two-thirds of which subside spontaneously before five cases are noted.'[24] Floods or cyclone disasters do not necessarily intensify such outbreaks, but they do make them more apparent to relief workers. Relief workers are faced with the difficulty of determining whether such threats do or do not deserve to be considered as part of a relief priority. Only too often, time, energy and funds are spent on mass inoculation programmes, when, as John Seaman, medical officer for Save the Children Fund (UK) argues:

With the overwhelming majority of diseases which may pose a hazard after disaster, mass vaccination, particularly when this is hastily and inadequately organised, plays no part in control (the subject of a large literature). The vast sums and efforts which have been and continue to be lavished on typhoid and cholera vaccination programmes have brought little but temporary increase in the survivors' confidence in authority; there is no reason to suppose that they have prevented much disease. Control rests with the simple, cheap and effective method of surveillance, case findings and treatments.[25]

Similarly, misconceptions about the needs of victims in the rehabilitation phase of relief can also skew priorities and involve needless time and funds. Satish Jacob, a former relief official for the Indian agency, CASA, regarded the misconceived rehabilitation efforts made in the wake of the 1978 cyclone in Andra Pradesh as typical:

Those affected by disasters are extremely poor people with few assets. Nature has taught them how to be resilient; they bounce back. It is stupid for outside people to undertake the kind of aid they do. These people (disaster victims) do not need emergency relief except for perhaps the first 48 hours. By the third day, these people manage, somehow, some things on their own. Maybe just two banana leaves over their heads, but nevertheless it is a shelter. What is desperately required is something between immediate relief and intermediate relief, something to get back their tools, their clothes. Suddenly we got a telephone call: 'Please choose sites for 6000 houses in areas where you are working.' Initially we objected, but then, OK, we compromised, 6000 huts. Still everything went wrong. We were buying hundreds of pounds of nails; prices in the area went shooting up and there was no participation from the affected community. If there was anyone in the village who complained, we said, 'Stuff it!' . . . The biggest hindrance to the man who has been hit is that he never got the kind of aid he wanted; he was never consulted.[26]

So, too, during the post-rehabilitation phase, are good intentions too often underpinned by misconceptions. During attempts to restore the shattered Italian communities destroyed by earthquakes in November 1980, the United States Congress appropriated $50 million for rehabilitation projects. The criterion for the assistance was that the funds had to be expended upon something 'visible and permanent', and it was decided to build twelve school houses. No matter how grand the gesture, the fact was that a significant proportion of the affected population had moved elsewhere and many of the schools were redundant.[27]

While in many instances it is easy to criticize the failings of relief intervention, it is important to remember that disasters are not only often shrouded in uncertainty but they also very often pose extraordinary operational difficulties. In the Sudan in early 1985, plans to transport food to starving refugees and local people in Darfur went awry when roads were washed away by rain. As one United States Agency for International Development (USAID) official commented on the African emergency in 1985, 'In these countries, indeed in most of sub-Saharan Africa, the transport infrastructure is under stress at the best of times. In a food crisis like this one, it becomes a nightmare.'[28] Land-locked nations such as Chad, the steep mountain areas of northern Ethiopia, the marshy lowlands of southern Bangladesh all create extraordinary barriers to mobilizing relief effectively.

Who is to Decide? The relief culture

In outlining the dilemmas posed by disaster relief, one must ultimately confront one of the single most fundamental sources of those dilemmas, the relief culture: the attitudes and motives of the components of the international network which seek to assist.

The Economist's 'Development Report', in March 1986, described a January meeting in Swaziland between European Parliamentarians and delegates from African, Caribbean and Pacific states that receive aid under the Lomé Convention. The 'jamboree' was lavish, but not totally without a degree of culture strain.

Katarina Focke, the German socialist chairwoman of the European Parliament's Development Committee, could not conceal her irritation at the heat, the discomfort and being required to watch a performance by refugee children from Mozambique at a refugee camp in the dusty lowveld. 'This is too tedious. We have a schedule to keep to. And they can't even sing.' In this group, it seemed that many had packed their prejudices with their tropical gear and were determined not to have them challenged—not by real discussion in the conference hall, not by 'impertinent' questions from the press, not even by the real Swaziland beyond the luxury complex.[29]

This incident is not necessarily typical of the interactions between the international relief community and governments and peoples of disaster-afflicted states. However, in an exaggerated form, it does emphasize what O'Neill calls the 'monsters of concern'. 'They can be called monsters because their doing good, their wanting to save, is done in the interests of experiencing themselves as above or outside the lives of those for whom they care.'[30]

Harrell-Bond believes, based on extensive observations of emergency assistance to refugees, that a basic failing in the relief process 'lies with the ideology of compassion, the unconscious paternalism, superiority and monopoly of moral virtue which is built into it.'[31] O'Neill's and Harrell-Bond's condemnations are harsh, but unfortunately they are not that far off the mark when assessing the relief culture. One problem for those involved in emergency relief is that many of their relief solutions are based on innovative developments which they, the relief workers, see as appropriate. Oxfam, for example, had been convinced in the early 1970s that polystyrene sheeting would provide excellent material for emergency housing. The advantages of polystyrene were its low cost, resilience, and transportability. The technological fix, however, came to a sticky end when those who were to inhabit them tried to assemble them. As Oxfam's Jim Howard and Robert Mister were later to explain, the 1975 Turkish earthquake relief operation demonstrated that one of the problems was that these shelters involved 'high technology using sophisticated equipment requiring trained men, and novel materials which were unfamiliar to the recipients.'[32]

Hewitt sees what he calls the 'natural science-technological fix' approach to hazards as 'essentially a sociocultural construct reflecting a distinct, institution-centered and ethnocentric view of men and nature.'[33] This sort of fix too often becomes manifestly evident in emergency assistance to refugees. Relief camps are organized in straight rows of tents or huts, with centralized cooking and lavatory facilities. 'Democracy' is imposed by insisting on the election of camp representatives—all seemingly quite sensible in terms of logistics and communications. Neither, however, necessarily reflects the social structures of the refugees themselves. Rather, they reflect the most effective means of camp design and distribution from the perspective of outside relief workers.

If one takes most disaster relief situations, and observes how often and in what ways outside relief workers actually talk to the afflicted, rarely does the relief official actually discuss the needs of the afflicted with the afflicted themselves. Normally, the assumption of needs is sustained by the 'monologue' of the outsider. Those stricken by disasters are assumed to be hapless and helpless. Their knowledge of local conditions, their traditional coping mechanisms and their own sensitivity to what is needed are ignored as they are condemned to the encapsulated realm of 'the victim'.

The fact that this monologue continues during most disaster relief operations is not solely the fault of the outsider. Cultural norms may dictate that assistance should be received politely and with gratitude. To question the relevance of assistance may well conflict with standards of courtesy. Furthermore, the sophisticated equipment—ranging from helicopters to two-way radios, the presumed expertise underscored by hypodermic needles and clipboards—can all be extremely intimidating to people not used to such paraphernalia. When the international community first began to intervene in the East Pakistan cyclone relief operation in 1971, many of the villagers in the delta had never seen an airplane before. Some were reported to wonder whether or not the relief plane was actually of this world![34]

The relief culture, based so fundamentally on scientific positivism, also tends to over-extend its use of comparability in assuming that relief is required.

Famine conditions in one country are assumed to be evidence that similar conditions will lead to famine in another. Hence, as Waddell's investigations into the 1972 frost 'disaster' in New Guinea suggest, American and Australian officials assumed that the conditions that had led to famine in Biafra were applicable to the conditions confronting 150,000 people in New Guinea's highlands. No one had bothered to consider the coping mechanisms of the local population. Crop levels and migration patterns relevant to Biafra were assumed to be relevant in New Guinea. Humanitarian instincts won the day in relieving 'a famine that never was'.[35]

To assume from the above that disaster relief is unnecessary or consistently inappropriate is not, however, the message. During the first stage of an emergency, food, clothing, medicines, blankets, etc. are very often urgently needed. Stages two and three also very often require outside funding and technical expertise. Yet the relief culture too often fails to take into consideration the consequence of its assistance. It too often imposes its normally well-intentioned assistance with little regard for the psychological, social and economic contexts of the afflicted. It reflects compassion without consideration, ignoring the fact that the afflicted are human beings, not just victims.

The point is suggested in a more personal anecdote: at a meeting in Oxford in 1984, a panel of four 'experts' was assembled to discuss the mounting refugee crisis in Ethiopia and the Sudan. Two were from the United States, one from Great Britain and the fourth was an Eritrean refugee. The first three led the discussion, made pleas for the case of long-term solutions, and delved into the complexities of being a refugee. The fourth member of the panel was only belatedly asked to make comments. Neither the panel members nor the audience really ever asked the Eritrean what it was like to be a refugee, what his interpretation of the situation was. Perhaps his contribution was not really needed. The three 'experts' knew what was needed; they had all done their research; they could mobilize the compassion of the audience. What could the fourth member of the panel contribute? . . .

Towards What End?

(a) *Righteous indignation and the relief culture.* Most discussions about the problems of disaster relief inevitably include the sagas of corruption. These sagas fuel the righteous indignation of many donors, and perpetuate the condescension that permeates many aspects of relief work. Donors are the purveyors of acceptable values; governments of the afflicted and even the afflicted themselves are frequently viewed as betrayers of fundamental articles of faith.

Corruption, however, poses a definitional problem. Corruption for one society may not be the same for another. Corruption is also a perceptual matter. Its significance in a relief operation may often be exaggerated far beyond its practical effect. Nevertheless, corruption is indeed real. It does exist—amongst donors as well as recipients. In early 1952 floods destroyed an extensive area and homes and left local inhabitants in need not only of shelter but of food and clothing also. The government of the country, local officials and private voluntary organizations responded quickly and generously. However, as the relief operation swung into action, relief officials began to note an unanticipated increase in the number of people seeking help. To their dismay, they discovered that people from areas untouched by the flooding were joining the distribution

queues to take advantage of free food and clothing. The afflicted area was the east
coast of England.[36]

A certain moral superiority often imbues dealings engaged in by the developed
world with those in the developing world. Yet, corruption is by no means the sole
prerogative of either. If corruption can be defined as intentionally deviating from
a norm of acceptable behaviour, then one is confronted with the problem of
determining what is indeed acceptable behaviour in a disaster relief operation.

The picture of a relief operation which most organizations provide is one of
orderly queues of people lining up for their hand-outs. The assumption
underlying such pictures is that the recipients are grateful for the help, and
quietly return to their tents to await the next distribution. If this were the reality,
the lives of the relief workers in the field would be considerably easier; but the
image belies reality. Very often relief supplies arrive unpredictably, and by the
time an assumed priority delivery has arrived, that priority item is no longer
needed. Furthermore, what is delivered as relief may be totally unsuitable for the
disaster victims.

One official from the joint United States Somali Emergency Logistics Unit
organized by CARE complained that 'donors were still sending supplies of dried
skimmed milk and beans. But refugees don't like DSM or beans. Why waste
your money?'[37] Often in relief camps that are near towns, recipients take items
that they do not need, and trade them for more familiar foods or other items.
This is in fact a frequent occurrence. A woollen blanket that a Bengali might
drape over his head becomes too sodden to use in the heavy rains. He takes the
blanket and trades it for more appropriate cloth in the local market. The trader,
in turn, sells the blanket in Calcutta. Is that corruption? It is corruption only to
the extent that the donor assumed the blanket was to be used in the manner that
the donor felt appropriate. To the recipient, the blanket, though inappropriate,
could at least be used to acquire what he needed. This one example is indicative
of a more general pattern. Tins of relief food, blankets and clothing found in
commercial market-places are by no means unusual. It may prove an embarrassment for relief officials anxious to prove that they have accurately distributed
and accounted for all goods. On the other hand, the supposed corruption that led
to those goods finding their way to the markets is only too often the only way in
which recipients can get what they feel they need. One might even argue that
donors, who are unwilling or unable to assess and provide what victims require,
are practising a form of corruption. For inappropriate and poorly-timed assistance is controlled not by the disaster victim but by those who have the resources
to help. On one level, corruption is often a question of who is defining the term.

The impact of corruption is also often exaggerated. In part this is due to the
fact that the media are too anxious to apply what has been called 'Kamm's first
law of journalism'. Kamm's law, according to Nelson, is that 'news is the
difference between what the government says is happening and what is in fact
happening'. Perhaps the principle is useful in the hot-house atmosphere of
post-Watergate Washington, but it can be crippling when applied to relief
operations in disaster-prone countries: 'Government officials are startled to find
that reporters treat sceptically—or ignore—the facts [that] are presented to
them, even true facts, presented in good faith. Reporters will question death
tolls, and accuse officials of either exaggerating them or underestimating them.'[38]
Kamm's law very often focuses the attention of the media on what has gone
wrong, and an easy target is invariably actual or perceived corruption. The point
here, however, is not to condemn the press, but rather to suggest that this kind of

attitude tends to distort the effect of real or generally defined corruption. It is not the press alone that perpetuates the moral superiority of donors in the face of recipients' 'corruption'. Corruption is assumed to be an inherent failing of the relief process.

One official from the World Food Programme with fourteen years' field and headquarters experience emphasized that corruption was:

a subject that should not be overlooked. Where there's smoke, there's fire, and in my experience with the WFP, there is always something that is skimmed off the top. However, the amount that is taken would make a significant difference to the life of an individual who has taken it. Assuming that butter oil sells for $2600 per ton, ten tons from a large shipment will make little difference to the overall supply, but it adds $26,000 to somebody's Swiss bank account.[39]

While no one can condone corruption, its impact on most relief operations is generally accepted to be of limited consequence.[40] The real issue is the impact of corruption not upon relief operations but upon the perceptions of the relief culture.

One can argue that corruption may be a definitional and perceptual matter, but there can be no doubt that it does exist in most relief efforts. The reason that those people of good-will are often so disappointed that their own humanitarian values do not permeate throughout the entire relief process is due in no small part to the way that disaster victims are viewed. Shawcross quotes one relief official's assessment of the 1979 Kampuchean relief operation as being 'like sex on a tiger skin'. 'It had everything—temples, starving brown babies and an Asian Hitler figure.'[41] The operation had everything, in the sense that right and wrong, innocence and evil could be portrayed in stark black and white. Relief is provided to helpless victims. Relief would not in fact be required if the institutions of the victims' governments were less inefficient, less callous and less corrupt.

The definition attempts to isolate victims from their overall social context. In most instances, the majority of victims are not helpless in the sense that they lack judgement about what is best for themselves. Nor do they undergo instant post-disaster metamorphoses that change their attitudes about what they want or need as individuals. The theme may appear cliché-ridden and obvious, but it is too often forgotten in images of the disaster relief process: people are people.

In this same sense, disaster relief operations create many opportunities for those people outside the disaster-afflicted area. For trucking firms in the Sudan in the 1985 famine relief operations, international intervention meant that there was a new source of custom that could be tapped. For food merchants in Ethiopia in mid-1984, the prospect of higher prices as the famine intensified led them to hoard grain. The Sudanese trucker and the Ethiopian grain merchant, too, are forms of corruption, at least for those who see disasters as diversions from a norm. What such people fail, however, to take into account is the parallel form of corruption that takes place on the donor side. Of course, corruption takes place on the donor's side, in forms equally as blatant as on the recipient's side. The arrest of a WFP official in 1983 who was profiteering in relief grain in Thailand is but one example.[42]

In the same way that a relief operation in an afflicted area cannot be divorced from the societal context in which the disaster has taken place, nor too can the provision of relief be divorced from the societal context of donors. A Norwegian official admitted that he often had to contend with 'a certain pressure from the fish industry and the pre-fabricated housing sector in times of (foreign) disasters.

There are enormous surpluses of dried fish and salted fish, and we are under certain pressure to use them.'[43] Similarly, a British official in the United Kingdom Disaster Unit commented that 'when a disaster strikes, there are frequent phone calls from businessmen trying to make a fast buck.'[44] Such inclinations are not infrequently supported by discreet pressures from members of Parliament with a clear eye to their constituents.[45]

Righteous indignation may well be deserved, but it should be aimed at both sides of the network—donors as well as recipients. Corruption is a factor in the relief process, but its importance and consequences are determined by the dynamics of a relief culture too prone to isolate disasters from society at large.

(b) *Cure or cover?* The relief culture's propensity to view disasters as a deviation from normal life is a convenience. It provides a well-defined construct in which compassion can be demonstrated without durable commitment. The problem with this view is that it poses a very profound dilemma for those involved in the relief process: towards what end is one providing relief? There is a natural and understandable inclination for most people to justify aid to victims of a disaster solely on the assumption that, without such assistance, victims' lives would be in danger. Without food, clothing, blankets, without help to rebuild shattered lives, obvious suffering would not be avoided. The point is compelling, and is not easy to deny. Nevertheless, in certain important respects this assumption as it is put into practice avoids the essence of both care and purpose. At what stage do helpless victims become 'normal human beings'? What ultimately is the purpose of relief intervention?

Many relief agencies see disasters as a kind of 'foot in the door' to undertake longer-term development work. This reflects the increasingly recognized need to deal with the true sources of disasters, namely, the economic and social conditions that make people vulnerable. However, despite the increasingly recognized link between disasters and development, the relief process *per se* perpetuates a division between the two which is difficult to close. The kind of commitments that might be required to marry relief and development pose complex issues for both donors and recipients. As one USAID official made clear:

We cannot become embroiled in every area that might require our longer-term assistance. One of the hazards of becoming involved in a disaster relief operation is that it might be assumed that we shall follow on relief with major development undertakings. There is always the danger of becoming trapped.[46]

Similarly, governments of the afflicted might be willing to accept short-term assistance, but may not wish this ultimately to involve programmes that might disrupt an acceptable status quo or undermine their authority. Thus, the relief process becomes encapsulated into a distinct and isolated effort which, in turn, raises two practical issues.

The first issue arises from the problem that, if the goal of relief is to return the afflicted to a state of normality, then what does one mean by normalcy? To rebuild homes on slopes prone to earthslides, for example, is doing little more than creating the scene for the next disaster. Similarly, to re-establish agricultural communities on land worn out by soil erosion, inaccessible to water and overworked just paves the way for the famine next time. These are the practical consequences of 'sticking-plaster' approaches to malignant cancers.

Secondly, by treating disasters as an encapsulated problem—separate from a more abiding social and economic context—the full implications of external intervention become a secondary or tertiary consideration. In other words, the economic impact of prolonged free food on agricultural economies or the mini-economic booms created to service the relief operations are rarely considered as the relief process gears itself up to deal with a crisis that is conceptually isolated.

The impact of this kind of hazard inherent in disaster relief has not been lost on many of the institutions and individuals seeking to assist the disaster-stricken. The levels of understanding about the impact of external intervention have greatly increased. Even the very factors that promote and compound disasters are far more clearly recognized now than they had been just a decade ago. Accumulative experience, an increasing sensitivity on the part of social scientists and the more focused attention of those in the 'hard sciences' have enhanced the potential capability of the relief process. Given that 'convenience' will most likely continue to sever the natural link between disasters and development, one can at least see an emerging guideline for more effective relief. Indeed, one might even say that a criterion of response can be suggested that would mitigate some of the worst aspects of relief intervention and might prevent the full impact of a disaster even occurring.

Criteria for Relief

There are six crucial aspects of disaster relief that ultimately determine the strengths and weaknesses of any single operation: preparedness, prediction, assessment, appropriate intervention, timely intervention, and coordination.

Preparedness

The international community, certainly as reflected in the growing body of professional literature,[47] is increasingly attuned to the benefits of pre-disaster planning. The United Nations Disaster Relief Organization has sought to promote preparedness measures in many disaster-prone countries. It has provided extensive literature on practical ways to organize relief units, to prepare paramedical facilities and to establish effective early warning systems.[48] Some of this work ('everyday implementable improvements such as using 6" bolts instead of nails')[49] has been incorporated into development projects funded by the United Nations Development Fund.

Jamaica's Office of Disaster Preparedness and Emergency Coordination, established in 1980 with UNDRO assistance, is a model of the kind of preparedness activities a national disaster focal point can take. Designed to prepare for emergencies caused by earthquakes, hurricanes, oil spills and transport incidents, the disasters office put into action a 'National Disaster Plan'. This plan includes a wide variety of measures which mitigate the impact of disasters. Critical resource lists are maintained and updated, emergency simulation exercises are undertaken, high-risk areas are closely monitored and early warning systems have been developed.[50] This kind of preparedness programme ensures that when disasters do strike some structure will at least be in place to respond.

The fact that the Jamaican example has not been imitated by many similarly disaster-prone states will be considered in Chapter 3. However, the important point in establishing a criterion for disaster responses is that there is at least an increasing capability to limit the impact of a disaster, to control a degree of its unpredictability, and to approach relief in a coordinated and coherent manner.

Prediction

Among the growing number of people who are professionally interested in disasters, there is a general consensus that 'disasters are not unforeseen events and technology now exists to identify the hazards that threaten a community and to estimate the areas and settlements that will be affected.'[51] Yet, despite this conclusion, one must not fall prey to the belief that disaster prediction is necessarily easy, nor is it solely a matter of technology. There is no doubt that technology can and will play an increasing role in disaster prediction, but effective prediction requires the interplay of technology with sensitive social and economic understanding.

Given the millenniums in which famines have visited societies throughout the world, it is perhaps surprising that only recently has mankind developed methods of successfully anticipating the onset of famines. Perhaps it is equally surprising that the most effective methods of prediction do not stem from such sophisticated means as satellite observation. Famine indicators can be gleaned from social and economic patterns that, in theory, have always been available to analysts. The fact that such patterns have only recently come to the notice of the international community is merely a demonstration of the fact that increased professionalism has made analysts look more deeply into causation.

Famines, as Sen has concluded, are in many instances only indirectly caused by crop failures. They are more often the result of people's lack of 'entitlements' (i.e. whether they can find employment, what they can earn).[52] Thus, in most famine disasters, those with resources can still buy food. It is those without the resources—those who have to sell their land or their cattle and, as a consequence, lose their entitlements within their local economies—who lose any chance of gaining access to food.[53] This was demonstrated in Ethiopia, though unfortunately only on an experimental scale, by the United Nations Children's Fund. There, UNICEF established a highly successful 'cash for food' project in which peasants were given cash (the equivalent of $17 per month) to buy not only food but sheep, oxen and farm tools. With the cash, they were able to buy sufficient food for their own survival in what was labelled a 'famine area'. More than food, however, they were also able, by purchasing tools, etc., to regain their entitlements through their ability to generate income.[54]

Sen's analysis and UNICEF's experiments reinforce Seaman's and others' important findings that famines provide clear indicators. Livestock sales, grain prices and stages of population movements give clear indications of famine onsets.[55] However, such grass-root indicators in no way mean that more sophisticated technology cannot join in the prediction battle. Satellite observation, for example, provides a further way of ascertaining the possibility of famine. Satellites can assess weather patterns; they can provide some indication of ground cover. They can only be used, however, in conjunction with on-site surveys. There is always a need for 'ground truthing'.[56]

The hazard of relying solely on satellite observation was evidenced in Ethiopia in mid-1984. Despite clear indications on the ground that famine was intensifying, UNDRO maintained there were signs that conditions in Ethiopia were improving. UNDRO's assessment was principally based on satellite observations.[57] The fact that the 'green' spotted by the satellite was that of acacia trees was missed, leading one Oxfam official to comment that all the satellite had uncovered was 'green starvation'.[58]

Predictive capabilities have nevertheless increased; and despite the dangers of over-reliance on sophisticated technology, satellites, for example, do play an important role. Data from synchronous meteorological and global observing satellites can track developing and mature hurricanes in the Western hemisphere. TIROS satellites can now trace the step-by-step progress of cyclones and typhoons in the Indian Ocean and Western Pacific, monitored by centres in Australia, China, Guam and Japan.[59] Such prediction capabilities have earth-based counterparts. Seismological instruments have become more sophisticated in determining the likelihood of earthquakes and other related earth disturbances.[60] Hydrologists have developed more effective means of estimating flood propensities, and both hydrologists and seismologists understand the need to combine their sciences with sensitivity to local culture, knowledge and even folklore.[61]

There are many disasters that are not predicted, which for reasons that go to the core of this work are missed or ignored. However, in determining a reasonable criterion for effective relief, one can certainly conclude that predictive capabilities have been steadily enhanced. The ability to prepare for the impact of a disaster agent and to intervene in time has increased significantly.

Assessment

It is only too understandable that the chaos following a disaster makes the needs of victims extremely difficult to determine. For outsiders, lack of familiarity with the local culture and even the language of those caught up in a disaster can prove barriers to accuracy. Conversely, for those who are part of the affected group, assessments are 'often influenced by their personal involvement, either due to loss of their loved ones, property loss, or shock over the magnitude of damage and destruction.'[62] Yet, it is this kind of extreme difficulty that has led more and more analysts to focus on the problems of assessment. Since the late 1970s, greater attention has been paid to practical assessment techniques, and this attention has resulted in a relatively large outpouring of manuals, guides and academic analyses concerned with survey and evaluation procedures.[63]

Perhaps one of the most important aspects of such work is that it makes clear demarcations between types of disasters and their impacts. For example, the fact that earthquakes very rarely result in significant crop losses means that the afflicted do not normally require massive food aid. However, in disasters caused by tidal waves or floods, food aid is usually a vital requirement. High winds that do not result in floods normally lead to a 'moderate' section of the population requiring extensive care for injuries. On the other hand, food scarcity for high-wind victims is rarely a problem.[64] The fact that there have emerged over the past decade more sensitive bases upon which to determine needs means that the relief worker has a clear starting-point to undertake accurate assessments. Equally important is the fact that, with such clear categorizations in hand, priorities are easier to determine and defend. The inclination of outside interveners to send what they feel might be appropriate or what they feel able to donate can be constrained by the weight of appropriate guidelines.

In other words, the growing capability to foresee what is required to deal with various types of disasters means that much of the randomness that pervades assistance can be eliminated from the relief process. In turn, the elimination of randomness also means that the afflicted as well as the governmental institutions of the afflicted can be spared the 'relief invasions' that have traditionally followed many calls for assistance. Airports and sea-ports no longer need be cluttered with goods that prove inappropriate to the needs of victims.

This greater professionalism in dealing with emergency assessments has spilled over into the world of refugee assistance as well. Not until the end of 1982 had there been a single source that outlined 'an organised systematic response to improving the management of refugee emergencies.'[65] With the introduction of a *Handbook for Emergencies* by the United Nations High Commissioner for Refugees, relief workers now have a tested step-by-step set of procedures upon which to determine the needs of those who fall within their charge.

Such assessment guides designed to help those on the ground to determine needs can often be supplemented by information based once again upon technology. Satellites (for example LANDSATS and meteorological satellites) and low-, medium- or high-altitude aircraft can supply wide-coverage images and conduct aerial surveys with camera or radar equipment. These kinds of technology mean that damage assessment as well as population movement estimates can be greatly enhanced. As with prediction so, too, with assessment. Technology and more sensitive assessment guidelines are ultimately only successful if the afflicted themselves are active participants in the relief process. The fact that 'community participation is valuable and necessary in all the major aspects of first aid'[66] is a lesson increasingly grasped by relief workers. Greater stress is being placed on the need of those involved in the relief process to use the knowledge and the social structure (for example a village headman) of the stricken community to determine relief requirements.

Appropriate intervention

Linked with more sensitive assessment procedures is the increased awareness of what might be called more 'appropriate intervention'. Along with assessment guidelines have emerged appropriate lists of supplies that should be used during an emergency. These supply lists specify the types of foodstuffs that different cultures and nationalities find acceptable, the kinds of clothing and shelter appropriate for different parts of the world, and the kinds of medicine and medical assistance required for different disasters.[67]

Moreover, the relief network has shown increased awareness of the economic and social complexities involved in external intervention. For example, one way of ensuring that appropriate food aid can be provided is to attempt to purchase food locally or regionally. Jackson makes this point when he criticizes the extensive use of imported, low-calorie dried skimmed milk in a situation where people require a high-calorie intake. Local or regional food purchases, notes Jackson, 'is an approach to disaster relief increasingly favoured by both the European Economic Community and the World Food Programme. The EEC refers to this method as "triangular operations" because it makes money available to buy food in a country near to the afflicted area rather than sending out food of its own.'[68]

In the aftermath of the 1976 earthquake in Guatemala, relief workers were careful not to take over the design and construction of housing themselves. They made a specific point of marrying local techniques with their own more earthquake-resistant methods, and even more importantly worked through 'the people already respected in the community as builders who in the long run would be asked for advice and whose recommendations and actions would be followed.'[69]

Appropriate intervention in the case of refugees has undergone intensive analysis in the past few years. Again, the conventional assumption of helpless victims grateful for the mere security of safety and regular food has been fundamentally challenged. Anthropologists, sociologists and social psychologists view the plight of the refugee in terms of rebuilding community life and stimulating educational and economic opportunities. These evolving attitudes are reflected in the introduction of the *UNHCR Handbook for Emergencies* which states that:

indeed improvements in the techniques of relief alone that are not matched by an increased refugee involvement can be self-defeating. It is increasingly clear that a refugee's first reception in the country of asylum can critically determine his or her ability to become self-sufficient. Ill-considered assistance at the start, however efficiently delivered, can create a dependency syndrome which may last for years.[70]

Timely intervention

Appropriate intervention is timely intervention. However, it is worth making the distinction between appropriate and timely, to emphasize one basic point: no matter how accurately needs have been assessed or how appropriate the actual relief items are in themselves, unless such assessments and goods are provided in a timely way, they are of limited use or can even be destructive. Put in another way, if aid is not received in a timely manner, then it is no longer appropriate. Timely intervention involves not only an awareness of when aid is needed but also when aid is no longer needed. The horror stories of poorly-timed aid deliveries are legion: a World Food Programme relief operation began more than a year after famine broke out in Bangladesh in 1975; EEC skimmed milk powder requested for Grenada after flooding in 1976 arrived in 1979;[71] medical assistance to Burmese refugees in Bangladesh did not arrive until children began dying in large numbers.[72]

The conditions that often confront officials attempting to assist disaster-prone countries make timely deliveries an extremely complex logistical affair. Poor internal transport facilities and communications make deliveries and distribution hazardous. In a country like Chad, larger than any individual European state, there are only 100 miles of paved roads! And, as in the case of the Sudan, when relief transport began to operate on the major road from Port Sudan in 1985, the flow of lorries actually destroyed much of the surface of this vital link between the port and the relief camps. Added to this are the complications presented by recipient countries' import controls and customs duties. Even in times of serious emergency, officials in many countries are reluctant to bypass restrictions that are seen as economically necessary for the nation as a whole. Hence, timing, too, may become subject to the delays caused by the need to change import regulations or, at least, to agree on exemptions for the purposes of relief goods.

While inadequate infrastructures and even official regulations present problems that cannot be easily remedied during times of disaster relief operations, the possibility of more timely intervention has been enhanced in several ways. The World Food Programme has experimented with pre-positioned stocks of food in several areas in Africa and South Asia in order to cut down on the amount of time required to bring food from developed countries to disaster-afflicted countries. Special units, such as the Swedish Emergency Force, can provide military-type logistic solutions such as pontoon bridges and temporary airstrips. Although extremely expensive and normally a last desperate solution, air-drop techniques by helicopters and conventional aircraft of relief materials have also been perfected.

However, these kinds of developments may increase the delivery capabilities of relief, but they do not alone answer the fundamental question of what is timely. Timeliness is not always a question of speed. There is a general belief that 'quick aid is double aid'.[73] This assumption does not always hold true. Quick aid can be as disruptive as no aid at all if it is not carefully determined beforehand. To rush in assistance just at the point when the affected community is restoring itself through its own coping mechanisms can destroy local self-confidence. This applies to refugees as much as it does to those stricken by natural disasters. As the Emergency Officer for the United Nations High Commissioner for Refugees stated in 1984, 'To undertake an emergency relief operation for refugees in every case might hamper voluntary repatriation or integration into the local community [of the host country].'[74] Knowing when to turn aid on requires a keen sensitivity. Similarly—and equally as important as knowing when to turn aid on—is the problem of knowing when to turn it off. Even in disasters where the impact might be of a relatively long duration, the timing factor must be carefully considered. The Dominican Republic in 1979 offers a relevant case:

> In the devastated south-west of the Dominican Republic following Hurricanes David and Frederick in 1979, food stocks were largely destroyed . . . Swift international response enabled food to meet the needs of 300,000 people over a five month period. From the beginning, people were told that the food would be provided only for those five months; thus false expectations of continued food assistance were not created and no institutionalisation of the programme followed. The programme was designed and run locally and its success was largely due to these factors.[75]

Coordination

Like inappropriate or untimely assistance, uncoordinated relief efforts have also generated a store of disaster legends. Duplication of aid, double deliveries to one community and none to another, competition amongst relief agencies, are but some of the unfortunate events in international relief responses. The problem has not gone unnoticed. Mechanisms on a variety of levels have been created to enhance the coordination of relief assistance. Efforts to create 'relief cells' in disaster-prone countries are in part a recognition that in the final analysis the government of the afflicted must be the focal point for determining what aid is needed and which agencies should be doing what, when and where. Nevertheless, the international community has also attempted to enhance relief coordination at the donor level.

The United Nations 'family' has sought to improve its internal coordination of relief aid. The creation of the Office of the United Nations Disaster Relief Coordinator, designed to act as an information and monitoring channel for assessments and deliveries, is evidence of this awareness. Voluntary agencies have created international, regional and domestic coordinating mechanisms. On the international level, the International Council of Voluntary Agencies, which comprises the majority of major private voluntary groups, established the Voluntary Agency Steering Committee as far back as 1972 'to provide an on-going forum for exchange of experience and techniques in disaster preparedness and management, but more particularly to share information on specific disaster situations and coordinate the response from appeals.'[76]

Regionally, the voluntary agencies within the member states of the European

Community established in 1982 an 'Emergency Coordinating Committee' under the Liaison Committee of Development Non-Governmental Organizations to the European Communities. Great Britain and the United States offer two important examples of domestic coordinating bodies. In Britain, the Disasters Emergency Committee acts not only as a forum for agency discussions, but also serves during large-scale emergencies as a central point for the receipt of funds. InterAction in the United States facilitates the coordination of activities of 105 diverse private voluntary bodies, and throughout 1984-5, helped seventy-five of its members to pool their resources for aid to emergency-stricken Africa.

Such developments reflect the growing awareness that without more effective coordination at both 'country level' (i.e. in the country where the disaster has taken place) and at the international donor level, relief will continue to suffer from what one former United States official called 'a considerable degree of efficiency losses'.[77] Despite these continued 'efficiency losses', one can at least point to the fact that over the past decade there has emerged a greater understanding about the dilemmas and difficulties posed by disasters. The need for greater coordination is at least appreciated as an important aspect of effective relief . . . although, in the heat of the moment, coordination is certainly one criterion that is too often forgotten in practice. The six-point criteria of effective relief provides a target, a goal that—by the nature of disasters themselves, and the dilemmas they pose—can never be fully attained. Perfect prediction, perfect assessment or coordination can rarely be achieved in disaster-prone countries. Yet, in looking towards these criteria as a target, a more abiding guideline must not be lost.

In the final analysis, disasters are about vulnerability, and vulnerability—whatever the disaster agent—is created by mankind. The real solutions to disaster prevention, preparedness and relief can only come from addressing the basic problems that create the very vulnerabilities that render human beings prone to disasters. Disasters cannot be divorced from normal life; they are a reflection of it. So, too, are the immediate responses to relief.

If one views disasters as isolated phenomena, if one treats 'victims' as a distinct category somehow separate from that of 'normal' people, in a very basic sense one perpetuates the attitudes that have too often made relief ineffective. One falls into the trap of the relief culture, the realm of technological fixes, all at the eventual expense of those who are suffering. In many respects, the international community is becoming increasingly aware of the technical problems that have for so long hampered relief. For reasons to be discussed in the following chapter, the attitudes and approaches towards international relief assistance have evolved considerably over the past seventy years. That international assistance too often falls well below what earlier were discussed as acceptable relief criteria can be understood from two perspectives. The first, suggested in Chapter 3, concerns the particular characteristics of the four main components of the international relief network: governments, inter-governmental and non-governmental organizations, and the media. The second perspective concerns the dynamics of the relief process itself, and the impact of those dynamics upon the institutional processes of all involved in international relief assistance. This will be considered in Chapters 4 and 5.

However, the technical problems considered in these chapters are ultimately far more amenable to solutions than the fundamental issue of the way in which we view disasters and disaster-afflicted peoples. Chapter 6 will offer some ways of approaching the periphery of the more institutional problems faced by the major components of the international relief network. What must be done to alter the way we view the causes of disasters and our attitudes towards the afflicted is left to the individual reader to decide.

Notes

1. Office of US Foreign Disaster Assistance, *Annual Report FY 1985*, Washington, DC, US Agency for International Development, 1986.
2. Ferrara, G.M. (ed.), *The Disaster File: The 1970s*, London, Macmillan, 1980, p.150.
3. Tazieff, H., 'La menace croissante des catastrophes naturelles et technologiques', *UNDRO News*, September/October 1985, p.6.
4. Linear, M., *Zapping the Third World: The disaster of development aid*, London, Pluto Press, 1985, pp.120–3.
5. Cuny, F., *Disasters and Development*, New York, Oxford University Press, 1983, p.14.
6. Wijkman, A. & Timberlake, L., *Natural Disasters: Acts of God or acts of man?*, Washington, DC, Earthscan Paperback, 1984, p.11.
7. Material for these statistics has been provided by the United States Agency for International Development, Washington, DC, and the Office of the United Nations Disaster Relief Coordinator, Geneva.
8. See, for example, Brown, B., *Disaster Preparedness and the United Nations: Advance planning for relief*, New York and Oxford, Pergamon Press, 1979, p.5. However, the Swedish Red Cross, in *Prevention Better than Cure* (Stockholm, May 1984, p.49), states that there is 'no universal well-established definition upon which all agree . . . Definitions vary widely from one source to another with the consequence that the statistical records show numerous discrepancies in the kinds of events that qualify as disasters.'
9. Hewitt, K. (ed.), *Interpretations of Calamity*, Boston, Allen & Unwin, 1983, p.10.
10. A consistent theme of many government officials in what normally are considered 'donor countries' is the fear that intervention in disasters may lead to politically and economically expensive long-term development projects. The term 'mousetrapped' arose during an interview with Hunter Farnham, USAID, Washington, DC, 15 September 1983.
11. Waddell, E., 'Coping with frosts, governments and disaster experts: some reflections based on a New Guinea experience and a perusal of the relevant literature', in Hewitt, K., op. cit., p.35.
12. One official from USAID told this writer in September 1983 that 'Ethiopia always had chronic famines' and that 'there seems nothing unusual' about the food shortfalls that the Ethiopian Relief and Rehabilitation Commission were announcing.
13. Wallerstein, I., 'The Range of Choice: Constraints on the Policies of Governments of Contemporary African Independent States', in Lofchie, M., *The State of the Nations: Constraints on development in independent Africa*, Berkeley, University of California Press, 1971, p.28.
14. Green, S., *International Disaster Relief: Toward a responsive system*, New York, McGraw-Hill, 1977, p.15.
15. United Nations Disaster Relief Office, *Disaster Prevention and Mitigation: A compendium of current knowledge*, Vol.2, 'Hydrological Aspects', New York, United Nations, 1978, p.3.
16. Chambers, R., 'Mass Distress, Migration and Rural Development in Sub-Saharan Africa', *Famine in Africa*, House of Commons, Foreign Affairs Committee, London, Her Majesty's Stationery Office, April 1985, p.143.
17. Ultimately, what is normally regarded as 'post-rehabilitation' and development are difficult to distinguish. As Cuny's discussion of post-rehabilitation work in Guatem-

ala after the 1976 earthquake clearly demonstrates, effective rehabilitation, like development also, can only take place in a broad politically and economically acceptable context. This broad context was absent in the Guatemala case, and, hence, post-rehabilitation efforts were fundamentally impeded. See Cuny, op. cit., Chapters 10 and 14.

18. Local relief officials often find themselves in a clear 'double-bind' situation in the aftermath of a disaster. If they do not provide figures that cohere with assumptions of outside observers they are frequently accused of minimizing or exaggerating the figures for unsavoury motives. Brig. Iqbal M. Shafi, who was sent by the Pakistan government to assist in setting up relief operations after the 1970 East Pakistan cyclone, said that when he tried to brief the international press on the situation, he was immediately accused of lying. His figures of fatalities were below the number the press had assumed were killed. They said he was suppressing the figures for political motives:

> One gentleman stood up and said, 'You are a West Pakistani, aren't you?' 'Look,' I replied, 'when I go to the UK, I don't ask you whether you come from Scotland or England.' But the chap persisted. I finally said, 'If you really want to know, I am an Indian but I chose to live in Pakistan'. They [the press] were critical; they were already conditioned. [Interview with Iqbal M. Shafi, Islamabad, 14 December 1982.]

On the other hand, when certain countries provide figures for post-disaster dead or afflicted, they are assumed to be 'crying wolf' or exaggerating. (See, for example, interview with George Beauchamp, USAID, Washington, DC, 19 November 1980.) This dilemma is discussed in greater detail in this book in Chapter 4 under 'Perceptual Variables and Persuasive Communications'.

19. In the Sudan in late 1984, this writer received information about the prospect of refugees from Ethiopia coming into Sudan that ranged from 'perhaps a few thousand' to over 400,000. Various estimates were given by the Office of the United Nations High Commissioner for Refugees, the International Committee of the Red Cross, the Relief Society of Tigray and the Sudanese Commission for Refugees. No one had any clear idea of how many refugees to expect.

20. Interview with Hugh Goyder, Addis Ababa, 13 October 1984.

21. Cuny, op. cit., p.99.

22. Cuny, op. cit., pp.98–9.

23. This factor has become increasingly recognized by relief experts, and applies to children as well as adults. UNICEF's *Emergency Handbook* makes a special point of noting that malnutrition is often due to 'ignorance and or taboos preventing children and mothers from eating certain available foods'. United Nations Children's Fund, *Assisting in Emergencies: A resource handbook for UNICEF field staff*, New York, UNICEF, 1986, p.58.

24. McCormack, W.M. & Curlin, G.T., 'Infectious Diseases: Their Spread and Control', in Chen, L. (ed.), *Disaster in Bangladesh*, New York, Oxford University Press, 1973, p.70.

25. Seaman, J., 'The Effects of Disaster on Health', in Davis, I. (ed.), *Disasters and the Small Dwelling*, Oxford, Pergamon Press, 1981, p.59.

26. Interview with Satish Jacob, formerly a relief official with the Indian non-governmental organization CASA, and now with the BBC, New Delhi, 16 March 1983.

27. Interview with Frances D'Souza, Director, International Disaster Institute, London, 25 November 1982. D'Souza had undertaken considerable research into the response to the Italian earthquake. See, for example, 'Recovery following the South Italian Earthquake, November 1980: Two contrasting examples', *Disasters: The International Journal of Disaster Studies and Practice*, Farnham, Surrey, Foxcombe Publications, 1982, pp.101 ff.

28. 'The Nightmare of Logistics', *Africa Emergency: A Monthly Update on the Crisis*, UN Office for Emergency Operations in Africa, New York, July 1985, p.3.

29. 'EEC Junketing', *The Economist Development Report*, March 1986, p.5.

30. 'Monsters of Concern' is a term taken from O'Neill, J., *Making Sense Together: an Introduction to Wild Sociology*, London, Heinemann, 1975, p.64, as quoted in Harrell-Bond, B., *Imposing Aid: Emergency Assistance to Refugees*, Oxford, Oxford University Press, 1986, p.363.
31. Harrell-Bond, B., op. cit., p.363.
32. Howard, J. & Mister, R., 'Lessons learnt by Oxfam from their Experience of Shelter Provision, 1970-1978', Davis, I., op. cit., p.165.
33. Hewitt, op. cit., p.8.
34. Interview with M. Mokammel Haque, who in 1970 had been seconded from his government post in Dacca to assist relief operations in the delta, London, 28 October 1982.
35. Waddell, op. cit., p.33.
36. For a detailed description of the causes and consequences of the Essex disaster of 1953 see, Whittow, J., *Disasters: The Anatomy of Environmental Hazards*, Harmondsworth, Penguin, 1980, pp.115 ff. A more recent example of this kind of corruption arose in the wake of the Zeebrugge ferry disaster in 1987 when it was discovered that people were making financial claims for fictitious 'relatives' who had never been on board the ferry. (BBC Radio 4 broadcast, 31 March 1987.)
37. Interview with Stafford Clarry, *ELU/CARE*, Mogadishu, 18 October 1984.
38. Nelson, L.-E., 'Disasters and the World Press: Being both a Redundancy and a Gloomy Sermon', unpublished paper.
39. Interview with Claudio Chavez, World Food Programme, Rome, 5 July 1984.
40. This assumption is impressionistic, based upon my own experiences and those of the vast majority of people interviewed for this book. No one denies that corruption exists. The point is the extent to which it significantly deprives disaster victims of much-needed assistance. My general conclusion is that, based on that criterion, the impact of corruption is exaggerated. In saying this, I am referring to most relief operations; I am certainly not suggesting that certain operations such as those that took place on the Thai border in the late 1970s and early 1980s fit the general rule!
41. Shawcross, W., *The Quality of Mercy: Cambodia, Holocaust and Modern Conscience*, London, Andre Deutsch, 1984, p.423.
42. George Warner, seconded from USAID to the World Food Programme, was charged with demanding a kickback of $7/ton of seed purchased through the Bangkok-based company Suisindo. Warner was arrested in Washington in September 1980; he pleaded guilty to a lesser charge and was fined $40,000.
43. Interview with an official from the Natural Disasters Section, Norwegian Ministry of Development Cooperation, Oslo, 5 June 1984.
44. Interview with official from the Disaster Unit, British Overseas Development Administration, London, 7 July 1981.
45. Interview with official from the Foreign and Commonwealth Office, London, 21 August 1984.
46. Interview with Alfred White, US Agency for International Development, Washington, DC, 18 November 1980.
47. From the mid-1970s to the present, there has been a tremendous outpouring of literature from a wide range of disciplines on various aspects of disaster relief. What is interesting, if not striking, is the recent emergence of disaster relief manuals produced by governments, inter-governmental organizations and non-governmental organizations. Note, for example, UNICEF's *Assisting in Emergencies* (ibid.), or United Nations High Commissioner for Refugees, *Handbook for Emergencies*, Geneva, 1982. The United Nations Disaster Relief Office has also provided a series of authoritative volumes on disaster prevention and preparedness since 1977. Non-governmental organizations have also been responsible for similar manuals. See, for example, Caritas Internationalis, *Manual des Secours en Cas de Catastrophe*, Rome, 1983, or, Catholic Relief Services *et al.*, *When Disaster Strikes*, Geneva, 1980.
48. See, for example, United Nations Disaster Relief Office, *Disaster Prevention and*

Mitigation: A compendium of current knowledge, Vol.8, *Sanitation Aspects*, New York, United Nations, 1982.

49. Interview with John Tomblin, Office for Preparedness, United Nations Disaster Relief Office, Geneva, 21 March 1984.

50. Office of Disaster Preparedness and Emergency Relief Coordination, Office of the Prime Minister, *National Disaster Plan*, Kingston, Jamaica, 1981.

51. Wijkman and Timberlake, op. cit., p.122.

52. See Sen, A., *Poverty and Famines: An essay on entitlement and deprivation*, Oxford, Clarendon Press, 1981.

53. One observer who had little experience in disaster work commented to this writer in Addis Ababa that he had been impressed with the ingenuity of people in Wollo province who were selling wood to earn money to purchase food. What the observer did not realize is that the wood that was being sold was the remnants of those peoples' homes. In desperation they had to dismantle their homes to get at the wooden supports which ultimately would be their last source of revenue.

54. 'Cash Projects Save Lives, Money', *Africa Emergency Report*, Office for Emergency Operations in Africa, April–May 1985, No.1, p.6.; Interview with Alan Court, UNICEF, Addis Ababa, 29 September 1984.

55. This general conclusion, however, does not imply that there are not inconsistencies and disputes over specific indicators. See, for example, Cutler, P., 'Famine Forecasting and Peasant Behaviour in Northern Ethiopia', *Disasters: The International Journal of Disaster Studies and Practice*, 8, No.1, 1984, p.48. Cutler discusses the differing interpretations about the significance of price rises in Ethiopia's Wollo province between Sen, A. (op.cit., pp.94–5) and Seaman, J. & Holt, J., 'Markets and Famines in the Third World', *Disasters: The International Journal of Disaster Studies and Practice*, 4, No.3, 1980, pp.283–97. However, as Cutler concludes that 'on the other hand, Sen, Seaman and Holt would all agree that under famine conditions prices of assets such as livestock and utensils will decline as desperate people rush to sell animals, farm goods and household goods to get money for food'.

56. Interview with Hunter Farnham, USAID, Washington, DC, 15 September 1983; see, for example, Abend, C.J., 'Problems in the Application of Technology in International Disaster Assistance', in *The Role of Technology in International Disaster Assistance*, The National Research Council, Washington, DC, National Academy of Sciences, 1978.

57. Cable from Panis (UNDP, Addis Ababa) to Wiersing (UNDRO, Geneva), 25 September 1984: 'Obliged to reiterate our . . . objection to paragraph one of UNDRO Sitrep 7 which is highly misleading. Please note that crop assessments cannot repeat cannot be based exclusively on satellite info and pluviometric data. . . .'

58. This remark was attributed to Marcus Thompson of the British agency, Oxfam.

59. For a good discussion on such satellite potential, see The National Research Council's *Assessing International Disaster Needs*, Washington, DC, National Academy of Sciences, 1979.

60. V. Karnik, 'Are earthquake disasters increasing?', *UNDRO News*, Geneva, March/April 1986.

61. Ibid., p.9.

62. Caritas Internationalis, Catholic Relief Services, LORCS, LWF, Oxfam and WCC, *When Disaster Strikes*, Geneva, 1980, p.11.

63. Ibid., p.47.

64. Cuny, op. cit., p.60.

65. United Nations High Commissioner for Refugees, *Handbook For Emergencies*, Geneva, UNHCR, p.v.

66. United Nations Disaster Relief Office, *Disaster Prevention and Mitigation: A compendium of current knowledge*, Vol. 11, *Preparedness Aspects*, p.69

67. For example, World Health Organization Emergency Health Kit: Lists A, B and C.

68. Jackson, T., *Against The Grain*, Oxford, Oxfam, 1982, p.13.

69. Cuny, op.cit., p.171.

70. UNHCR, op.cit., p.vi.
71. Both the WFP and EEC examples come from Jackson, op.cit., p.11.
72. Interview with A. Aurora, World Food Programme, 5 July 1984.
73. 'A third myth says that the quickest possible disaster response is always the best. Thus, without always assessing the needs and preferences of the victims, unnecessary or inappropriate items may be flown by expensive charter flights to any place in the world, which suffers from any type of disaster.' Swedish Red Cross, *Prevention Better Than Cure: Report on human and environmental disasters in the Third World*, Stockholm, May 1984, p.64.
74. Interview with Philip Sargisson, Emergency Unit, Office of the United Nations High Commissioner for Refugees, Geneva, 20 March 1984.
75. Jackson, op. cit., p.12.
76. Stephens, L. & Green, S., *Disaster Assistance: Appraisal, reform and new approaches*, New York, New York University Press, 1979, p.14.
77. Interview with Victor Palmieri, former Assistant Secretary of State, Bureau for Refugee Programs, US Department of State, New York, 23 September 1983.

2 The Evolving International Response

> Assistance to people stricken by calamities is, under present conditions, slow, poorly organised, and in a great degree, inefficient. The money allocated is so often badly distributed. Frequently the materials provided for purposes of relief are not adapted to the requirements of the people and the local climatic conditions. In many cases those who come to the assistance of the sufferers lack an expert knowledge of the technique of relief work. The offerings made by governments of the countries which are safe to those of affected nations are rather in the nature of charitable donations tending to embarrass the givers and humiliate the recipients.[1]

So wrote Senator Giovanni Ciraolo in April 1921, as he began to lay the foundations for an International Assistance Union to introduce 'international solidarity in face of the dangers and troubles of the world.' International assistance to the disaster-afflicted was by no means an invention of the post-World War I era. However, Ciraola's proposal reflected a growing belief that practical measures had to be taken as a 'human right of nations, stricken by calamities which could not be foreseen, to be assisted by international solidarity, if the entire mobilization of their own powers is found insufficient to succour the sufferers within their territory'.[2]

The forms that this 'international solidarity' has taken are the subject of this chapter: the evolution of international responses to disasters. If there is any single feature of this evolution that stands out most dramatically, it is the apparent fact that the evolution of international responses has generally lagged behind the growth in scale and frequency of disaster phenomena. This is not to say that the international community has remained indifferent to the problems posed by disasters. As this chapter seeks to demonstrate, there have been a variety of attempts to improve the responsive capabilities of the international community. However, as will be discussed in Chapter 3, the components of what shall be called the 'international relief network' face complex institutional problems in being effective relief actors; and the very dynamics of international relief, as will be considered in Chapters 4 and 5, explain why only too often the international community falls below an acceptable standard of response.

The evolution of international responses to disasters from 1945 to the mid-1980s can be separated into five very general phases. The first, that between 1945 and the beginning of the 1950s, reflects the international community's concern with mass disruption and distress following the Second World War. That period is marked by a significant growth in the development of private voluntary and inter-governmental organizations. There were two important assumptions that underlined this first phase: (1) that relief and rehabilitation for all intents and purposes meant Europe; and (2) that the majority of organizations created to deal with post-war relief and rehabilitation were essentially temporary.

Phase two began as the need for European post-war relief and rehabilitation rapidly receded, by the beginning of the 1950s. Many post-war relief organizations were pressed to find more permanent, stable roles. This search found many of these institutions turning towards the growing field of development. Development in what will eventually be called the 'Third World' offered an institutional *raison d'être*, but, it also diverted attention away from the issue of disasters.

While this development orientation relegated disasters and disaster relief to very low institutional priorities, the need for relief was not totally ignored. There were various organizational adjustments made to accommodate relief requirements, but rarely were these allowed to interfere with the growth industry of development. In a very limited way, the early 1960s began to reveal some changes in the attitudes of the international community. The problems of newly independent states had led to a series of disasters that shocked many. The assumption that states—whether newly independent or not—had the capabilities to deal with their own disasters was frequently and radically challenged. Phase three of the evolution reflected the acknowledged need for specialist disaster relief bodies. From the mid-1960s through to the early 1970s, one witnessed a spate of institution building within governmental, inter- and non-governmental sectors.

Equally important were the efforts made during this period to impose some kind of coordinating structure on the growing number of disaster relief actors. Yet, despite these efforts, the bevy of actors who now might become involved in relief did not prove particularly amenable to overall coordination. Phase four reflected the attempts made to deal with this reality. From the mid-1970s into the early 1980s, solutions were sought to revamp the relief process such that coordination could be engendered in ways that were ostensibly less dependent upon formal structures.

Attempts to revamp the relief process from the early 1980s to the present pointed to a reality that the international community felt it could now no longer ignore. The myriad of actors with relief roles could not easily be honed into a system, either informal or formal. The diversity of interests and approaches alone meant that greater systematization was an elusive if not impossible goal. The evolution's fifth phase is marked by the international community's increasing acceptance of what, fortunately or unfortunately, had always been the underlying reality: the plural capacities option.

While the spur to major international intervention in disasters arose out of the Second World War, it is worth bearing in mind that significant steps had been taken to organize more effective international relief even before World War I. The single most important step was the creation in 1863 of J. Henry Dunant's Red Cross movement. Born out of the horrors Dunant had witnessed at the Battle of Solferino in 1859, the Red Cross movement initially sought to establish national Red Cross societies that could mobilize volunteers to tend to the wounded on and off the battlefield. In 1864, the Geneva Diplomatic Conference adopted the first 'Geneva Convention for the Amelioration of the Condition of the Wounded in Armies in the Field', and with this international recognition, national societies began to proliferate.[3] By the end of the First World War, the International Red Cross movement comprised three distinctly separate but related entities:

(i)   The International Committee of the Red Cross, a private committee whose members must be Swiss citizens, seeks principally to act as an intermediary between belligerents. Its main concern is 'to endeavour at all times that the military and civilian victims of such conflicts and of their direct results receive protection and assistance, and to serve, in humanitarian matters, as an intermediary between the parties.'[4]

(ii) The National Red Cross, Red Crescent and Red Lion and Sun Societies are nationally-based societies, though independent of their own individual governments. A national society seeks to provide appropriate relief to disaster victims in its own country and, when so requested, to assist other national societies.

(iii) The League of Red Cross Societies is the world federation of the national societies. It attempts to coordinate the activities of national societies in the event of disasters requiring international assistance and also seeks to assist in the development of national societies' activities.

During and after the First World War, the Red Cross movement remained the single most important landmark in the evolution of humanitarian relief. However, its importance should not obscure the extraordinary wartime and post-war efforts which to some extent governments but, more dramatically, private groups, had made. One prominent example was the wartime Commission for Relief in Belgium which, according to Macalister-Smith was 'an organization without precedent'.

It appeared to be an *ad hoc* private international organization on a temporary basis, but in the performance of its functions the Commission possessed many of the attributes of state institutions. It negotiated and concluded agreements at the highest level, and enjoyed important immunities granted by the belligerents. Its representatives in military-occupied regions operated with wide powers and privileges, and it flew its own flag and issued its own passports. The CRB operated a large fleet of ocean-going vessels and canal boats, and by its existence and in the actual discharge of its relief functions it assumed the fundamental responsibility of providing for the basic needs of a whole population.[5]

Between 1914 and 1924, the American Relief Administration, the successor to the CRB, together with the European Children's Fund and the European Relief Council, had been responsible for delivering over $5 billion worth of relief to the peoples of Europe. Governments had directly and indirectly supported these private initiatives, but their principal relief preoccupations had been in the field of refugee assistance. In 1921 they established through the League of Nations an Office of the High Commissioner for Refugees, initially mandated to deal with peoples fleeing from Russia, but eventually to include Armenian, Assyrian and Turkish refugees. The International Labour Organization, created after the war, was also assigned the task of providing material assistance to these refugees. By 1938, at the Evian Conference, an Inter-governmental Committee on Refugees was set up to assist those escaping from Austria and Germany.[6]

Despite these important, albeit piecemeal, war and post-war activities, few in the international community showed any inclination to establish more permanent or systematic ways of dealing with disasters in general. Major potential donors—namely, nation-states—had fundamentally failed to introduce an effective framework to organize their own responses. Six years after Ciraolo's 1921 proposal had been translated into an International Relief Union, few practical changes had taken place in the interntional community's approaches to disaster relief. Camille Gorgé, reflecting on the work of the IRU up to 1938, not only bemoaned the niggardly financial contributions that participating governments had made but, even worse, he saw that what held true for the international response to Japan's 'disastrous earthquake' of 1923 remained true fifteen years later:

No one was shocked at the haphazard and chaotic way of giving help. On the contrary, it seemed quite natural that, after receiving due messages of sympathy or even gifts on a more or less generous scale, all the afflicted country had to do was to repair the loss and devastation by its own unaided efforts. Neither pity nor interest might intervene to too great an extent in its purely domestic affairs. This was a shrewd and convenient interpretation of the respect of sovereignty.[7]

It was only in the midst of World War II that governments began to fully appreciate the need for greater international intervention in the plight of disaster-stricken peoples. The trickle of refugees fleeing from persecution and the crisis of mass starvation that confronted Greece by 1943 all signalled the enormous problems that they would have to face after the termination of hostilities. Private organizations during the latter half of the war were already becoming embroiled in relief, and the sensitive collaboration between these private groups and wartime governments were the first signs of a relationship that would develop much more strongly over the next four decades.[8]

Recognizing the need to prepare for the inevitable relief requirements after the conclusion of the war, forty-four states signed a convention in 1943 to create the United Nations Relief and Rehabilitation Administration. UNRRA was 'seen as a partial answer to the inevitable consequences of the conflict—devastation, famine, pestilence, despair and perhaps a modern-day fifth Horseman of the Apocalypse, the exhaustion of foreign exchange capital in the Axis-overrun countries which would prevent them from importing needed supplies once the fighting stopped.'[9]

The Post-War World

The plight of the war-afflicted was principally viewed in terms of Europe. Given the devastation that that continent had suffered, it is hardly surprising. This preoccupation, however, had significant consequences over the next two decades for the ways in which disasters in general were perceived. In dealing with the famine, disease and social disruption that abounded in much of Europe, relief and rehabilitation were underscored by two very fundamental and inter-related assumptions. The first was that, with adequate assistance, Europe could be restored to normalcy quite quickly. In other words, relief and rehabilitation required quick though extensive inputs. Relief measures and the institutions that provided relief were both temporary in nature. Once adequate resources had been provided, the states of Europe would be able to stand on their own feet once again.

This view of relief as a short, sharp injection of assistance was sustained by a second assumption. The second assumption was that in the final analysis governments of the afflicted had the capability to deal with their own crises. Clearly, a considerable portion of national infrastructures had been destroyed and, as in the case of Germany, new governing institutions had to be put in place. Nevertheless, despite the considerable political turmoil in post-war Europe, the inherent structure of the state was still regarded as capable of guiding national recovery. Governments had it in their power to determine what was required and where. They had the administrative resources and the trained manpower to establish priorities and distribute relief and, ultimately, to determine the course of recovery.

Between the war and 1949, 192 private or non-governmental organizations (NGOs) sprang up to relieve the misery of war victims. Their sights for the most part were fixed upon Europe, as were those of their new inter-governmental counterparts. In terms of resources and influence with governments, the new inter-governmental organizations(IGOs), again created in large part to restore the millions of dislocated and malnourished peoples of Europe, had considerably more weight than NGOs. They were the new vanguard of relief: all were experimental in design and function; some were temporary in purpose and objectives.

These new inter-governmental organizations emerged out of the effort, first at Dunbarton Oaks in 1944 and subsequently in San Francisco in 1945, to create a United Nations Organization. Two years after the United Nations Charter was signed in San Francisco, the United Nations Relief and Rehabilitation Administration was dissolved and replaced by four separate United Nations agencies: the United Nations International Children's Emergency Fund; the International Refugee Organization; the Food and Agriculture Organization; and the World Health Organization.

While these four were ostensibly part of a 'United Nations family', each was given considerable autonomy within the United Nations system. Such autonomy would eventually have considerable, though not necessarily positive, consequences for the coordination of future international responses to disasters. However, in the context of the immediate post-war period, the independence given these agencies reflected both the hopes and fears of the UN's founders. Their hopes, as described by Luard, 'reflected the so-called "functionalist" theory under which international cooperation could not be imposed by some universal world organisation, but had to be built up by the experience of cooperation in individual fields where nations had common interests.'[10] Their fears centred principally around the political problems that threatened the work of the United Nations from the outset. Concerned that political problems would inevitably seep into the functional activities of the agencies, the founders sought to separate the activities of the United Nations from the UN's specialized agencies. Autonomy seemed to provide an appropriate solution.[11] Furthermore, the United Nations founders were worried that if the UN's Secretariat were placed in direct control over the agencies, the result would be an unwieldly and overly bureaucratic tangle.[12]

Hence, onto the stage of international relief were introduced four specialized agencies, each with its own councils and each with its own decision-making machinery:

(i)   The United Nations International Children's Emergency Fund was founded in December 1946 as a three-year temporary body principally aimed at post-war reconstruction. Its mandate covered two main tasks: aid for children and adolescents who were living in countries that were the victims of aggression or who had previously been receiving UNRRA assistance, and for child health in general. UNICEF's mandate was unique in the world of IGOs in three respects. Firstly, it can operate in any country without the approval of other governments. Secondly, it can operate in countries whose governments the UN's General Assembly has not recognized. Finally, UNICEF can actively seek funds from non-governmental sources, and has established over the years a wide network of private support groups.

(ii) The International Refugee Organization was set up in 1948 to take over the work of the 1947 Preparatory Commission for the International Relief Organization. The IRO from the outset had to sail very close to highly sensitive political winds, particularly with the influx into Western Europe of a large number of East Europeans. The West maintained that refugees and dislocated peoples could choose between repatriation to their countries of origin, while the East maintained that the IRO was obliged first and foremost to promote repatriation. In its four and a half years of existence, the IRO assisted over 1,619,000 displaced persons and operated over 670 refugee centres. By 1951, the IRO succumbed to political controversy and was replaced by the functionally more restricted Office of the United Nations High Commissioner for Refugees;

(iii) The Food and Agriculture Organization was established in October 1945 to rehabilitate farm, fishing and forestry production ravaged by the war. It also organized limited food emergency operations for seriously afflicted war victims.

(iv) The World Health Organization was the only one of the newly-formed specialized agencies that had a 'clear-cut reference to the principle of universal emergency assistance'.[13] Created in July 1946, WHO's constitution states that it is 'to furnish appropriate technical assistance and, in emergencies, necessary aid upon the request or acceptance of governments.'[14]

During this period, other UN specialized agencies involved in broadly defined emergency operations also appeared. The United Nations Relief and Works Agency, established after long debates in the UN General Assembly, was finally created in 1949 to assist refugees who had fled their homelands after the 1948 formation of Israel. The United Nations Korean Reconstruction Agency was but another example of a post-war specialized agency created to deal with the plight of disaster victims, in this instance those who were caught up in the Korean War.

Yet, neither the emergence of UNRWA nor of the UNKRA negates one very fundamental point, namely, that the institutions that were established after World War II were focused on relief that was conceptually restricted in terms of time, geography and approach. Relief as a concern for governments, IGOs and NGOs alike was orientated towards post-war Europe, and their experiences arising out of that involvement determined the nature of relief responses elsewhere for almost a generation.

Relief assistance tended to be ethnocentrically specific, dominated by Western cultural assumptions because these 'worked' in Europe. Relief requirements could be viewed as isolated, short-term injections of aid, since this approach had resulted in success in Europe. Relief, too, needed no external coordination, *per se*. The assistance and expertise proffered by governmental, non-governmental and inter-governmental agencies could be guided by the administrative structure of recipient governments.

In Search of Roles

The early 1950s posed institutional dilemmas for many, not only in the inter-governmental sector but in the private voluntary sector as well. The success of post-war reconstruction had ostensibly eliminated the need for emergency relief; and while there were still refugee problems and occasional disasters, neither of these appeared sufficient to justify the continued existence of the bevy of actors that had emerged during the post-war period. The crisis facing the British NGO, Oxfam, towards the end of 1948 epitomized the problem facing many IGOs and NGOs by the end of the decade. A strong body of opinion within Oxfam felt that, having fulfilled its initial purpose of aiding war-torn Europe, the organization should close down. Finally, by September of that year, after considerable soul-searching, Oxfam 'decided against closing down just because Europe was on the road to recovery . . . It resolved unanimously that . . . Suffering caused by the war had opened the way for a flood of goodwill which must try to meet need anywhere however caused.'[15]

The outlet for Oxfam's good-will, as well as that of many others, was in the field of development, principally in the southern hemisphere. Ironically, the more aid institutions became immersed in the problems of development, the more rapidly waned their interest in disasters and disaster relief. What appears ironic almost four decades later, is nevertheless understandable in the context of the times.

The early 1950s appeared to offer few challenges to the assumptions carried over from the post-war period about the nature of disaster relief. While less-developed nations (LDCs) were seen to require development assistance from international donors, relief aid was still principally a matter for governments of afflicted countries to handle. Disasters still, of course, elicited sympathetic responses and a degree of material assistance, as in the case of Ecuador's earthquake in 1949. However, the organization of relief and the bulk of relief assistance were responsibilities to be assumed by the government of the country in which a disaster had occurred. This attitude was not only consistent with post-war experience, but also reflected in large part the attitudes of governments and IGOs towards the issue of development. Development aid was initially regarded by developed states as a poor substitute for the benefits of trade expansion:

Domestic efforts in Southern states and domestic, not external, capital, it was argued, would have to be the primary means of economic development. Such domestic efforts would be enhanced and the need for external capital reduced by trade liberalisation. Expansion of trade would substitute for capital inflows.[16]

This Northern argument foundered on the all too evident fact that in most LDCs there was just not sufficient domestic capital to stimulate economic development and growth. The recourse to private banking institutions proved to be an inadequate alternative to meet the needs of LDCs, and the LDCs turned to multilateral organizations to plead their case. A variety of proposals appeared before the UN General Assembly, such as the International Development Authority (1951) and the Special United Nations Fund for Economic Development (1953). None of these LDC-sponsored initiatives led to any significant increase in aid, but they at least kept the issue before the public eye.

Disasters, too, played a part in keeping the causes of development before the public. Conflict in Korea and a large-scale famine in India in 1950 required considerable international assistance. Much of the funds for such emergencies came from the Technical Cooperation Administration, established in the United States to carry out Truman's 'Point Four' programme.[17] Significantly, a portion of this relief was distributed by American voluntary agencies which, under the United States 1949 Agricultural Act, were authorized to use surplus farm produce for relief and development purposes.

Yet, debates over development and occasional relief interventions were insufficient, in and of themselves, to sway the opposition of developed states to a change of stance. It was not until the mid-1950s that development began to emerge as a major institutional growth industry. One can point to three reasons for the increased attention given to development. The first is the tremendous transformation of the international system, reflected at least in the forum of the United Nations. Over a period of ten years since its formation, the United Nations had admitted seventy-two states to its original membership. By 1955, of 122 members, eighty-seven were developing countries. The change in complexion of the United Nations was particularly important in light of the second reason, namely the Cold War between East and West, which had intensified since 1948. Soviet involvement in the developing world, the socialist rhetoric of newly independent states and their turn towards 'non-alignment' brought East–West competition into areas well beyond the borders of Europe. Development aid became enmeshed in geo-political struggles. From the vantage point of donors it was a means both to lure and reward prospective allies.

A third reason for the take-off of development aid during the latter half of the 1950s was the general levels of affluence that were being attained throughout much of the Western world. Charity was affordable. As the media focused more and more on events in the developing world, the consciences of a growing number of people in developed nations were pricked by reports of poverty and misery elsewhere.

The transformation in attitude towards development was reflected both bilaterally and multilaterally. Bilateral aid grew very rapidly. In the United States, for example, a Development Loan Fund was launched in 1958 with an initial allocation of $300 million. Two years later, the United States provided one-third of the funds required to establish a $1 billion dollar Inter-American Development Bank. British and French aid also increased significantly. French aid rose from $648 million in 1956 to $863 million five years later. Similarly, British aid increased from $205 million in 1956 to $414 million in 1963.

New multilateral development funding agencies were also created. Under the International Bank for Reconstruction and Development, a subsidiary was established—the International Finance Corporation—to provide hard loans for private investment in underdeveloped countries. The lending capacity of the IBRD itself was doubled by 1958, from $10 billion to $20 billion, and two years later, again attached to the IBRD, the International Development Association was set up to provide soft loans to the LDCs. This trend was also reflected in the creation of the European Development Fund, established by the European Economic Community in 1957.

Aid was becoming big business, at least when compared with its paltry beginnings just a few years before. Specialist government and United Nations agencies and a host of voluntary organizations all began to have vested institutional interests in development. The development orientation, however, pushed disaster considerations even further down the scale of institutional priorities. If development was a growth industry, disaster relief was a no-growth area. Not only were disasters perceived as being the responsibility of affected governments, but for the development agencies they were an interference in their preoccupations with development. The big money was in the major infrastructural projects—dams, road networks, airports, turn-key industries—which marked governmental and IGO approaches to development of the late 1950s and 1960s. 'You can't build a career on disasters' was a statement that summed up the attitude of many.[18]

While careers may not have found firm roots in disaster relief, disasters were nevertheless increasingly seen as serving more abiding institutional interests. This was a fact appreciated as much by NGOs as by their IGO counterparts. Between 1950 and 1959, the numbers of private voluntary organizations had grown by almost 50 per cent.[19] Although the NGOs as a collectivity spanned a wide range of interests and activities, many of them found themselves competing for resources that relied upon public acceptance and recognition. The big development funds remained either in the hands of the major IGOs or were passed on through governments on a bilateral basis. For resources to fuel the different development interests of the burgeoning number of NGOs, the general public remained the major source of revenue.

In a very fundamental sense, throughout the early 1950s and 1960s, disasters provided a convenient device to reach potential donors. In no sense is this to suggest that the broad group of NGOs concerned with development saw disasters as purely an institutional convenience for raising funds. Most were fully and morally committed to assist those stricken by disasters, but in acting as focal points for the outpouring of public sympathy, they became increasingly aware that the drama of disasters could be turned to their advantage.

One key advantage was that disasters provided a means of promoting the image and funds of private voluntary organizations. Another was that the plight of disaster-afflicted peoples did to some extent underscore the poverty and despair that lay at the heart of the development message that NGOs were beginning to promote. Few in the NGO sector would deny the perverse reality that disasters did provide private voluntary organizations with a level of recognition and funding far more dramatic than their concerns with development. The public wanted channels for the outpouring of their sympathy for the disaster-stricken, and NGOs—either Church-based or non-sectarian—served as just that. There was no doubt in the words of one long-serving United States' NGO administrator that 'disasters filled the coffers' of the agencies.[20] Naturally, in so doing, disasters not only allowed agencies to exist, but they also gave agencies the resources to continue with their principal objectives, i.e. development.

The types of development activity that they undertook were essentially small scale. Education projects, water wells, health care and special feeding programmes in isolated rural areas, in small villages, were the development approach of the NGO sector. Small-scale projects providing direct assistance to the poor would eventually become a byword for appropriate assistance for a growing number of donor governments, IGOs as well as NGOs. For NGOs in the 1950s and early 1960s, scale was principally a reflection of the paucity of NGO resources.

Although NGOs served as convenient channels for public sympathy, few such private agencies differed in the assumptions and approaches that they took to disaster relief from the rest of the international community. Similarly to donor governments and inter-governmental organizations, private agencies assumed that governments of afflicted countries had the capability to deal with the process of relief distribution and assistance. Few agencies had extensive experience in those countries where disasters were now becoming manifest; few had any network of established contacts—save for some Church-based agencies—that could enhance the relief process; and few in fact had any expertise suitable to the types of disaster that were being faced. Nevertheless, as outlets for public concern, they were useful. And the role that disasters played in fostering their individual images and institutional interests would eventually be translated into valuable relief experience over the coming decade.

Inter-governmental organizations, also, had begun to accept an institutional interest in disasters; but, like NGOs, the relevance of disasters was but a marginal concern when compared to their preoccupations with development. To no small extent, such preoccupations reflected the attitudes of potential donor governments. These governments seemed hesitant to expand the relief roles of IGOs. The Food and Agriculture Organization (FAO), for example, had sought to establish an emergency relief capacity for over two years, between 1951 and 1953. However, the voluntary contributions that would have been required to set up such a fund were not forthcoming, and the initiative died.[21] The FAO, until the early 1960s, restricted its activities to development.

The United Nations International Children's Emergency Fund became the United Nations Children's Fund in 1953, a change in name that once again reflected not only institutional priorities but also the preferred orientation of governments. While its mandate was extended to include emergencies outside Europe, particularly in underdeveloped countries, UNICEF rapidly expanded into general health and welfare programmes directed towards long-term development needs. The World Health Organization, too, despite the fact that in 1954 a special fund was created to deal with emergencies, focused its efforts upon long-term development.

Of all the inter-governmental organizations that sought roles in the 1950s, the Office of the United Nations High Commissioner for Refugees was the one whose fate was most precarious. There was no development role *per se* for UNHCR. As Macalister-Smith points out, the fact that UNHCR did not inherit the role of the post-war International Refugee Organization 'reflected both States' weariness with the vast scale of the relief tasks of the predecessor organisations and the fervent hope that the need for exceptional, urgent or temporary relief measures was past.'[22]

Despite states' hopes, the problems of refugees did not of course disappear. Divisions in Europe during the early and mid-1950s increased the need for an inter-governmental body to provide both protection and assistance for Eastern Europeans flocking to the West. Furthermore, it was increasingly obvious that 'certain countries were facing particularly heavy burdens as an accidental result of their geographical situation'[23] and, by 1954, an emergency fund was established within UNHCR to provide a programme of permanent solutions. Incrementally, the authority and activities of UNHCR increased. Hungarian refugees in 1956, Chinese refugees in Hong Kong a year later, and refugees in North Africa during the late 1950s all led to an expansion of emergency activities on a level never anticipated five years before.

Yet, for the majority of IGOs, development was the institutional answer in their search for roles after the end of post-war rehabilitation. Development did not preclude disaster relief; but IGOs were wary of involvements that would not only divert resources from their main programmes, but also draw them away from the institutional security of development. From the perspective of the majority of IGOs, relief depended upon the voluntary contributions of donor governments or the diversion of resources from established programmes. Some organizations, such as UNICEF and WHO, sought to resolve the conflict by successfully appealing to their executive councils to establish special contingency or emergency funds.[24] Yet, no matter how relief funds might be made available, the demands that disasters could potentially make upon the resources of IGOs tended to keep the importance of disaster work as a low institutional priority.

To a significant extent, this attitude was sustained by governments upon whom the IGOs depended. Governments tended to view the role of inter-governmental institutions as principally one of development. They therefore merely confirmed the general IGO reaction that there were few interests to be served in becoming involved in relief activities for which the IGOs lacked expertise, resources and manpower.

Of course, like the NGOs, there were on occasion pressures for IGOs to become involved in disaster relief, particularly when a member state called for assistance. Not to be seen to be responding to the requests of the afflicted would diminish an IGO in the eyes not only of the requesting government but for other donor governments in the international community. The failure of one inter-governmental agency to respond to such requests also offered opportunities for other agencies to make their mark at the expense of the former. The latter would be seen to receive the kudos and good-will that ultimately could be translated into increased resources for institutional growth.

However, in the final analysis, disaster relief was not in fact part of the institutional role that IGOs had carved out for themselves during the 1950s. Their efforts were turned towards large-scale and well-funded infrastructural development. To some extent, this explained the distance, if not disdain, that separated the IGOs from non-governmental organizations.

As Willetts suggests, the involvement of non-governmental organizations in the activities of the United Nations was never greeted with much enthusiasm by the majority of the UN's founders, nor eventually by the UN Secretariat itself. It was really only pressure by the American delegation at the San Francisco conference in 1945 that led to Article 71 of the United Nations Charter, providing for NGO consultative status within the UN's Economic and Social Council. The type of consultative status that was provided depended upon the category of the particular NGO,[25] but in general terms the UN Secretariat showed little inclination to open its doors to the private agencies. The attitudes of the United Nations agencies towards private voluntary groups were only marginally different from those of the Secretariat. The kinds of development in which the specialized United Nations agencies were involved rarely offered opportunities for collaboration. The development approaches of the IGOs appeared to be beyond the scale of NGO capabilities to implement; and, paradoxically, the publicity that NGOs were learning to generate towards the end of the 1950s was seen as a potential threat to the interests of the United Nations specialized agencies.

In their dealings with IGOs, NGOs found it difficult to shrug off what some have referred to as their 'inferiority complexes'.[26] Lumbered with their image of eccentric do-gooders and blue-rinsed matronliness, the private voluntary agencies were regarded only too often as amateurs. Clearly, when it came to a comparison of available resources, the NGOs were in a league far apart from that of the relatively wealthy IGOs. Inevitably, both sides tended to keep their distance. The IGOs dealt with governments and concentrated on mega-projects, and the NGOs made do with their small projects and local contacts. It was not a healthy situation, but in the context of the interests and aspirations of both sides during the 1950s, it was understandable.

The results in terms of assistance to disaster-afflicted peoples were that relief was provided with few attempts at coordination either between donors and recipients or amongst donors themselves. Every relief operation in one way or another was marked by a degree of *ad hoc*ness, reflecting little institutional memory and uncertain, last-minute scrambles. Organizations—governments, IGOs and NGOs alike—each took their own routes to offer assistance. They approached each new disaster with little or no recollection of past mistakes or systematic analyses. Each new event was just that—new, requiring what one

LORCS official recalled as 'always reinventing the wheel'.[27] There were no focal points within any organization that concentrated solely upon disasters or disaster relief. Every new appeal necessitated a search for experts who might know at least something about the afflicted country or who had had some experience with relief measures, and similarly each such occasion meant for most donor institutions a scramble to see where relief funds could be found.

Responses on the whole were distinguished by some of the worst features of *ad hoc*ness: little coordination or systematization; minimal knowledge of appropriate measures; a cacophony of well-intentioned voices that viewed the problem of disaster relief from individual institutional perspectives. Compounding the uncertainty and unpredictability of international responses to disasters, there was a certain degree of 'benign neo-colonialism' as well. There was a lingering assumption that relief and spheres of influence and interest would coincide. It was assumed, for example, that the United States would help its disaster-stricken neighbours in Latin and South America, that the British would normally respond to the needs of its emerging Commonwealth, that Francophone Africa would receive assistance from its former colonial masters, and so on. Yet, in practice, responses in these 'spheres of concern' were by no means predictable. The assumption nevertheless disinclined those governments, IGOs and NGOs that could in theory form part of an international relief community to view either themselves or the relief process as a potential whole.

Institutional Answers

The 1960–4 crisis in the Congo was a revelation. The 'winds of change' blowing across the continent of Africa reflected the tragic side of independence. The aspirations of newly-independent states frequently foundered on the great gulfs between their goals and the availability of resources to attain them. Only too often, leaders of these new nations found that the solidarity that liberation struggles had instilled in their peoples rapidly dissipated after independence in the face of tribal and ethnic tensions, caused in no small part by the lack of resources to satisfy conflicting interests. As ill-prepared leaders grappled with economic and political complexities in their socially divided states, civil wars, mass dislocations, even famines became the reality of post-independence Africa.

The 1960s witnessed the fragility of an increasing number of new nations. Initial assumptions and aspirations for development had to be dramatically revised, and the search for new solutions was reflected in the creation of many new institutions to present the problems of the less developed world to the international community. Of greatest symbolic significance was the emergence of the Group of 77 in 1963. Given its numerical weight in the councils of the United Nations, this group or bloc of developing states was determined to use its strength to raise a broad range of trade and development issues in order to press for fundamental international reforms. Northern states were initially opposed to the initiative, but in light of the growing unity and sheer numerical strength of the Southern states, the North finally agreed to participate in the proposed United Nations Conference on Trade and Development, eventually held in Geneva in 1964. While the UNCTAD conference fell far short of meeting the objectives of its initiators, less developed nations at least established before the eyes of the world a level of bloc solidarity that few could have previously imagined.

As the results of UNCTAD showed, there was a limit to the type of reforms the developed world was willing to concede. Significant general preferential treatment in international trade was one of the broad-based reforms that proved a persistent barrier. Development aid, however, was to some extent a less divisive issue. The North felt that aid—particularly aid tied to its own industries—at least offered areas in which to make acceptable concessions.

Such aid concessions were by no means stimulated by magnanimity alone! The bloc of Southern states that had promoted the UNCTAD initiative were a force to be reckoned with in the United Nations and their territories still remained a lively arena for Cold War competition. The developing world was no longer isolated in a framework of 'colonial interests', but had emerged as a collectivity of nations that in one way or another influenced the course of global relations. To that extent, the South gained greater visibility. What happened in Africa, South or South-east Asia was no longer relegated to the affairs of empire; it was part of an increasingly complex global nexus, and increasingly their failings, strengths, weaknesses and aspirations came under the scrutiny of a widening international community. The same factors that heightened the attention of the industrialized world to the longer-term problems of underdeveloped nations also increased awareness of those nations' short-term crises, their disasters. It became increasingly apparent that many of the assumptions that underlay international attitudes about relief in the 1950s were being challenged by grim reality.

Disasters were indeed not intermittent events that could be described as 'localized acts of God'. They were persistent and societally erosive, all too often involving vast numbers of people and gnawing at the very stability of the state.[28] Nor, as it increasingly transpired, did the governments of less developed nations necessarily have the capacity to deal with their nations' disasters. The picture of post-war European states ultimately taking charge of their own disasters and guiding the relief resources of outside donors had little relevance in the context of the 1960s. The less developed world too often lacked the infrastructure, the administrative depth, the resources or the technical ability to deal with the emergencies it faced.

These grim realities were reflected in a spate of 'institutional answers' proffered by governments, IGOs and NGOs alike. For over a decade, from the early 1960s to the early 1970s 'relief cells', specialized agencies, and new departments emerged within governmental, IGO and NGO sectors to give specific attention to the problems of disasters and disaster relief. The focus of institutional attention, in other words, had evolved. No longer was the disaster field of little organizational consequence. Disasters inched up the ladder of institutional priorities, for reasons both humanitarian and pragmatic.

In humanitarian terms, one could not avoid the increased level of suffering owing to a whole range of different types of disasters that were being presented through the media. More pragmatically, however, the more such suffering was presented to the public in the developed world, the greater was the pressure on institutions with relevant roles and resources to respond. Disaster relief—the way in which an organization could mobilize its responses—became linked even more than in the 1950s to the way that an organization was assessed by potential supporters. Disasters provided organizations, non-governmental and inter-governmental organizations alike, a battlefront over which they could wave their institutional banners. Increasingly, it became important not only to be in the forefront of relief . . . where the cause was popular, but also to be seen to be there. The resources that organizations possessed to pursue their longer-term goals and to ensure their very survival and growth were intertwined with the new attention that disasters were receiving.

Paradoxically, while institutional interests in development as well as in their own survival were increasingly linked to disasters, the conceptual link between disasters and development was by and large ignored. The former remained isolated, a fact that explains why, from an operational perspective, the relief units and specialist agencies that were developing over the decade were poorly integrated into the general developmental work of the organization of which they were a part. Relief was handled as a separate and distinct aspect of aid. It was essentially a technical matter, involving the transfer of appropriate materials and resources and—on occasion—expertise to the afflicted nation. The idea that disaster prevention and preparedness could be linked with development was a perspective that was generally ignored. Development by and large was about mega-projects; disasters were the nuisances that now only too often interfered with the process of 'Westernizing' the less developed world.

The number of organizations in the voluntary sector increased quite considerably. Between 1960 and 1970, 289 major new non-governmental organizations were created, an increase of 26 per cent of the total that existed in 1959.[29] The vast majority of these had some form of developmental role, and directly or indirectly contributed to disaster relief. The rapid growth of the voluntary sector led many NGOs to feel the need for a more harmonious and coherent approach to the problems facing less developed nations. They needed, as far as possible, to turn their growing number towards influencing the approaches of donor governments and IGOs to development issues. In order to generate coherence and harmony amongst themselves as well as to create some semblance of united pressure upon the big governmental contributors, they formed the International Council of Voluntary Agencies in 1962. ICVA, however, proved to be little more than a talking shop, and certainly did not present the unity of focus for which it had initially been designed.

The difficulty of generating a united front or even of establishing a degree of harmony amongst its own diverse membership was made only too clear when, in 1965, ICVA set up a Commission on Emergency Aid. Here, one hoped at least that, in the face of serious, short-term disasters, the growing legion of NGOs might demonstrate a greater willingness to cooperate. Hope and practice, however, were separated by seemingly insurmountable hurdles. Members of the emergency aid commission appeared reluctant even to exchange information about their relief plans or activities, let alone cooperate together in relief operations. The good intentions underlying the ICVA could not circumvent voluntary organizations' mutual suspicions, their different orientations, and the simple fact that—with greater numbers—individual agencies had to intensify their competition for available resources.

It took the shattering experiences of the Nigerian civil war (1967–70), the Peruvian earthquake (1970) and the East Pakistan cyclone and subsequent civil war (1970–1) to awaken some of the larger voluntary organizations to the need to work more actively together. A vigorous effort to harmonize interests meant that not all agencies could necessarily be included, but at least if the major agencies could agree on a basis of cooperation, then the climate would be set for others. This attempt 'to get our house in order' led to the creation of the LORCS-Volag Steering Committee in 1972, comprising the League of Red Cross Societies, Catholic Relief Services, the Lutheran World Federation, Oxfam and the Church World Service.

'The Steering Committee was', according to one of its members, 'initially a fencing match amongst us, but when we got to know each other, discussions became increasingly frank.'[30] Whether that frankness really translated itself into useful exchanges of information, let alone a unified approach to disaster and development policies, is a question that to date remains very much open to debate.[31] Yet, what the Steering Committee did reflect was a growing self-awareness that the activities of voluntary agencies were increasingly under public scrutiny.

Increased public awareness about the activities of the voluntary agencies during the mid- to late 1960s had provided them with a growing degree of influence in government corridors. Agencies were learning how to become pressure groups, and governments were being forced to listen. That is not to suggest that elements of disdain for the 'do-gooding' activities of the voluntary agencies were totally erased from the minds of government and IGO officials. Certainly, a few USAID officials who had seen some of the dramatic disasters of the 1960s and 1970s felt that relief operations were frequently cluttered by the 'stuff from people's junk closets' that was passed on through voluntary agencies.[32] Yet, public awareness and intelligent use of the media were indeed giving voluntary agencies greater influence, and, to that extent, the agencies were listened to, if not actually heard, in the corridors of power.

Private agencies, despite the 'junk', did serve some practical purpose for officials within government and inter-governmental bodies. The fact that they did work at the 'grass-roots' level meant that they often knew better what was happening inside the countries where they were involved than accredited diplomats, sometimes even better than the bureaucrats of the host country. NGOs were gaining a reputation for understanding local conditions and, in times of disasters, the problems of the afflicted often better than most other outside observers; and in many instances they were able to transmit this information more quickly to the outside world than their IGO and governmental counterparts.[33]

Thus, public awareness, the very growth of agencies, their increasing usefulness, the concomitant inter-agency competition for public as well as government resources all led to a number of formal and informal institutions that were designed to promote more effective NGO–government liaison. This form of institutionalization can be seen from Table 2.1.

If governments were increasingly reconciled to their involvements with NGOs, the situation for the inter-governmental sector was perhaps more complex. Functionally, relations between IGOs and NGOs had logical divisions. The former were generally not 'operational', in other words they were funders, they were the multilateral outlets for relief assistance, but they did not actually work at the ground level of development or disaster assistance. For IGOs, the implementation of relief, for example, was the responsibility of the government of the disaster-stricken country and the non-governmental sector, both domestic and international.

But, despite this seemingly clear-cut division, there were points of overlap, potential conflict and, indeed, even competition. As IGOs became more involved in disaster relief, they were expected more and more to be alert to the onset of disasters and to be able to assess damage and needs. These activities to some extent overlapped with the warnings and assessments that voluntary agencies were also giving. The voluntary agencies, however, did not have to receive the formal assent of host governments to make their views known. They did not have

Table 2.1 Government–NGO liaison forums

Country	Forum	Date Est.
Belgium	Geographical sections in Service du Cofinancement et de l'Aide d'Urgence (SCAU) deal directly with NGOs and SCAU Personnel Department has section specifically for NGOs.	1976
Canada	Canadian Council for International Cooperation	1968
Denmark	DS-1 Danida Secretariat [*Restructured with sole concentration on NGOs]	1986*
Great Britain	NGO Section of the Overseas Development Administration	1982
Netherlands	NGO Coordinating Group	1973
Norway	Catastrophe Committee	1984
United States	Office for Private and Voluntary Cooperation, US Agency for International Development	1972
West Germany	Regular liaison meetings in Section 301, Ministry of Foreign Affairs	1978

to confront governments which, because of administrative problems or political sensitivities, were frequently reluctant to announce a disaster or, alternatively, insisted upon exaggerated reports of disaster impacts.

The greater constraints faced by IGOs, when compared with the freer NGOs, led to sharp differences over approaches and findings. NGOs criticized the cloistered world in which international civil servants lived. They berated their diplomatic niceties and their seeming unwillingness to leave for any period the confines of their comfortable offices and homes in capital cities. The NGOs were in so many instances first on the scene of a disaster because that was where they worked.

Such criticism, and in varous instances it was well deserved, did little to bridge the gulf between NGOs and IGOs. Despite the fact that an increasing volume of resources was being channelled from the IGO sector to NGOs in the field, a sense of distance, frustration and competition continued to mar their relations.

In his study of United Nations decision-making, Kaufmann has remarked that 'papers submitted by non-governmental organisations or speeches delivered by their representatives, with rare exceptions, receive scant attention'. He notes, however, from an assessment by H.A. Jack, that by 1974 at the World Food Conference where special meetings took place to discuss the blatant problems of food and famine, the voices of NGOs could no longer be ignored by the United Nations or its specialized agencies.[34]

However, the greater attention being received by NGOs by no means eliminated the strains between NGOs and IGOs. Indeed, the more publicity that the former received, the more the latter felt a sense of threat. NGO complaints that the international community was slow in responding to the needs of disaster victims were frequently interpreted as criticisms of the inter-governmental sector.[35] But the inter-governmental sector felt trapped between the inclinations of donor governments upon whom it depended, and the posturing of potential recipient governments who rarely deal with the IGOs in a consistent manner. State governments—be they donors or recipients—were both judge and jury of the IGOs, and it was upon them that their survival depended.

One such organization was the World Food Programme, established in 1963 as a joint responsibility of the United Nations and the Food and Agriculture Organization. The objectives of the WFP were to use food provided mainly by government donors for relief and emergency purposes as well as for social and economic development. Yet, after its trial period from 1963 to 1966, WFP, like most of its sister organizations, found greater institutional stability by devoting the vast majority of its resources and manpower to development. In part this reflected the very obvious fact that development was a much more time- and resource-consuming endeavour than periodic emergencies. However, it also reflected other realities, namely, that potential recipient governments were frequently loathe to admit that their countries faced food crises and that donor governments preferred to give emergency food aid bilaterally.

The WFP's potential role as a major actor in the relief process was shunted to a relatively unimportant position within the relief network. This would eventually begin to change over the subsequent decade in line with general international concern about emergency relief. Nevertheless, the World Food Programme's ability to respond to disasters continued to depend principally upon the resources (for example, in the case of the European Economic Community, the level of surpluses) that governments would make available.

Throughout the 1960s and early 1970s, an array of new organizations—private and governmental—had been created that could contribute to emergency relief. Few, however, had shown any tendency to coordinate their efforts or to professionalize the relief process beyond their own institutional boundaries. The ad hocness of the 1950s merged with the wave of new institutions of the 1960s and 70s, and the results were only too often more of the same unpredictable and disjointed responses. The failings of the system were apparent to many.

Certainly within the United Nations itself, there was a keen sense that, beyond platitudes of sympathy, the Secretariat played little part in the relief process. The General Assembly would commiserate with the disaster-afflicted and would urge the world community—including the specialized United Nations and private agencies—to provide assistance; but, 'needless to say, these resolutions did not necessarily commit any UN body to action in the particular country but merely served to demonstrate international concern for the plight of disaster victims.'[36]

By 1964, however, after a series of seven major disasters, attempts were made to assess the type of role that the Secretariat should have in the relief process.[37] For reasons not dissimilar to those which prevented effective collaboration amongst the NGOs, the idea of an overall coordinated United Nations approach to disaster relief met with a mild but by no means enthusiastic response. Many within the Secretariat were not convinced that relief assistance, let alone coordination, should be a role of the United Nations. Securing international stability and peace were sufficiently onerous responsibilities, and the practical constraints of manpower, resources and priorities seemed to leave little room for assuming an additional role in the highly technical area of disaster relief.[38] The specialized agencies within the 'United nations family' were more than willing to concur with the Secretariat's sentiments; so, too, for that matter did the League of Red Cross Societies, representing the world's largest NGO network, see that its own *raison d'être* and that of their national societies would be reduced by an enhanced United Nations role.

Major donor governments, while promoting the need for the United Nations to reassess its role in the field of emergency assistance, were lukewarm when it came to any responsibility that went significantly beyond a symbolic one. Governments were wary of losing the effect of the goodwill that bilateral relief assistance afforded them, and, anyway—so they argued—speed of response to the disaster-afflicted, though often disjointed, should not be sacrificed to a vague concept of internationalism.[39] Even the lukewarm interest shown by governments in providing the United Nations with a larger relief role waned rapidly, soon to be replaced by a much more modest interest in providing the Secretary-General with a 'disaster relief fund'. This was a proposal that was relatively cheap, and would avoid the complications and threats that a United Nations focal point might pose for governments, and agencies, both inter-governmental and voluntary.

Nevertheless, even this simple proposal was seen to present difficulties; for the United Nations Secretariat, funding for disaster relief *per se* was not regarded as a major problem. More often than not, in the estimates of the Secretariat, the resources of private voluntary organizations, governments and the specialized agencies were sufficient to meet the funding needs of most serious disasters; and there was concern among the Secretary-General's staff that the presence of a United Nations disaster fund would lead to a diminution of funds from donors who would expect the resources of the UN fund to carry the burden of relief. Furthermore, as Stephens points out, if any United Nations fund were to be made up of voluntary contributions, the spectre of the fund-starved International Relief Union of 1927 was a pervasive image.[40] The United Nations shied away from a role that seemed to be merely symbolic, and demonstrated little inclination to pursue responsibilities that it felt tangential to its main purpose.

As a compromise between the disinclinations of the United Nations and the essentially symbolic role that major donors sought to impose upon it, the Secretariat suggested in 1965 that a fund be established that would theoretically not overlap with the donations of other contributors. It was agreed that the United Nations could draw up to $100,000 per annum, with a maximum contribution of $20,000 for any single disaster. The self-imposed contribution criteria would be difficult to follow, but the limited size of the amount available for any single disaster clearly demonstrated that no matter how the United Nations' contributions were utilized, its practical impact would indeed be generally symbolic.[41]

The creation of an emergency fund by no means ended discussions on an appropriate United Nations disaster relief role, but the issue was allowed to simmer gently on the institution's back burners throughout the latter part of the 1960s.[42] As others have very ably described, it took three major disasters, between 1969 and 1971, to bring the simmering issue of the United Nations' role in emergency operations to the boil.[43] The civil war in Biafra, 1967–70, demonstrated a profound unwillingness and inability of the agencies as well as the Secretariat to intervene in a highly sensitive political situation involving all aspects of a complex disaster: famine, refugees, and threat to civilian populations. Conversely, the earthquake in Peru in May 1970 underscored another failing for, in this instance, the United Nations agencies—together with the massive intervention of other donors—'invaded' Peru's afflicted northern mountain region. Massive volumes of aid of all types—inappropriate and appropriate— inundated the affected areas, and the Peruvian government's attempts to control the situation were thwarted by the sheer weight of external pressures.[44] Less than six months later, in South Asia, the international community, including the United Nations' specialized agencies, found itself embroiled in another series of major natural and man-made disasters. Once again, the spectre of a relief siege appeared, this time over the cyclone-devastated delta of East Pakistan; and once again, faced with the complications of Pakistan's 1971 civil war, the United Nations and the rest of the international community found itself perplexed as to the appropriate response.[45]

For the United Nations system and the donor community at large, the experiences of the late 1960s and early 1970s were catalytic. In one very general sense, disaster phenomena were regarded more and more as a distinct and well-defined area of concern which demanded far greater concerted attention than had been the case at any time since the World War II. Less and less were disasters to be treated as problems that disrupted the vital business of development. Disasters, as reflected in various important institutional adjustments, were gaining a foothold in the priority concerns of the donor community and, similarly to the sudden increase in NGOs in the 1960s, relief 'cells' began to blossom in governmental and inter-governmental sectors. These 'cells'—either wholly new and independent structures or fixed focal points within established organizations—were designed to provide contact points for information, for assessment evaluation, for speedy intervention in disasters, and even in some instances to assist in disaster prevention and disaster preparedness. In the overwhelming majority of cases, the mandates of these cells were far more extensive than the funding and manpower available to fulfil them. Nevertheless, if institution-building at least reflected a search for solutions, then the developments noted in Tables 2.2 and 2.3 below do suggest an ostensible commitment to improving the responsive capabilities of various governments and inter-governmental agencies.

It would be naive to suggest, however, that the growth of specialist relief cells, particularly in the inter-governmental sector, was solely due to a sudden awakening to the growing dimension of disaster problems. Much of the stimulus to strengthen the individual relief roles of the specialized United Nations agencies was spurred on by institutional insecurities. Not only did the voluntary organizations frequently show up the failings of IGOs, but initiatives within the United Nations itself were threatening the boundaries of established specialized agencies. The growth of relief cells, in other words, was fuelled in no small part by inter-agency competition. No agency with even a residual role in relief could afford to be outdone by another. It became axiomatic that relief competence and organizational security went hand-in-hand.

Symptomatic of the specialized agencies' concerns was the emergence of the Office of the United Nations Disaster Relief Coordinator in 1972. Born out of the simmering discussions that lasted throughout the mid- and late 1960s on the United Nations relief role and the very apparent problems that had emerged by the end of that decade, the UN's Office of Inter-Agency Affairs had prepared an extensive document which, among other things, reintroduced the possibility of a role for the Secretary-General as an initiator of relief coordination.[46]

Almost two years of arduous discussions preceded the creation of UNDRO. Some nations, up to the weekend before the General Assembly was to vote on the proposal, were still adamantly opposed to the creation of a United Nations disaster relief office. Others, while accepting the need for a UN office that could

Table 2.2 Disaster units in United Nations Organizations

Organization	Unit/function	Date
Food and Agriculture Organization	Office for Special Relief Operations (arose out of the Office for Sahelian Relief Operations–1973)	1975
United Nations High Commissioner for Refugees	Emergency Office	1980
United Nations Children's Fund	Office of the Emergency Operations Coordinator	1971
World Food Programme	Emergency Unit	1975
World Health Organization	Emergency Relief Operations Office	1974
United Nations Development Programme	Role of Resident Representatives to coordinate relief operations on country level designated in UN Res. 2816 (XXVI) December	1971
United Nations Disaster Relief Office	Main activity to mobilize, direct and coordinate relief activities of UN system as stipulated by UN Res. 2816 (XXVI) December	1971
Pan-American Health Organization	Emergency Preparedness and Disaster Relief Coordinator	1977
United Nations Office of the Coordinator for Special Economic Assistance	Concerned with economic emergencies threatening economic viability of member states	1977

Table 2.3 Disaster units established in major donor governments

Country	Name of unit & ministry	Date Established
Belgium	Section C-25, Service Catastrophes Naturelles Service du Confinancement et de l'Aide d'Urgence Ministry of Foreign Affairs	1978 1982
Canada	International Humanitarian Assistance Division, Canadian International Development Agency	1978
Denmark	DM-1-DANIDA, Ministry of Foreign Affairs [Disaster relief was part of DANIDA's main role when it was established in 1962. DM-1 resulted from reorganization which took place in 1986]	1962/86
France	La Cellule d'Urgence et Veille, Ministry of Cooperation	1985
Great Britain	Disaster Unit, Overseas Development Administration	1974
Netherlands	Emergency and Humanitarian Aid Section, Ministry of Foreign Affairs	1975
Norway	Coordination of Disaster Relief Section, Ministry of Foreign Affairs	
Sweden	Section for Emergency Relief Assistance, Swedish International Development Authority	1975
Switzerland	Directorate for Cooperation Assistance and Humanitarian Aid, Federal Department of Foreign Affairs	1972
United States	Office of US Foreign Disaster Assistance, Agency for International Development	1964
West Germany	Section 301, Ministry of Foreign Affairs	1978

intervene in natural disasters, did not want to extend the proposed office's mandate to man-made disasters. But even more fundamental was the question of what UNDRO should really do: what was the purpose—and more important—the authority, of this new institution?

The initial draft resolution called for a United Nations organization that would 'mobilise, direct and coordinate relief activities of the various organizations of the United Nations system in response to a request for disaster assistance from a stricken country.'[47] There was considerable resistance to the term 'direct' from a variety of quarters, from UN agencies (e.g. UNICEF), from voluntary agencies (the League of Red Cross Societies) and from various governments, including the Soviet Union and France, all of whom felt that 'direct' imperilled their freedom of choice and action.[48] Nevertheless, with the assurance from American and British delegates to the United Nations that 'direct' would be more analogous to a 'traffic cop' speeding up the flow of traffic rather than determining which car was to go where and when, Resolution 2816(XXVI), creating UNDRO, was finally approved in December 1971. The resolution allowed the Secretary-General to appoint a Disaster Relief Coordinator, who would refer to and consult directly with the Secretary-General. In the same resolution the Secretary-General's allocation to provide disaster assistance was increased (i.e. $200,000 a year and $20,000 to any single disaster), but in reality UNDRO's mandate—no matter how ambiguously drafted—significantly outstripped its actual capacity to fulfil it.[49]

This fact was clearly understood; but, as many embroiled in the discussions were fully aware, creating an institution was one thing, the implications of allowing it to fulfil its mandate were, however, another.[50] The desire to maintain control over the reins of relief had entrenched proponents throughout the relief community. Even with significant adjustments in its financial resources and manning levels, five years later UNDRO continued to meet an all-too-apparent resistance to using the organization as some had at least in theory intended.[51]

Given the propensity for inter-governmental organizations to keep the voluntary agencies at a distance and, conversely, the more than ambivalent attitudes of the NGOs to the IGOs, it was remarkable to see the assistance that voluntary agencies—principally the League of Red Cross Societies—provided the newly-formed United Nations Disaster Relief Office.[52] While the League provided the main bulk of practical assistance to UNDRO, other voluntary agencies clearly gave it their support.[53]

To a significant extent, such assistance and support marked not only the private agencies' general acceptance of the need for greater international relief coordination, but also their growing self-confidence and acceptance in the international community. For all the failings of the international relief community in Nigeria/Biafra, Peru and East Pakistan, the voluntary agencies' contributions and efforts—when compared with those of others—seemed more effective. This is not to absolve them on their continued tendency to compete with each other or of their frequent willingness to conform to the dictates of public pressure—in conflict with the needs of the afflicted. It is instead to suggest that, when compared to assistance provided directly through donor or recipient governments or United Nations organizations, their approaches appeared to a growing body of opinion to be more relevant, imaginative, and appropriate.[54]

Part of the reason for this increased appreciation of the work of voluntary agencies stemmed from the more professional attitudes of donor governments themselves. More and more governments in the donor community were instituting relief cells which, like their counterparts in inter-governmental organizations, sought to monitor and coordinate relief assistance; and these responsibilities led to increased links with the voluntary sector and a growing acceptance of the latter's professionalism.

Professionalism alone, however, did not explain these evolving links. Much of the driving force that established increasingly close contacts can be ascribed to the complex nexus of the media, public pressure, interest groups and government. The media, as both consumer and producer of news, became an integral part of the rush to justice. Voluntary agencies became adept at putting their points of view to the press, radio and television; and governments found themselves more and more called upon to justify their own responses to disasters through the media in the wake of media-aroused public interest and outcries; and the public—increasingly exposed to the horrors of disasters through the growth of the media—seemed to respond. All depended upon the perceived intensity of disaster victims' plights, as determined by what the media presented.[55]

The media proved more than adept at stimulating the concerns of the public. It also proved extremely adept at unveiling apparent deficiencies in the relief process. Indeed, a disaster litany was begining to evolve—in part justifiable, in part irresponsible, in part based upon a profound lack of understanding about the nature and problems of disasters—which became the glossary of the media's analysis of disaster management. Governments of the afflicted were frequently portrayed as 'callous' or 'indifferent' to the plight of their peoples; 'corruption' normally abounded, 'politics' and 'bureaucratic delays' explained the vagaries of relief assistance ('relief never reached the needy'), duplication, and lack of coordination. These were just some of the characterizations constantly conveyed about a large proportion of disaster relief operations.[56]

Such criticisms contained more than an element of truth, but, more often than not, they failed to take account of the complexities of responding to disasters and providing relief. Yet, despite the fact that the litany suffered on more than a few occasions from over-simplification and exaggeration, certain issues hit home: one was inter-agency competition; another was lack of coordination.

Discordant Cries for Coordination

The advent of video technology in the late 1970s changed the balance of disaster reporting from the printed word to television. Television could now provide viewers with instant visual displays of the full horrors of disasters and the terrible plight of disaster victims. And there was certainly no lack of possible stories. From 1976, the number of natural disasters increased and so, too, did the number of deaths and afflicted.[57] Man-made conflicts also began to generate hitherto unforeseen dimensions of tragedy. By 1980, 9,000,000 refugees from twenty-eight countries had fled conditions of searing violence to seek asylum and aid across national boundaries. By the end of the decade, there were approximately 7.5 million 'internally displaced' people who had had to abandon their homes and livelihoods to seek safety from civil strife elsewhere in their own countries.[58]

Despite the refocused interest in disasters and the relatively intense period of institution-building, the emerging horror and complexity of disasters required a more flexible, systematic and coherent approach to assistance. What was required 'were not more institutions, but greater willingness to coordinate the capabilities and resources of those already in existence. Existing institutions would have to demonstrate a capacity to share responsibilities for assessment and to adjust institutional boundaries where necessary to meet the crises at hand. From the mid-1970s into the early 1980s, governments, IGOs and NGOs all seemed to be acknowledging the need for greater coordination of the international relief network.[59]

However, beyond the level of platitudes, coordination posed innumerable problems, and found few adherents when it came to implementing a relief operation. Donor governments, as Kissinger was to remind the United States in 1973, increasingly viewed disaster relief as a means of consolidating bonds with friendly states.[60] If coordination meant a greater shift away from bilateralism towards multilateralism then, from the perspective of most government donors, relief would indeed be difficult to coordinate. On the other hand, if coordination was merely a matter of providing information about the nature of a donor's commitment, then—with the appropriate mechanism in place, for example UNDRO—coordination under most circumstances could be improved.

NGOs, too, picked up the cry for greater coordination. They were not reluctant to point the finger at donor governments and IGOs for perpetuating disjointed approaches to relief, but they rarely provided an example from their own activities of how best to promote effective cooperation and coordination. It was not that the voluntary sector necessarily lacked the will. The Licross-Volags Steering Committee, as mentioned earlier, did attempt to introduce some coherence into the relief process. It had shown tremendous support for the United Nations Disaster Relief Coordinator, lending personnel and sponsoring a rapid exchange information system. To that extent, the major NGOs had certainly demonstrated far greater will than either the majority of governments or indeed inter-governmental organizations.

Nevertheless, such efforts were the result of a few agencies only, and did not necessarily represent the commitment of the vast majority. Nor could the efforts of these few even eliminate the practical pressures they faced when it actually came to undertaking a relief operation. Despite their concern to promote greater network-wide coordination, the realities of different institutional perspectives and the persistent demands of fundraising often meant that the voluntary agencies—at headquarters and field levels—were no more cohesive in their activities than those whom they criticized.

To a large extent, the ostensible determination of those who espoused the need for coordination was laid at the doorstep of the IGO sector. Having actively pressed for a more effective international relief network, governments had supported the efforts of the United Nations agencies to create specialized relief cells; they even established a separate agency, namely UNDRO, to direct international relief efforts. From the point of view of donors, if coordination was to have any meaning, it would be translated into the activities of the IGOs. Similarly, NGOs also saw that the cry for coordination would largely have to be picked up by the inter-governmental sector; for IGOs had direct access to both donor governments and governments of the afflicted, and it was at that level that coordination had ultimately to be agreed. Furthermore, IGOs, relatively speaking, had the power of the purse to foster cooperation and coordination among the NGOs. With the bulk resources that the former often had at their disposal, they could impose greater coherence on relief operations by determining which private agencies should do what with whose resources. Yet, all this depended on the inter-governmental community taking the lead, proving first of all that it could get its own house in order.

To many, the relief operation in the drought- and famine-afflicted Sahel in Africa in the early 1970s demonstrated not only the difficulties of coordination but also glimmers of hope that a cohesive approach to relief could be achieved. As early as spring 1972, the Inter-governmental Committee of the World Food Programme had recommended that six Sahelian states should be provided with emergency food aid. By September, the Food and Agriculture Organization intensified its warnings of the looming disaster, and by then various governments and NGOs had begun to provide assistance.

Yet, despite the FAO's warnings and evidently deteriorating conditions in the Sahel, United Nations' involvement at the outset was negligible. The United Nations Disaster Relief Office, the recently created coordinating mechanism, failed to become involved because of its youth, inexperience and inadequate staff and resources.[61] It was only because of the fact that donors recognized the need for greater operational coordination that any United Nations agency seemed initially to become involved at all. The World Food Programme (WFP), by March 1973, agreed to act as a focal point for information about shipping matters. It was an important role, for limited port and internal transport meant that accurate timing about arrivals became one of the critical factors in the operation's success or failure. However, the fact that the relief operation was already under way prevented the WFP from really gaining any control over even the informational aspects of the relief effort. It was evident, according to the United States General Accounting Office (USGAO), that 'the WFP lacked the necessary authority to insure an even flow of donor food shipments, and most donors had already made firm plans for shipping the majority of their committed food.'[62]

The lacklustre performance of the WFP came at a time when the true extent of the crisis was becoming a highly visible issue. In light of the increased expectations of a United Nations role in relief matters in general, the Secretary-General turned to the Food and Agriculture Organization to act as the UN focal point for all emergency assistance from the UN system to the Sahel. Unlike the WFP, the FAO at the time had the standing within the donor community to enhance the status of a single responsible coordinator. With the full authority of the UN Secretary-General and with the growing death-toll of the famine, the FAO could command the necessary clout.

The FAO set up a special office—the Office of Sahelian Relief Operations (OSRO)—to supervise the United Nations input. However, in its initial attempts, OSRO, like the earlier more restricted efforts of the WFP, found little cooperation. Agencies within the UN system were acting independently of OSRO, and donor governments themselves were only too often failing to provide OSRO with information on consignments and transport schedules.

OSRO's problems were quite simple. It lacked staff, experience and effective field organization and communications systems. Basically, in its early form, it had little to offer donors, and was but an additional appendage to an increasingly chaotic relief venture. The only way for OSRO to fulfil its intended mission was to find ways to compensate for its weaknesses. It could not acquire its own resources, systems or experts in sufficient time to make an impact on the operation, but it could use those of others to achieve its aim.

OSRO set about persuading the donor community to focus on three important issues. The first was to determine what were the key problems affecting the operation. Rather than rely on its own very limited expertise, OSRO officials convened a series of donor meetings in 1974 to get the donors to define and discuss the various aspects hampering relief measures. One result of such meetings led, in June 1974, to the creation of coordinating committees composed of donor representatives to monitor the flow of relief traffic in every major Sahelian port.

The second issue that OSRO persuaded donors to consider concerned information. Since information was so important, OSRO set out to establish with all those making contributions what sort of specific information they required. By April 1974, an agreed informational format was devised in conjunction with all donors. In having agreed on what they wanted, donors also committed themselves to supply the type of information on which they had all agreed.

Finally, there was the question of assessment. Once again, OSRO accepted that it had neither the manpower nor the resources to determine the individual damage and needs generated by the Sahelian drought. However, if it could rely on experts from other organizations, then OSRO's assessment functions could be expedited. Of course, the question of which experts—in a jealous international grouping of agencies—would be chosen remained to be resolved. The solution, in one sense, was patently obvious: multi-donor missions. Those who had major contributions to make to the relief operation were to be combined into a single assessment unit, and through such multi-donor missions, they could arrive at not only commonly accepted assessments, but also generally accepted relief standards.

The Sahelian experience for many in the international relief network provided an interesting revelation. Emerging out of all the mishaps, the failed initiatives and the initial complacency, came at least a demonstration that in the end a semblance of coordination could be generated. In many instances, IGOs, NGOs and governments eventually showed considerable institutional flexibility; they were willing to act in concert in terms of providing information and assessment procedures; they demonstrated a degree of constraint in adhering to shipping and transport schedules.

It was not the case that the overall operation could be described necessarily as a success. Monitoring of deliveries, accountability, deliveries themselves, all were aspects that were open to severe criticism. But, in the wake of all these complaints, there was at least a glimmer of systematization. Did this have any implications for the future?

The answer began to emerge in the form of United Nations Resolution 3243, proposed late in 1974 by thirty nations. The resolution called upon the Secretary-General to increase the effectiveness of the United Nations Disaster Relief Office to coordinate international disaster relief. By March 1975, based on the conclusions of a panel of experts, a series of measures was proposed to enhance international coordination. Among these, two proposals are of particular relevance to appreciate the hopes of the drafters. UNDRO itself was to be significantly strengthened. Additional funds, providing for more sophisticated communications equipment, a tripling of staff and increased operational resources, were proposed and eventually approved later in 1975.[63] UNDRO was to be enlarged in such a way that the mandate it had been given three years earlier might actually become that bit more realistic.

Of equal significance was the recommendation that negotiations be undertaken among the United Nations agencies to institutionalize 'present informal understandings' about the roles and responsibilities of each in times of disaster. These arrangements were to specify not merely agreed institutional boundaries, but also the specific contributions, i.e. procurement, transportation, special staff, that each would provide for disaster relief. The implication for the agencies was that coordination was to be fostered through formalized arrangements. If the agencies were unable to demonstrate an ability to cooperate through informal understandings, then they would have to order their affairs through pre-arranged and formal agreements. In a sense, coordination was to be imposed. It was expected, and the agencies would have to concur.

The efforts made by UNDRO between 1976 and 1980 to regularize its relations with other UN agencies and the League of the Red Cross reflected in large part the wishes of the major donors. Beyond that, however, it also reflected a general assumption that coordination could be structured and that careful delineation of responsibilities—confirmed by precise agreements—would be the major step in that direction. Of such agreements, perhaps the most important was that signed between UNDRO and the United Nations Development

Programme in 1979.

Since its creation in 1966, the United Nations Development Programme had become the single largest specialized body within the United Nations family. It had grown fast, and its involvement was extremely wide. With offices in the capitals of most developing countries, UNDP carried a lot of institutional weight, and this was reflected in the responsibility given to UNDP resident representatives in the capitals of these countries to bring together their colleagues from other agencies to discuss issues of mutual concern. According to the resolution which created UNDRO in 1972, UNDP resident representatives were accorded a 'key role' in coordinating emergency assistance at the local level. UNDP, however, had shown little predisposition 'to give disaster work a high development priority', for such work—from UNDP's perspective—often raised sensitive issues for both donor and recipient governments that could complicate the all-important longer-term relations between UNDP and host governments.[64]

Hence, given seven years of UNDP reluctance to wear an UNDRO hat, the memorandum of understanding between the two in 1979 could well be regarded as something of a breakthrough, demonstrating, if nothing else, that the agencies were attuned to what was being expected of them by a good portion of member states. The key feature of the agreement was that UNDP formally acknowledged that its resident representatives should take an active part in acting on behalf of UNDRO to head 'relief committees' in disaster-afflicted states. What in practical terms the resident representatives could do within such *ad hoc* committees to foster cooperation and coordination was another matter, but in principle an important formal mechanism was created.[65]

The tentative steps taken on the inter-governmental level towards a permanent disaster focal point were momentarily halted by the beginning of the 1980s with the publication of the UN Joint Inspection Unit's (JIU) 'Evaluation of the Office of the UN Disaster Relief Coordinator'.[66] The evaluation was damning, leaving little that had been achieved to date untouched. However justifiable the criticisms of UNDRO's administrative structure and its inability to coordinate, the real issue that the JIU inadvertently exposed was the extent to which member states were determined to have a single UN disaster relief focal point. All the arguments that ensued during the conception of UNDRO in 1971 arose again, only this time with nine years' evidence to sustain arguments of proponents and opponents alike.

Should UNDRO deal solely with natural disasters; should its functions be brought directly under UNDP; what was really meant by coordination, let alone direction? The JIU's recommendations, which were supported by many highly experienced officials within and outside the United Nations, were to restrict quite dramatically UNDRO's responsibilities. UNDRO, it concluded, should only deal with 'sudden natural disasters'. The UNDRO voluntary trust fund should be dismantled, and UNDP's Governing Council should oversee that of UNDRO. For all other areas of disaster activities, the JIU proposed that an inter-agency Emergency Assistance Committee should be created to:

respond to the broader humanitarian issues necessitated by disaster of all kinds and to preparedness and prevention needs . . . The Committee should not oversee or be required to approve humanitarian and related emergency assistance work by UN system organisations when their mandates clearly specify their responsibilities.[67]

The JIU's evaluation created an authority vacuum that many of the specialized agencies were not unhappy to exploit. The evaluation's recommendation of an inter-agency Emergency Assistance Committee would inevitably mean that each agency would be fully represented on such a committee. Within the formal structure of such a committee, each agency would be equal to the other, a fact greeted with enthusiasm by all other than UNDRO. Even more important was the recognition that the proposed committee would not oversee work by 'UN system organisations when their mandates clearly specify responsibilities'. To all intents and purposes, that phrase would put paid to any attempt by any other organization to have a permanent coordinating and directing role . . . whatever those terms actually meant.

The agencies' sense of liberation from the spectre of formal coordination by a single UN focal point was short-lived, however. A larger body of opinion—representing key donor governments as well as a broad spectrum of developing countries—was still unwilling to abandon its aspirations for UNDRO. Whatever UNDRO's experiences to date, few governments appeared willing to return to the *ad hoc*ness that a truncated UNDRO seemed to foretell.[68]

Consistent with member states' general inclinations and contrary to the Joint Inspection Unit's recommendations, the UN Secretary-General proposed a new plan at the end of 1982 'for all governments and relevant agencies to cooperate with the United Nations Disaster Relief Coordinator'. The 'experiment' was to continue, and UNDRO was to receive an increased trust fund, a higher disaster assistance ceiling (from $30,000 to $50,000), and a reaffirmation of UNDRO's role as the 'focal point' of the United Nations system for disaster relief coordination.

The almost unanimous endorsement by member states of the December 1982 resolution was clear evidence that a formal mechanism for international relief coordination was still deemed essential. In this respect the UNDP Administrator's instructions of October 1983 to headquarters staff and field offices can be regarded as an important step back on the trail which many agencies hoped would be abandoned after the JIU's 1980 report. In the words of the instructions, 'many resident representatives have been appointed UN resident coordinator [for UNDRO], their responsibilities in relation to disasters have, if anything, been increased.' Resident representatives were to assume more active roles, not only in the coordination of emergency operations, but also in equally sensitive matters of disaster preparedness and prevention.[69]

The reassertion of UNDRO's important coordinating role and the seeming acceptance of it by many of the network's key components were not sufficient to ensure practical compliance. While yet another General Assembly resolution, in 1984, called for even further enhancement of UNDRO's responsibilities,[70] there were practical realities that eroded formal resolutions and agreements. These realities reflected the complexities of a new spate of disasters in the early 1980s and continuing institutional determination to maintain relative autonomy, neither of which could easily be laid to rest through formal understandings.

The new spate of disasters and a resurgence of institutional independence fed on each other: they were interactive forces. The disaster which befell Kampuchea in 1979–82 was but one example. The horrors instigated by Kampuchea's Pol Pot regime had led to an exodus of refugees leaving Kampuchea for the safety of the Thai and Vietnamese borders. With the overthrow of that regime in 1979, the Heng Samrin government was installed in Phnom Penh by invading Vietnamese forces. The civil war that ensued intensified the flight of hundreds of thousands of Kampucheans to Thailand. Furthermore, the civil war, combined with the mass destruction of Kampuchea's agricultural structure by Pol Pot, was reportedly taking Kampuchea to the brink of virtual starvation. Kampuchea was a horrifying example of all the potent elements of a complex disaster at play.

Thailand was concerned that to accord the Kampucheans on its borders the status of refugees would be regarded as a hostile act by Vietnam. The government in Bangkok chose instead to take the position that the Kampucheans were 'economic migrants'. This position, in turn, led the United Nations High Commissioner for Refugees to accept that 'economic migrants' were outside its mandated authority to provide assistance. During the same period, the growing alarm about famine within Kampuchea posed another dilemma. The Pol Pot regime was still the officially recognized government of Kampuchea, and the *de facto* government of Heng Samrin was not. Hence, it was only the former that could formally request international assistance, while, ironically, it was the latter that had control of the machinery of state that could assist in the organization and distribution of aid.

To outsiders, witnessing the massive emergency on both sides of the border, the situation was absurd. International means of assistance were being thwarted by international rules and procedures that—when faced with millions of suffering people—made little sense. The situation was left open for those who had the capacity to respond to take up the cause. The United Nations Children's Fund was able to begin operations because of the relative flexibility of its mandate which allows it to operate in any country without the approval of other governments. The International Committee of the Red Cross could also respond, because of its internationally accepted role of helping all who are victims of conflict. Private voluntary agencies could also undertake relief measures, since they fell outside any official restraints imposed by governments.

While UNHCR and other IGOs, for example the WFP, eventually entered into the relief fray, it was only too apparent from the initial stages of the relief operations that systematic and well delineated relief efforts were only too vulnerable to the disruptive impacts of more abiding interests. It was all very well to talk about an international focal point and to accept the principles of coordination and mutually acceptable spheres of responsibility; but when it came down to the practical realities of implementing relief, too many variables entered into the picture.

Kampuchea, both within and along its borders, was in one sense a unique disaster. Few disasters have been of equal proportions, both in terms of dimension and complexity. Nevertheless, for all its extreme features, it did point to what seemed to be certain basic truths. No matter how one might try to systemize the behaviour of IGOs, the different tendencies of donor and recipient governments will always add uncertainty and unpredictability to inter-governmental behaviour. No matter how formal the understandings between IGOs, the opportunity costs for individual agencies of not responding to a disaster in terms of their own institutional interests are too high to make them adhere consistently to any pre-arranged agreements.

NGOs, too, have to react in terms of institutional opportunity costs; and since there are few formal means of meshing their responses on a systematic basis with other relief components, coordination and cooperation also depend on the externalities of any particular situation. Governments, for all their insistence on international coordination, are in fact the worst violators of systematic and regularized responses. If, for example, the wife of the President of the United States had not in 1979 personally become involved in publicizing the plight of the Kampucheans, an American response might have been delayed for many more months than it had already.[71] Governments pick and choose how and when they will react to calls for or offers of assistance; and their inconsistent responses perpetuate unsystematic behaviour throughout the entire relief network.

The Plural Capabilities Option

George Davidson, a former UN Under-Secretary for Administration and Management, had considerable experience in the basic functional, day-to-day affairs of the United Nations. He was one of those who felt that the United Nations should not really have disaster relief responsibilities; yet when, in 1980, he was called upon by the Secretary-General to consider what the United Nations required 'to meet humanitarian needs in emergency situations', he responded with his usual dedication and efficiency.

In Davidson's view, the goal of an effective UN relief effort from the point of view of coordination and cooperation should be that the 'systems' speak with one voice. However, 'if the components of the United Nations system and the cooperating inter-governmental and voluntary agencies are not to speak with "one voice", the least that can be expected of them is that they perform as a harmonious chorus and not as a babble of dissonant and discordant voices.'[72] In Davidson's view, there were too many impracticalities in seeking to impose an overall coordinating agency on the various relief sectors; similarly, there were just too many factors that tended to erode formally instituted coordinating and cooperative arrangements. Davidson believed that realism demanded a looser, more flexible approach that emphasized agencies 'sharing their common burden.'[73]

In other words, continued pursuit of more precisely defined mandates or more formal coordinating mechanisms would inevitably lead nowhere. One had to live with the realities of an inherently competitive system, and let cooperation flow from perceived mutual interests. One such way was a greater emphasis upon 'joint assessment procedures' that would not necessitate overt coordination, *per se*, but offered a means by which agencies could each proffer their specific potential contributions to a relief operation without relegating their individual institutional interests to an overall authority. A team comprising representatives of interested agencies would be sent to a scene of disaster, and would individually suggest the type and level of assistance that each would provide. It was hoped that all agencies would channel updates on the assistance they were contributing through UNDRO; but beyond this procedure, there was a general de-emphasis on formal coordinating structures.

Joint assessments seemed to be relatively effective as long as certain conditions applied. In Chad in 1983, joint assessment proved effective. This was due to several important considerations: the food disaster was being managed away from the glare of publicity; the government of Chad felt that it was in its interests to work with the IGO joint assessment team; there were only a few small non-governmental organizations involved in the emergency operation. The resources required for the first stages of the operation were relatively small, the problems facing the country relatively defined and sufficient time had been available to structure the joint assessment procedures at headquarters level.[74]

However, Chad represents a relatively unusual case. In disasters of the sudden-onset variety, there is a propensity for organizations to respond to immediate information in ways governed by their own interpretation of events.

Where they feel compelled to be seen to be responding, the time for 'joint assessment' is sacrificed to perceived urgency. Hence, in the 1985 Mexico City earthquake disaster, ninety-one special aircraft had been despatched from countries all over the Northern and Western hemispheres, and 'the American Red Cross was forced to divert a planeload of medical supplies to an airport 150 miles away because Mexico City's airport was jammed with "junk".[75]

The long gestation period of creeping disasters such as famine also does not necessarily lend itself to any greater tendency towards joint or cooperative assessments. Chad was 'unusual' in the sense that the operations involved few vested institutional interests, that the problems were relatively clear-cut and that it attracted limited publicity. If one takes the emergency operation in Ethiopia between 1985 and 1986, one sees a far more 'typical' example of the definite limitations of coordination and joint assessment.

Despite the deserved acclaim for its efforts, the UN's Office for Emergency Operations in Ethiopia was never able to bring the separate operations of inter-governmental and non-governmental organizations to an agreed assessment of need and requirements in that famine-stricken country. It was clear that organizations—despite the UN's officially-acknowledged coordinating role——were disinclined to seek basic agreement on priority areas or requirements.[76] Of course, all the conditions that Chad offered were absent in Ethiopia. Under the glare of international publicity, agencies sought to demonstrate their individual capabilities and undertook whatever measures they felt inclined to.[77] The resources that were available to provide assistance made the operation attractive to a wide range of actors, and harmony of purpose was all too often forgotten in the rush to partake of the relief cake.

In reflecting on the evolution of international responses to disasters, one finds a sad irony. There is no doubt that humanitarian concern for the disaster-afflicted—as represented by the growth in the numbers of potential relief actors—has significantly increased over the past century, and certainly since the end of World War II. And yet, despite such growth, there are all too few instances when these humanitarian concerns are reflected in basic changes and approaches to the failings of the relief process. Why this might be so has to be seen from the particular pespectives of the kinds of actors involved in what in Chapter 3 we shall describe as the 'international relief network'. It also has to be understood from a more systemic perspective, that of the relief process itself, which we shall consider in Chapters 4 and 5.

Notes

1. Quotation from Italian Senator Giovanni Ciraolo in Elia, G., *The International Assistance Union*, Geographical Congress of Cambridge, 1928, p.3..
2. Ibid.
3. At the end of 1877, there were thirty National Red Cross Societies in Europe, including Russia and Turkey. The first National Society in Latin America was established in Peru in 1879, and in Asia the first National Society was created in Japan in 1886. The first African National Society was set up in the Congo in 1888. Today there are 143 National Societies.
4. Statutes of the International Committee of the Red Cross, Article 4, adopted in 1952 by the XVIIIth International Conference of the Red Cross.
5. Macalister-Smith, P., *International Humanitarian Assistance: Disaster relief actions in international law and organisation*, Dordrecht, Martinus Nijhoff, 1985, p.11.
6. Ibid., p.16.

7. Gorge, C., *The International Relief Union: its origins, aims, means and future*, Geneva, International Relief Union, 1938, p.12.

8. A fascinating example of the kind of wartime collaborative efforts between governments and private agencies is given by Dr Marcel Junod in *Warrior Without Weapons* (Geneva, International Committee for the Red Cross, repr. 1982, Chap. 5). In one instance, in 1941, the ICRC negotiated with both the German and the British governments to allow relief supplies and parcels for prisoners of war to enter Continental ports in special Red Cross ships.

9. Stephens, T., *The United Nations Disaster Relief Organisation: The politics and administration of international relief assistance*, Washington, DC, University Press of America, 1978, p.32.

10. Luard, E., *International Agencies: The emerging framework of interdependence*, London, Macmillan, 1977, p.265.

11. For an analysis of the problems that this autonomy has caused, see UN Doc. JIU Rep/85/9, 'Some Reflections on Reform of the United Nations', Geneva, 1985.

12. Luard, op. cit., p. 10.

13. Stephens, op. cit., p.41.

14. Article 2(d), Constitution of the World Health Organization.

15. Whitaker, B., *A Bridge of People*, London, Heinemann, 1983, p.18.

16. Spero, J., *The Politics of International Economic Relations*, London, Allen & Unwin, 1980, p.132.

17. President Truman stated during his 1949 inaugural address that a fourth point of his programme would be to make assistance available for development. This 'Point Four' was implemented in the US International Development Act of 1950.

18. Interview with an official from the US Agency for International Development, Washington, DC, 15 September 1983.

19. Lissner, J., *The Politics of Altruism: A study of the political behaviour of voluntary development agencies*, Geneva, Lutheran World Federation, 1977, p.59.

20. Interview with Alfred White, US Agency for International Development, Washington, DC, 18 November 1980.

21. Macalister-Smith, op. cit., pp.102–3.

22. Macalister-Smith, op. cit., p.39.

23. UN Doc. A/Res/832 (IX) 154.

24. For UNICEF, see E/RES 44(IV) and A/res 417(V); for the World Health Organization, see Resolution 24, Seventh World Health Assembly, May 1954.

25. For an excellent discussion on the three categories of NGOs within the UN structure and the consultative procedures within these three categories, see Willetts, P. (ed.), *Pressure Groups in the Global System: The transnational relations of issue-oriented non-governmental organisations*, London, Frances Pinter Publishers, 1982, Chap. 1.

26. Interview with Stanley Mitton, Director for Foreign Emergency Response, Church World Service of the National Council of Churches, New York, 15 December 1981.

27. Interview with Jurg Vittani, League of Red Cross Societies, Geneva, 19 March 1984.

28. See Table 1.3, Chapter I.

29. Lissner, op. cit.

30. Mitton, see n. 26.

31. Interview with Michael Harris, former Overseas Director, Oxfam, Robertsbridge, 25 June 1985. See also, Harris, M., *Ethiopia Before and After*, Geneva, International Council of Voluntary Agencies, 1985, p.76.

32. Interview with Curtis Farrar, US Agency for International Development, Washington, DC, 18 November 1980. The 'junk' issue still remains very much a feature of international responses to disasters. See, for example, Charles Schmitz's study of the 1985 Mexico City earthquake disaster in *Disaster: The United Nations and interntional relief management*, New York, Council on Foreign Relations, 1987, p.13.

33. It is perhaps symbolic that the first signs of the largest refugee movement that the world has seen to date, namely, the flight of 10 million East Pakistanis to the borders of India, were transmitted by an Oxfam official, Alan Leather, while serving in a

remote village in Western India. For all the mixed reactions to the NGO sector, the rapidity of their responses has normally found favourable comment. See, for example, *Development Cooperation Review, 1979*, Paris, 1979, p.113.

34. Kaufmann, J., *United Nations Decision Making*, Rockville, Maryland, Sijthoff & Noordhoff, 1980, p.94, in which the author refers to Jack, H.A., 'A Persistent Species at Rome: NGOs', *America*, 1 March 1975.

35. The criticisms by many NGO representatives of international responses to disasters fall into two basic stereotypes: governments are 'too political' and IGOs are 'too bureaucratic'. IGOs frequently complain that NGOs fail to appreciate the complexities that international civil servants have to face.

36. Stephens, op. cit., p.67.

37. UN Doc. E/Res 766(XXX), Earthquake in Chile; A/Res 1753 (XVII), Earthquake in Iran; E/Res 930 (XXXV), Earthquake in Libya, Floods in Morocco, Volcanic eruption in Indonesia; E/Res 970 (XXXVI), Earthquake in Yugosalvia; A/Res 1888 (XVIII), Hurricane affecting Cuba, Dominican Republic, Haiti, Jamaica and Trinidad and Tobago; and E/Res 1014 (XXXVII), Volcanic eruption in Costa Rica. See Stephens, ibid., p.66.

38. Interview with Diego Cordovez, Under-Secretary General for Special Political Affairs, United Nations, New York, 16 December 1981. Cordovez did not necessarily support this view, but suggested that this was an attitude that permeated the Secretariat. This opinion was certainly supported by Ismat Kittani, President, UN General Asembly in an interview on 16 December 1981, in New York, as well as by Eric Jenson, a UN official who had played a major role together with Martin White in seeking ways to coordinate UN responses to disasters in the early 1970s.

39. UN E/4036, Para.4.

40. Stephens, op. cit., p.71.

41. Stephens, op. cit., p.71.

42. Very basic issues about the UN's disaster relief role, for example coordination, were not addressed for almost four years, from 1965 to 1969, despite concerns expressed by certain member states such as Italy.

43. Most writers see the 'take-off' of persistent UN interest in disasters emerging from the Biafran, Peruvian and East Pakistan experiences of the late 1960s and early 1970s. It is this period that seems to be the consistent starting-point for most analyses of major developments in the area of international disaster assistance.

44. Interview with Diego Cordovez, see n. 38.

45. UN Secretary-General U Thant was seen by his colleagues to be extremely frustrated by the bureaucratic snags that member states, such as France and the Soviet Union, created during his attempts to come to grips with the complex East Pakistan refugee crisis. This was certainly brought out in interviews with Diego Cordovez, Sir Robert Jackson, Eric Jenson and Ismat Kittani.

46. UN E/4853.

47. UN Draft Resolution E/L 1438.

48. UN E/SR 1787 & E/SR 1790.

49. Schmitz, op. cit., pp.27 ff.

50. Stephen Tripp, former Relief Coordinator for the US Office for Foreign Disaster Assistance, maintained that he approached the US Ambassador to the United Nations, Mr George Bush, during the formation of UNDRO, to express certain concerns about the new organization's operational capacity. Bush seemed, according to Tripp, to indicate that the United States was not particularly concerned about the actual capability of UNDRO. Interviews with Stephen Tripp, 15 and 16 September 1983.

51. This is clearly one important conclusion arising out of the UN Joint Inspection Unit's 'Evaluation of the United Nations Disaster Relief Coordinator', Geneva, October 1980, JIU/Rep/80/11.

52. Given the initial concern, if not hostility, with which the LORCS greeted the proposal to create UNDRO, the LORCS eventually became one of its staunchest

supporters. The cordial relations which arose during the early stages of UNDRO's existence were due to the willingness of key personalities in Geneva to work together. However, as one observer noted, when the League's Secretary-General, Henrik Beer, retired, relations between the two organizations became more strained.

53. Compared to the 'arms-length' treatment received by UNDRO from many within the United Nations family, non-governmental organizations have on the whole been quite supportive. In fact, according to Michael Harris, then Oxfam's Overseas Director, the NGOs expended considerable energy in pushing for an UNDRO-type organization in 1971.

54. The image is in many respects true. However, it was one that was fostered by the NGOs themselves, through public appeals and advertising which emphasized NGOs' abilities to get aid directly to the 'poorest of the poor'. This niche in the market, however, posed and continues to pose conceptual problems for the non-governmental sector, problems that are discussed in Chapter 3 of this book.

55. 'Television's appetite for the extreme had not helped in the more complex business of alerting people to the build-up of famine', writes Peter Gill. 'Save the Children Fund press officers quoted an ITV reporter in 1984 as apologising for having concentrated on political rather than humanitarian questions during a visit to Ethiopia early in the year. "There were no acute cases of starvation to film," he said, "so it wasn't news" '. Gill, P., *A Year in the Death of Africa: Politics, Bureaucracy and the famine*, London, Paladin, 1986, p.92.

56. Interview with Peter Gill, Robertsbridge, 19 May 1985.

57. Shah, B.V., 'Is the environment becoming more hazardous? A global survey 1947 to 1980', *Disasters: The International Journal of Disaster Studies and Practice*, 7, No.3, 1983, p.203.

58. Newland, K., *Refugees: The new international politics of displacement*, Worldwatch Paper No.43, Washington, DC, Worldwatch Institute, March 1981, p.10.

59. Harris stated before the general conference of the International Council of Voluntary Agencies in May 1985, 'This need for closer liaison has been said before, but little has come of it. ICVA itself spoke of the need for "improved coordination" . . . and surely the whole purpose behind ICVA from its inception has been for closer working relationships between NGOs . . . Whilst the majority would agree with the idea in theory, few appear to implement practical proposals.' Harris, op. cit., p.76. Similarly, the Davidson Report (UN Doc. E/1981/16, 9 March 1981) refers to the various past attempts to get the United Nations family to coordinate its relief efforts. Governments' ostensible interest in coordination was reflected in their attempts to engender greater harmony among the United Nations agencies.

60. 'State/AID Response to General Accounting Office's Draft Report to the Congress: "Need to Build an International Disaster Relief Agency" ', Appendix I, Comptroller-General of the United States, *Need for an International Disaster Relief Agency*, Washington, DC, GAO, 1976, p.55.

61. Comptroller-General of the United States, ibid., p.19–20.

62. Ibid., p.19.

63. UN Doc. A/3243, 29 November 1974 and UN Doc. A/10079, 6 May 1975.

64. Interview with Richard Symmonds who had held a variety of senior posts with UNDP and UNRRA, Oxford, 3 November 1980. Despite this point, UNDP's Governing Council decided in 1980 to clarify UNDP's disaster role. In so doing, it established limits of $1 million per disaster and $2 million per year per country from the Programme Reserve for longer-term technical assistance only, supported Resident Representative efforts to encourage government contingency planning, and raised the UNDP emergency allocation limit from $20,000 to $30,000 per disaster. UN Doc. DP/432, 22 January 1980.

65. UNDP/PROG/FIELD/110, 28 December 1982.

66. UN Doc. JIU/REP/80/11.

67. JIU, ibid., pp.37–8.

68. UN Doc. A/Res/37/144; see also A/Res/36/225, 17 December 1981.

69. UNDP/PROG/Hqtrs/125/Rev.1.
70. UN Doc. A/Res/39/207.
71. This at least was the opinion of Sir Robert Jackson, the UN Secretary-General's Special Representative for coordinating all humanitarian programmes resulting from developments in Kampuchea. Interview with Sir Robert Jackson, New York, 21 November 1980.
72. UN Doc. E/1981/16, 9 March 1981, p.26.
73. Interview with George Davidson, New York, 23 September 1983.
74. Interview with Giles Whitcomb, Coordinating Officer, UNDRO, Geneva, 23 March 1984. In a very frank discussion, Whitcomb accepted the 'usual problems' that arise among agencies in relief operations, but was anxious to point to the Chad case as an exception that demonstrated the capability of agencies to work together.
75. Schmitz, op. cit., p.13.
76. Kent, R.C., 'The Office for Emergency Operations in Ethiopia: Enduring Lessons from a One-off Shot', paper prepared for the Nuffield Foundation, London, 1987.
77. Interviews with members of the UN Office for Emergency Operations in Africa, 14–17 October 1986. Interviews were conducted with representatives seconded to the OEOA from all the major UN agencies.

3 The International Relief Network: The Actors

Over a period of sixty-five years, the number of potential relief actors that can be mobilized to assist victims of disasters has grown significantly. However, despite this institutional growth, one might still ask whether Ciraola's complaint in 1921 that 'assistance to people stricken by calamities is . . . poorly organised and in a great degree inefficient' remains only too valid today.[1]

In posing this question, one must inevitably be struck by the fact that attitudes towards disasters have changed little. They are still regarded for the most part as aberrant phenomena, unpredictable, unprecedented, and distinct from 'normal life'.[2] There are few indications that disaster prevention or preparedness measures have found their way into the priority concerns of most governments. Lack of coordination, unpredictability and inappropriate assistance remain the hallmarks of most relief efforts throughout the world.

While it is easy to condemn such persistent failings, it is more important for our purposes to explore why these failings continue to occur. In Chapters 4 and 5 an explanation will be sought in what will be described as the 'relief process'. Here, however, in Chapter 3, our purpose is to consider the types of actors that form what we shall call the 'international relief network', and, by so doing, explore the structural and institutional constraints that hamper each of the network's components in their relief roles.

System Versus Network

The bevy of actors who may contribute to a disaster relief effort can scarcely be labelled a 'system', if by system one means a 'set of parts coordinated to accomplish a set of goals' in a consistent and regularised manner.[3] Following Bertalanffy's lead, Pettman suggests that a system has four basic characteristics. It must have a set of units that are sufficiently interdependent such that a change in the state of one unit has repercussions on the others; a system has a 'boundary' which separates it from an external environment; it also has a 'structure that depicts the pattern of relationships between the component units'; and finally, a system has goals, 'be they only the maintenance of its own stability'.[4]

One might argue that the League of the Red Cross, with its constituent national Red Cross and Red Crescent Societies, in itself forms a system. Yet, from a component-wide perspective, there is no international relief system *per se*. The diverse set of actors that has potential relief roles displays little structural interdependence, nor does it share a common boundary, other than the fact that each component may on occasion contribute to the relief process. There certainly is little evidence of a consistent pattern of relationships among the components, and, even when focused on a relief operation, these components rarely share a set of common institutional goals.

From all of this, is one to conclude that there is no coherence at all, no semblance of a system that catalyses the relief efforts of this disparate band of actors? Critics of international responses to disasters, such as the highly-experienced former UN Coordinator, Sir Robert Jackson, are inclined to point disparagingly to the 'non-system' where common values and purpose are denied by the extreme variations in attitudes, functions and approaches of those who become directly or indirectly involved in disaster relief.[5]

In a strictly definitional sense, critics such as Jackson are right to point to the non-system. Nevertheless, at the same time they too often ignore what might be described as a functional 'international relief network'. Over the past decade and a half, an international relief network has emerged that is loose, unpredictable, but at least reflects a consensus about the nature of disaster relief and which institutions might be available for relief work.

This network is devoid of any institutional framework, lacks coherent goals, reflects few patterned relationships, yet points to a variety of transnational and functional linkages that have emerged probably more out of informal contacts than from formal institutional arrangements. A senior USAID official on temporary assignment to Ethiopia during the 1984 famine relief operation remarked that if she had complaints against the way that Britain's Save the Children Fund was conducting its operations, she would just pick up the 'phone and speak to SCF's director in London. 'We all know each other', she said. 'The relief community is relatively small, and over the years most of us have gotten to know how each other operates.'[6]

The international relief network is an amalgam of non-binding contacts, sustained by various channels of communication and by an awareness of who is around. On occasion, various components of the network will align themselves to promote particular interests, and will also work in concert to assist in relief. However, such arrangements are rarely enduring and, when they do occur, create little more than short-term interdependencies.

While one can criticize the effectiveness of the international relief network, in historical perspective one cannot ignore the fact that much of the institutional isolation that marked earlier international relief efforts has been eliminated. Although international assistance in times of disaster is frequently disjointed, unpredictable and uncoordinated, the network lends a degree more coherence than was the case fifteen years ago. This may best be seen by looking at four features of the international relief network: (1) communications; (2) transnationalism; (3) specializations; and (4) alignments.

Communications

There has emerged an intense web of communications, to which most relief actors have access. It is by no means a perfect web; for reasons that will be discussed in the next chapter, the perceptual and organizational factors that tend to distort the communications process too often leave information unclear or ignored. Be that as it may, the components of the relief network are still tied into an increasingly intricate flow of disaster information.

On governmental, inter-governmental and non-governmental levels, an array of communication sources abounds. The United Nations Disaster Relief Office provides disaster warnings and 'situation reports' to a relatively large number of private, governmental and IGO relief offices. This telexed information covers all types of disaster, apart from those that normally fall within the purview of the United Nations High Commissioner for Refugees. Other IGOs also provide telexed communications to potential relief participants. The UN's Food and Agriculture Organization, the World Health Organization and the World Meteorological Organization, to name but three, make a practice of providing highly specialized disaster information to the network, reflecting their particular areas of expertise.

Governments, too, add to the density of the communications flow. The US Office of Foreign Disaster Assistance (USOFDA), perhaps the most elaborate governmental component of the communications web, distributes disaster information throughout major relief institutions, both within the United States and outside. USOFDA normally exchanges information with major IGOs and NGOs, and sees its unofficial role as an international clearing house for others in the network.

Similarly, the non-governmental sector abounds with a variety of communication links. The International Council of Voluntary Agencies in Geneva, through its special committee on disasters, transmits updates to its members on disasters. The League of the Red Cross, too, has a communications net that links Geneva with its national counterparts throughout the world.

There can be little doubt that access to information has increased significantly in a relatively short period. The fact that there are often serious flaws in the type of information that is transmitted and that information is ignored or distorted in the communications process[7] does not detract from the fact that a growing number of potential relief participants have access to an expanding global communications network.

Transnationalism

It has become only too evident that the fate of disaster-stricken peoples all too often becomes embroiled in the political calculations of governmental donors. The increased tendency to provide assistance bilaterally is clear evidence of the 'national interest' element entering more and more into the relief process.[8] Yet, despite such trends, it is interesting to note the transnationalism that underpins many of the activities of donor participants, including governments.

Donor governments, directly or indirectly, are not reluctant to use foreign non-governmental agencies to distribute relief. The British government was willing to use the offices of Norwegian Church Aid to assist famine victims in Ethiopia's Eritrea province. The United States, similarly, was willing to allow commodities which it provided to the American-based Catholic Relief Services to be distributed through foreign non-governmental organizations. While the issue of relief becomes increasingly politicized, functional aspects of the relief process demonstrate a relative degree of non-political transnationalism.

In some respects this reflects an earlier practice that had been established to some degree among non-governmental agencies. NGOs that did not have their own operation in a disaster-afflicted country would work through counterparts. These counterparts might be indigenous to the afflicted country or else from another foreign country. Nationality, in other words, is not an over-riding determinant of who works with whom. The transnationalism reflected throughout much of the relief network must be seen, like the factor of communications mentioned earlier, in the broader context of what had been the case two decades before. In comparison with the more nationalist orientation of relief participants in the past, there are more transnational relations among the relief network's components. For the most part, they do not engender enduring relationships, but they are nevertheless linkages that give some definition to the idea of network.

Specializations

In the chaos and confusion that follow a disaster, scant regard is often given to a systematic assessment of what is required and to who should be providing specific forms of aid. And yet, despite this all-too familiar picture, there is a significant degree of awareness that there are indeed specialist organizations that have particular capabilities to intervene in appropriate ways in the relief process. The increasing acceptance of specializations in the field of disaster relief is an important characteristic of the network. The fact that institutional specializations have gained greater recognition over recent years does not mean that the specialization of any particular organization constrains others from duplicating the former's efforts. Nevertheless, among an ever-widening body of relief actors, there is greater awareness of which particular actor or type of actor is best at achieving certain kinds of relief objective.

In light of the relative anarchy that makes the relief process so unpredictable, the emergence of recognized specializations is at least one step in the direction towards operational coherence. The consequence of specializations is not dissimilar to that of what in a different context we have referred to as 'plural capabilities'.[9] To some degree, there are, at least in theory, focal points towards which certain types of disaster and disaster relief operations can be directed.

The World Food Programme, for example, is regarded as the main coordinator for the international community in operations requiring large-scale food shipments. The World Health Organization is acknowledged for its expertise in the area of immunization programmes. The United Nations Children's Fund has particular capabilities in dealing with highly vulnerable groups such as children and lactating mothers.

These kinds of functional demarcation are to a lesser extent also to be seen at the non-governmental level. CARE's logistic capabilities in handling large-scale food distribution have been accepted in many major relief operations by IGO and NGO counterparts alike. The United Kingdom's Save the Children Fund's medical intervention programmes are generally considered to set standards worth imitating; the Lutheran World Federation's logistics expertise, like that of CARE, is generally well acknowledged; and Oxfam's clean-water schemes and camp operations are recognized as particularly well-established specialities.

If such specializations served as bases to determine who should intervene in a relief operation, one would really be able to argue that some semblance of a system could be seen emerging out of the disparate band of relief participants. However, specializations may be increasingly recognized, but they do not serve as a criterion for involvement in the relief process. They are essentially part of a general awareness of 'who is around, who might be available'—an awareness that characterizes a network of unobligated actors rather than a system of interdependent participants.

Alignments

The communications web, the pattern of transnationalism and the awareness of specializations that characterize the international relief network are features that generate few commitments or obligations. They merely suggest ways in which the network may be identified. Equally as ephemeral but with more practical bite is the alignment nexus which components of the relief network form on occasion to pursue particular objectives. This alignment process is transitory; nevertheless, it does reflect an important characteristic of the network. In instances where functional interests of relief components overlap, interesting, though normally temporary, linkages form.

One of the co-founders of the European Community's Non-Governmental

Liaison Committee and the head of the Dutch agency CEBEMO viewed these temporary alliances as part of a political process that enabled European voluntary agencies to gain greater resources from the European Commission. Agencies in different EC countries would question their governments about the relatively low level of funding they were each receiving from the European Commission. In turn, the governments, in pursuing the individual complaints of their respective NGOs, inadvertently became part of a larger pressure group orchestrated by NGOs from different Community states.[10]

Government departments that wish to alter their own government's policies towards a particular relief decision may dip into the network to align IGO and NGO support to bring external pressure for change. A USAID official responsible for assistance to Africa suggested that this kind of coalition-building enabled USAID to provide emergency aid to Mozambique and Angola despite the Reagan Administration's hostility to those regimes.[11] Similarly, IGOs may use the political influence of others, such as NGOs, to press for relief assistance from reluctant donors. A member of the World Food Programme's emergency office saw that a basic technique for mobilizing governments was to work through 'pressure points', i.e. NGOs and the press.[11] In the same way, UNHCR, according to Rizvi, seeks to overcome the resistance of donors to some of its more controversial operations.[12]

These kinds of temporary alignment are fostered by the increased familiarity that exists between many of the network's components. Familiarity has been spawned through the communications web and through the contacts that have often been made in the course of a variety of relief operations. Familiarity has for the most part not led to a fundamental change in the relative independence and operational autonomy of the components of the relief network, but it has led to a greater willingness of many in the network to rely upon the influence and capabilities of others when circumstances serve mutual interests.

The four characteristics of the international relief network suggest a body of diverse actors tenuously linked by a host of informal contacts and temporary commitments. These characteristics go some way to explain why the capabilities of individual relief actors have been enhanced over the past fifteen years. No matter how imperfect the communications flows, nor how tenuous the contacts, those within the relief network have gained a degree of shared experience. In essence, contacts and communications have generated a learning process that has in certain respects influenced the ways in which the relief network responds.

The four characteristics also account for the spasms of *ad hoc* coordination that one occasionally encounters in relief operations. To suggest that relief operations are always marred by lack of coordination and randomness would not be accurate. There are indeed many 'islands of coordination' that emerge in the sea of any single relief effort. When such islands do appear, they are very much functions of the network characteristics discussed earlier. Yet, the reasons for the lack of more extensive and consistent coordination are also due to the characteristics that underpin the network. The very components of that network are too diverse, their interests too disparate, to engender the interdependence, the boundaries, the shared institutional goals and values that would comprise a system. This becomes only too clear if one looks at 'who's who in the international relief network'.

Who's Who in the International Relief Network

There arises a very fundamental problem in attempting to describe the components of the relief network: who is a relevant actor? Take, for example, the East Pakistan cyclone disaster of November 1970. From the United States alone, over fifty-six private agencies and *ad hoc* committees raised within four months substantial contributions to relieve the suffering along the deltic coast-line of that province. Were all those fifty-six private agencies and *ad hoc* groupings truly 'components' of the relief network? Ultimately, establishing a criterion becomes a very arbitrary task. One must acknowledge that there is certainly a vast array of groups, committees, individuals and charities which, together, frequently provide an extremely supportive function in times of disaster. Nevertheless, one must distinguish between general supportive activities and relief roles.

For our purposes, relief actors will be defined in terms of their institutional roles and the predictability of their involvement. 'Institutional role' assumes that an actor has a degree of professional expertise, has established mechanisms of distribution either through its own organization or through other organizations, has access to relief resources and has some specifically-defined and permanent responsibility to intervene in disasters. Added to this criterion is the element of predictability. An *ad hoc* committee formed to collect relief supplies for a particular disaster relief operation cannot be regarded as either a permanent or predictable actor in the relief network. Its work may indeed be useful and supportive, but, conversely, when the next disaster arrives, the possibility of its intervention is unlikely. Hence, even the Geldof-inspired Band Aid organization cannot be assumed to be a relief actor within the terms of this definition; for, despite all its success, it was not created to have a long life-span.[13] Who, then, are the major components of the international relief network, and what are their strengths and weaknesses?

Governments and Their Contending Priorities

Governments of the Afflicted

While the focus of this book is on the 'international relief network', it is extremely important to emphasize the roles that most governments in disaster-afflicted countries play in the provision of relief. 'Disaster relief goes wrong when people forget about a nation's sovereignty', remarked the Norwegian Red Cross's Sven Kilde.[14] And though the point may be an obvious one, only too often international relief is provided with scant regard for the sensitivities and the implications of disasters for governments of the afflicted. Outsiders are all too quick to point to what they regard as governmental callousness and indifference without attempting to understand the complexities and resource constraints that major disasters pose for developing countries. In this respect, it is worth bearing in mind that, while the international community provided just over $8 billion dollars for disaster relief between 1970 and 1984, the governments of the afflicted provided almost $15 billion in self-help.[15]

This is not to minimize the role of international assistance, but rather to balance the impression that donors too often have about the relatively minor role of recipient governments in the relief process.[16] Such governments generally bear the major burden of relief in ways both direct and indirect. Disaster relief often requires much-needed resources to be redirected to areas of urgent need.

As so many foreign relief officials have observed, disasters not only reveal the precariousness of life for victims, but also the general wretchedness of an even larger section of society.[17] Disasters place enormous strains on the administration and infrastructure of most developing countries. Officials who are seconded to deal with relief operations leave gaps in ministries that at the best of times lack administrative depth. Road, rail and port facilities are requisitioned in activities that do little to ensure the country's economic survival.

There can be little doubt on the other hand that there is normally some substance to observers' criticisms of the particular approaches that governments take to dealing with disasters. Relatively few particularly disaster-prone countries have invested in any form of long-term disaster preparedness or planning.[18] Slim resource margins or predetermined resource priorities mean that relief may not be as forthcoming as it would in more developed societies. Rigid bureaucracies tend to ignore the full impact of a disaster until the situation has become overwhelmingly acute. Insufficient administrators, few of whom may have had specialist training, may be unable to provide an accurate assessment of the disaster to relevant departments. Communications between the disaster site and the nation's capital may well be poor. All these oft-repeated problems are just some of the constraints that hamper recipient governments' responses to disasters. And yet, the importance of the government is fundamental to the entire relief process.

Legally, it is only the government of the afflicted that can instigate international assistance for its people. The international community cannot formally respond to a disaster without the specific request of the recipient government. This applies to non-governmental organizations as well as to governmental donors and inter-governmental organizations. The importance of this principle to recipient governments cannot be overestimated.

Given the pressures that are posed by disasters in most developing countries, disaster relief is an extremely sensitive issue. An adequately handled relief operation may give the ruling government a modicum of kudos for the efforts it has made. More likely, however, a disaster normally leaves the government exposed to accusations from opposition parties of government indifference or incompetence. This tendency was clearly reflected in May 1985, in Bangladesh, when—despite a quick government response to a serious cyclone disaster—the opposition Awami League used the 'government's incompetent handling of relief' as part of its political platform.[19]

Closely linked to the general political sensitivities inherent in disasters and disaster relief is the matter of control. Governments are reluctant to relinquish their authority over relief operations to outsiders. In the event of their accepting outside help, this perceived abnegation of responsibility can be used to discredit the government at home and abroad. A government wants to be seen to be responsible. To this extent, international assistance can pose a difficult choice for recipient governments. International aid can overwhelm the resources and manpower of governments. It can undermine government control. Yet, as is so often the case, without such aid, governments cannot effectively respond to the crisis. Herein lies the ever-present dilemma, the dilemma between calling for assistance and possibly losing control.

Once having opted for international assistance, recipient governments frequently find that the relief process can generate problems which fall outside those associated with the relief operation *per se*. A disaster relief operation can breed discontent among the section of the population that has not been afflicted, or it can exacerbate already well-entrenched grievances. A former UNDRO Coordinator recalled the 'jealousies' that arose among villages affected by the Lice earthquake in Turkey in 1975. 'One village receives more than another village; someone says the Kurds don't receive enough; and all these jealousies are politically exploited.'[20]

From the point of view of a recipient government, there is always the potential problem that relief may create differences of life-style between assisted victims and the rest of the population. Sven Lampall of the League of Red Cross Societies could cite several instances where:

local villagers [who had not been affected by a disaster] set up roadblocks and threatened not to let relief goods pass unless we diverted some of the relief goods to them . . . You may know that a particular area was not hit by a disaster, but still there are needy people that require assistance. The government might say to the relief officials, 'Do it or we'll have problems.'[21]

In playing host to several hundred thousand Ethiopian refugees throughout the 1980s, the government of Somalia faces an embarrassing and difficult choice. Many Somalis not only near the refugee camps but also many miles away continue to suffer from acute food shortages. They come to the camps—some are even trucked in by the government—claiming to be refugees. In many instances the Somali authorities are complicit in this deception; in equally as many instances, they have no control over those who claim refugee status. The net result, however, is that in one way or another the government sees the refugee operation as a way of dealing with severe domestic shortages.

The fact that the government of Somalia did not seek assistance from the international community for its own domestic problems goes to the heart of another dilemma for many disaster-prone governments. Admitting to certain types of disaster, for example a food crisis, can have potential political repercussions. A government, in making a formal appeal for relief food, is opening itself up to criticism of the ways in which its agricultural policies have failed. It was not insignificant that the Sudan, during the onset of a famine in early 1985, in every way as severe as that in Ethiopia, refused to formally request international assistance until well after the famine had taken hold. As one of the most important 'breadbaskets' of the region, the Sudan was anxious not to have its image undermined. The image had both political and economic consequences. Politically speaking, a famine would demonstrate to many both inside and outside the country that government policies had failed. Economically, rumour of a Sudanese food crisis might lead buyers in the Middle East, for example, to look for alternative food suppliers.

Such blends of economic and political pressure frequently affect the approaches that recipient governments take towards disasters. A government may be reluctant to admit, for example, that a section of its population is suffering from a major cholera epidemic. Once such an event is acknowledged by the World Health Organization, the impact on overseas trade or tourism can be extremely costly. Furthermore, the fact that an acknowledged epidemic might frighten populations outside the affected areas is also a factor to be borne in mind, particularly when there are inadequate resources to deal with the problem in the first place.[22]

In 1983, the government of Peru was severely condemned by various private relief agencies for failing to assist the Indian population stricken by the climatic disruption caused by the notorious El Nino.[23] The Indian population, according to observers, was to be found predominantly in the south of the country, and the

Peruvian government's principal concern was the effect of El Nino upon the industrialized northern areas. It was not that the government 'consciously ignored' the south, as some have maintained, since it was more than willing to accept outside assistance for those non-industrialized areas. From the government's point of view, however, given limited available resources, priority attention had to be given to the country's economic heartland.

Major relief efforts assisted by outsiders also confront recipient governments with what might be described as a cultural dilemma. In distribution camps, foreign relief officials often complain that individuals try to cheat the system by registering for assistance several times under a variety of false names. Very often the individual who practises this form of deception is merely fulfilling his or her obligations to provide for an extended family. Yet, the deception disrupts the orderly distribution process which the relief official seeks to promote. Government officials who are faced with these different norms must either face the accusation of outsiders that they are perpetuating corruption or face local complaints that they are disrupting an accepted social practice.[24]

As with all governments, those of disaster-prone states are also extremely sensitive to the political implications of international assistance. Donor governments bearing largesse may not be politically acceptable to a recipient government. The latter may be suspicious of their motives, and may often feel threatened by them. Certainly, that was the case in Ethiopia in late 1984 when several key officials of Col. Mengistu's government were convinced that United States relief involvement was being used to undermine the regime.[25]

Yet, this kind of suspicion is by no means confined to governmental donors. Recipients have views about the intentions of non-governmental organizations or even those of the United Nations. Private voluntary agencies can often arouse serious doubts. The particular religious persuasions of some or the social orientation of others (for example fostering grass-roots democracy) may well be regarded as a threat to the established order.[26] The inter-governmental agencies of the United Nations are also not immune from such suspicions. Stanley Mitton from Church World Service was allowed a free hand to travel and study the emergency problems faced by Kurdish peoples in Iraq at a time when United Nations personnel were not allowed beyond a ten-mile radius of Baghdad. In this instance, Church World Service was trusted and the United Nations was not. Such sensitivities, too, play a major role in who is approached for assistance and when, if the approach is made at all.

Finally, one cannot ignore the question of pride, which is also a determinant in the approaches that recipient states take to disaster relief. One very experienced analyst felt that one reason why the Ethiopian Emperor did not respond to the 1973-4 famine more readily was because he did not want to have his own nation 'lumped in with all those other beggar states of Africa'.[27] India is a prime example of a nation that is reluctant to call for international aid in times of emergency. It prides itself on being an independent nation, capable of providing assistance to its own people. It is willing to accept assistance through its own relief structure, but very reluctant to let relief operations fall outside its control.[28] Even when ten million Bengalis fled from civil war to the eastern provinces of India in 1971, the Indian government did not formally call for international assistance. It assumed that the Bengalis were an 'international problem' to which the international community had a moral responsibility to respond. Yet, as host to those ten million, India would accept international assistance only if it went through the appropriate Indian channels established by the government.[29]

Donor Governments

In terms of the volume of resources that are provided for international relief efforts, donor governments are by far the network's most significant component. Donor governments use three basic channels to provide relief: bilateral assistance between donor and recipient governments; multilateral assistance provided, generally speaking, to recipient governments through the mechanisms of inter-governmental organizations; and indirect assistance provided either to recipient governments or directly to the afflicted through the operations of non-governmental organizations.

Most donor governments set great store by the distinction between disaster relief and development aid. The latter, they maintain, normally reflects abiding 'national interests', while the former is assumed to be 'apolitical'. From the United States point of view, Maurice Williams, the former Deputy Administrator of USAID, maintained that 'food and relief are above the battle',[30] and Joe Sisco, a former American Assistant Secretary of State, observed that 'humanitarian assistance is a governmental given. There is a difference between relief aid and development aid.'[31]

Yet, this broad-based distinction deserves to be treated with a modicum of scepticism. Generally speaking, development assistance is certainly more consistently and more overtly tied to the national interest of donors than is disaster relief. However, the distinction has never been a pure one, and it has become increasingly less so. It can readily be argued that disaster relief has always been a way in which donor governments have demonstrated their particular historical links, economic and geo-political interests with the governments of the afflicted. The fact that France responds more quickly to disasters occurring in states that were once within its former empire, that West Germany, given its Turkish connections, responds with alacrity to disasters in Turkey, that Great Britain focuses upon members of the Commonwealth is, in the words of a former British Prime Minister, 'all quite understandable'.[32]

Understandable though it may be, this tendency works against the assumption that humanitarian relief is unfettered by political motives. Far more fundamental, however, is the recent and more overt tendency to use disaster relief as part of a government's foreign policy arsenal. In the United States, it was a trend that the former Relief Coordinator of the United States Office for Foreign Disaster Assistance, Stephen Tripp, began to see emerge under the Nixon administration. 'The political twist was always there', said Tripp. 'It reached its ultimate in Peru[33] when a White House official was designated as the coordinator. The White House said that we [OFDA] weren't giving them enough political image. The White House wants governments to know what we [the US] are doing.'[34]

In part, such pressures stemmed from the domestic politicization of relief. As television increasingly brought disaster images into the homes of Americans, disaster relief struck a responsive chord, a chord that was used to full effect by the growing number of voluntary agencies that were increasingly willing to make representations to the Congress. The disasters of those around the world became domestic political issues.

When, in late 1970, the government of Pakistan had been slow in responding to American offers of assistance in cyclone relief, the State Department warned the American Ambassador in Islamabad by telex that there was a 'tendency discernible among the public here [in the United States] to begin [to] blame the US government for inadequacies of government of Pakistan relief measures and

insufficient response to needs of situation.'[35] Nixon kept prodding the State
Department to get Islamabad to respond so that he could 'keep [Senator
Edward] Kennedy off his back'.[37] Neither the Nixon administration nor subsequent American administrations were alone in the domestic politicization of
overseas disasters. This same pattern could be discerned in many other nations
that emerged as important contributors to the relief process. In the Netherlands,
for example, one minister felt that disaster relief offered an opportunity to do
'something worthwhile for the politically active, religious-based non-
governmental agencies in Holland'.[37] There was little doubt in the mind of one
senior official in Sweden's International Development Authority that 'disaster
assistance is frequently prompted by parliamentary pressure', as in the case of
Swedish aid to Vietnam.[38] Similarly, in Norway, the aid given to Afghan
refugees reflected the Foreign Minister's 'response to domestic pressure from
the Christian Democrats'.[39] In these countries, as in West Germany, Great
Britain, Japan and elsewhere, the same pattern emerges: overseas disasters have
increasingly found their way into domestic political debates.

This, of course, is not merely the consequence of the media's impact on the
public, nor is it solely due to the increased professionalism of non-governmental
agencies in mobilizing public support. Relief assistance serves as a domestic
political and economic tool, perhaps less overt but equally as dramatic as
development assistance. On the domestic front, governments often feel compelled to provide emergency relief for reasons that go beyond satisfying the
humanitarian instincts of their publics. Political parties in one nation use
humanitarian relief to demonstrate solidarity with similar ruling parties in a
disaster-afflicted nation. One Dutch observer felt that 'the links between political parties are often a better indicator of which countries receive relief than
government policies.'[40] While one must not exaggerate the point, intra-party
solidarity is a motive that is mentioned frequently to explain the provision of
relief by Western European governments.[41]

Relief aid is also often seen as a means of satisfying particular pressure groups.
Governments are always wary about the kind of pressure groups that might
emerge in response to a disaster. CARE knew that it could effectively mobilize
the Polish–American lobby if the United States government did not respond to
serious food shortages in Poland during 1982 and 1983. In Western Europe,
governments are particularly careful to ensure that a balanced proportion of
relief filters through denominationally-based relief organizations, since these
organizations indirectly represent important electoral elements.[42]

Closely tied to such domestic political calculations are the economic consequences of relief aid. As the dimension of emergency assistance increases, so, too,
does the economic potential of the domestic economies of donors. It is significant
that at least one-half of all American relief aid is provided through US Public
Law 480—the law that provides for the disposal of America's huge farm
surplus.[43] Such statistics do not necessarily deny humanitarian intentions, but
they do reflect the fact that what is good for the American farmer is also deemed
to be good for the disaster victim. One World Food Programme officer commented that

the WFP is a convenient mechanism for the US to offload surplus grains. In an
emergency the US might be willing to put up wheat as part of its emergency food
contribution. However, since the stricken area might be maize and not wheat eating, I
have to spend a lot of my time resisting these pressures.[44]

Beyond what one official in Britain's Disasters Unit described as the 'ambulance chasers', there is the inescapable fact that, when relief is needed, donor governments are pressured to think in terms of what their own domestic suppliers can provide. Hence, the Swedes acknowledge that over 40 per cent of the material assistance they provide is produced in Sweden.[45] In the Netherlands, an official recalled that one group pressing hard for assistance to Pakistan in 1970 was the Dutch shipbuilding industry, which wanted contracts to provide small river boats to deliver food to the cyclone victims.[46] OFDA in the United States found itself under similar pressure from automotive manufacturers who did not understand why 'US taxpayers' money should be used to buy foreign Volvos and Mercedes trucks' for the 1984 Ethiopian relief operation.[47]

As the foreign aid budgets of most major donors have stagnated or declined over the past decade, the difficulty of gaining extra resources to expend on overseas emergencies has become that much greater. The United States Office of Foreign Disaster Assistance, representing the world's largest international relief donor, is authorized to give up to $3 million for any single disaster before seeking additional resources from USAID. However, once further requests are made, USAID then has to convince the Office of Management and Budget and the Congress. This then embroils AID in a debate over a whole range of issues of priority, both domestic and international. Such financial limitations on relief intervention are faced by all major donor government departments that deal with emergencies. Although none has anywhere near OFDA's $3 million initial contribution level, they must all seek additional funding by competing in Cabinets or Parliamentary committees with other government priorities.[48]

To stereotype such economic considerations as essentially callous would be doing an injustice to the dilemma that governments face. Often the prospect of utilizing the resources of domestic industries, such as fishing or housing in Norway, is seen as a way of serving the needs of both donor and recipient.[49] The fact that the interests of recipients may not be best served by this kind of compromise should not suggest that the response is devoid of all humanitarian concern. Nor for that matter can one ignore the problems which such governments face in attempting to reconcile a host of competing demands on resources in the larger context of national budgets. While one may not agree with what governments determine as national priorities, one must nevertheless acknowledge the dimensions of domestic politics which overseas disasters bring into play.

'I am aware that the political side effects of disaster relief have to be avoided', remarked the Head of the North African desk in the Dutch Ministry of Foreign Affairs. 'I have to judge what the public might want and what is the most sensitive way to achieve it.'[50] The problem for this official, as for those in most donor governments, is the very difficulty of ensuring that balance. As the very complexity and dimensions of disasters increase, that balance becomes ever more difficult to determine. Disasters increasingly expose the vulnerability not only of victims but also of recipient governments. International intervention—sometimes overtly and sometimes inadvertently—plays a part in maintaining the authority of the recipient regime. It is this kind of calculation, noted a United Nations Assistant Secretary-General, that explained why donors were so responsive to Bolivia during the El Nino disaster. They felt that assistance would be one way of sustaining that country as a democratic government.[51]

The significance of foreign policy in disaster relief has become an increasingly important fact of political life. Traditionally, disasters were defined by most governments as those consequences of natural phenomena that required short-term inputs to assist the afflicted in relatively stable regimes. For this reason, it is interesting to note that, in most donor governments, there has always been a sharp institutional distinction between natural disasters and those that are man-made. The former were initially always handled by those officials on what might be described as 'the aid side', or what some call 'the soft side', of government departments dealing with overseas matters. The latter have consistently been placed under the direct supervision of foreign-policy makers. Man-made disasters—resulting from civil wars, boundary disputes and so on—were regarded as too sensitive a policy issue to be institutionally separated from political desks. Natural disasters, on the other hand, could to some extent be less tied to overall policy issues.[52]

While the same divisions still remain in most government structures, the latitude for responding to even ostensible natural disasters has become increasingly circumscribed. To the extent that disasters expose both the vulnerability of people and governments, a decision to intervene becomes by definition encapsulated in a political arena. 'I define 90% of our programmes as political so as not to offend the political section', stated the head of the Emergency Relief and Humanitarian Assistance Unit within the Dutch Department for Development Cooperation.[53] Certainly, throughout the governmental relief organizations analysed for this book, there is a general tendency to clear more and more relief decisions with foreign policy counterparts.[54]

Relief aid to Kampuchea, Angola, Mozambique, Ethiopia, Vietnam, Nicaragua and a host of other countries is difficult to separate from a more general political context. Sharp political differences divide not only potential recipients from potential donors but also divide potential donors themselves. The fact that the Helms-Kirkpatrick lobby in the United States felt that 'the Ethiopians should ask the Soviets' for famine aid in 1984 is but an extreme reflection of the difficulty of divorcing emergencies from a more abiding political context.[55] The fact that West Germany and the Netherlands were reluctant to provide emergency assistance to Nicaragua for fear of alienating the United States is but a further indication of the difficulty of separating a disaster from its political ramifications. Except in cases where the political context is, in the words of a USAID official, 'straightforward' (namely, little possibility of what that official termed 'negative fallout'), 'relief aid is political in the sense that you may look a lot harder if you're not getting on well with a particular country'.[56]

The very fact that a government may provide relief aid to a disaster-stricken nation bestows a degree of legitimacy upon the recipient. The importance of this is most clearly demonstrated in the context of disasters arising out of civil wars. For a government, even through the indirect channels of non-governmental agencies, to provide assistance to non-combatants in times of conflict is riddled with political overtones. When such assistance is used in areas held by rebel forces, the government of that country might view such aid as strengthening the opposition. Normally, donors will emphasize that such assistance is only for non-combatants, but the struggling government is rarely convinced that donors can really distinguish between civilians and rebels. Indeed, in cases such as Kampuchea and Ethiopia, the ruling regimes view such humanitarian assistance as unquestionably motivated by political considerations, and donors are hard-pressed to disprove that assumption.[57]

From the perspective of opposition forces, even reputedly neutral aid can very often be seen as a symbol of political recognition. In 1986, a member of a British voluntary agency told of the Eritrean Relief Association's irritation that too many donors tried to conceal the amount of assistance that the ERA was receiving under the umbrella of the Ethiopian relief effort. The ERA, the civilian arm of the Eritrean Peoples Liberation Front, felt that publicity about the relief aid it had received from donors would enhance its international standing in its attempts to gain independence from Ethiopia.

Governments' decisions to provide assistance, however, are based on more than mere symbolism. Great Britain and the United States both sought to distance themselves from assisting Biafran non-combatants because their paramount interest was to preserve the territorial integrity of Nigeria. Conversely, many within the Reagan Administration hoped that eventual assistance to Ethiopia might directly undermine the domestic support of Col. Mengistu's regime.[58] While these kinds of calculations are ever-present in one way or another, their very complexity often determines the routes that governments choose to funnel their assistance. Of the three mechanisms which donors use to provide assistance—bilateral, multilateral and through NGOs—it is the first that is ostensibly the most political, and certainly the increasingly preferred option.

When, in 1976, the United States General Accounting Office proposed ways to strengthen the coordinating capacities of the United Nations Disaster Relief Organization, the then Secretary of State, Henry Kissinger, strongly disagreed with the GAO's proposal. To expand the role of UNDRO, he felt, would devalue the bilateral effect of relief assistance:

US disaster relief is an important way for the American public, as well as its government, to express its humanitarian concerns for those adversely affected by natural and man-made disasters. Equally important, disaster relief is becoming increasingly a major instrument of our foreign policy. The assistance we can provide to various nations may have a long-term impact on US relations with those nations and their friends.[59]

Bilateral assistance, as Kissinger's reply to the GAO's proposal suggests, is generally provided to achieve a variety of objectives. Government-to-government assistance is clearly one way of demonstrating bonds of friendship. The alacrity with which the United States responded to the short-term famine in Kenya in mid-1984 and mobilized massive amounts of assistance for the famine-ravaged Sudan a few months later are clear demonstrations of the use of relief aid to bolster ties between friendly states. Clearly, such bilateral assistance is given by a government with an eye to its own public in order to enhance its own image of humanitarian concern before their eyes. Furthermore, a government uses bilateral assistance as a way not only of generating similar assistance from other potential donors, but also of demonstrating to recipients and the international community the meanness of governments that do not contribute. USAID's Administrator never failed to note throughout 1984 and 1985 how the Soviets had made little contribution to their Ethiopian client state.

Bilateral assistance can also be used as a means of gaining political clout over a recipient. The government of a disaster-afflicted state in many instances cannot avoid the pressures put upon it by a generous donor: the prospect that disaster assistance may lead to longer-term aid, or the sheer volume of relief itself may make the government far more amenable to donors' particular interests. Bilateral aid can also offer the advantages of speed, particularly when abiding political interests are at stake. For example, in June 1980, a severe food shortage in Uganda meant that cow-peas had to be urgently transported from Tanzania. The British Embassy in Kampala contacted the Disaster Unit in London for urgent assistance to charter an aircraft to transport the food. The response was extremely rapid, since the British government was concerned that, without its intervention, the Soviets would be asked to help instead.[60]

Beyond the very fundamental fact that political interests are an integral part of bilateral assistance, lies an equally important consideration. Certain types of assistance that are required during emergencies can only be offered by governments and require the close cooperation of the receiving government. The Swedish Stand-by Unit, a team of relief specialists, is composed of volunteers from the Swedish military. To be brought into action, the Stand-by Unit requires the full authorization of the recipient government in order to avoid the danger of being seen to send combatants.[61] In situations requiring cargo planes, helicopters or other forms of large-scale logistics assistance, donor governments have the resources—resources, however, which cannot easily be transferred to a multinational organization or voluntary agency. The use of such resources requires the approval of the recipient government.

The use of multilateral, or inter-governmental organizations, by donor governments equally reflects that peculiar *mélange* of humanitarianism and politics that marks bilateral assistance. 'We're not virgins', remarked an official of the United Nations High Commissioner for Refugees. 'We know why governments give us money, but what we try to do is to tack between donors' objectives and what we feel we are responsible for.'[62] This sentiment reveals more than a modicum of truth about the ways in which governments use the mechanisms of inter-governmental organizations. By channelling resources through IGOs, donor governments can 'legitimize' complex political/humanitarian issues; they can evade disagreeable domestic choices brought on by such issues; and through IGOs they can offload responsibility for monitoring and assessing the impact of aid.

The vast amount of assistance that the United States provided through the offices of the United Nations High Commissioner for Refugees to deal with Afghan refugees after 1979 was more than a humanitarian gesture. By utilizing UNHCR, the United States was able to emphasize that the plight of the Afghans was an international issue. In so doing, it added a degree of international legitimacy to its claims that the 1979 Soviet involvement in Afghanistan was an 'international crime against the peoples of Afghanistan'. To have assisted the refugees bilaterally—*vis-à-vis* the government of Pakistan—would have left the issue encapsulated in the context of East–West relations. To work through a major agency of the United Nations was to add international opprobrium to Soviet involvement.

Internationalizing humanitarian issues through the machinery of international organizations is an important feature of multilateralism from the perspectives of donor governments. Yet, not only does it serve to add legitimacy to points of political interest, it also serves to avoid difficult problems which humanitarian issues create on domestic fronts.

In mid-1983, before the full dimension of the Ethiopian famine crisis was fully accepted, USAID's Administrator, Peter McPherson, had to face a difficult choice. American relations with Ethiopia were poor: the regime's pro-Soviet orientation, the hostility it displayed towards the United States, the nationalization of American private property and the continued tensions which Ethiopia was seen to be generating in the Horn of Africa, all made the prospect of American aid of any kind highly unlikely. Key officials within the National Security Council and a bevy of conservative officials in Congress, in the United States UN delegation and within USAID itself, strongly opposed any United

States involvement. At the same time, however, there were officials within USAID, a coterie of Congressmen and Senators, and very strong private agency pressure groups, that were beginning to push for relief aid to Ethiopia. McPherson dealt with the dilemma by channelling funds through the United Nations Disaster Relief Organization. He justified his action by stating that the United States had to be seen by the international community to be participating in the international response, but could also satisfy his critics that the United States was not becoming directly involved with the Marxist regime.[63]

This was not an unusual tactic. Despite official hostility to the governments of Mozambique and Angola, USAID was able to contribute to emergency feeding programmes in those countries through the United Nations Children's Fund. Most major donor governments have recourse to the offices of United Nations specialized agencies when domestic pressures create similar kinds of domestic dilemmas. Even Sweden, which had proved to be an important bilateral aid provider to Ethiopia from 1983 onwards, had up to that point preferred the multilateral route for domestic reasons.[64]

For Sweden and other major donors, the multilateral route also offers the advantage of offloading what can broadly speaking be described as 'accountability' responsibilities. In providing assistance bilaterally, the donor must for obvious reasons be able to explain to Parliaments and various governmental accounting offices how and where resources have been spent. This can be a particular problem when one is dealing with recipients that have poor administrative structures or where the complexity of a disaster makes accurate accounting extremely difficult. The pressure for accurate accounting can also prove to be a thorn in bilateral relations, particularly when donors are not satisfied with the way a recipient might use relief aid. One WFP Programme Officer explained that a particular North American donor government knew that the government of Bangladesh was using relief supplies to supplement an urban rationing programme. Given severe food shortages in Dacca, the Bangladesh government's position was understandable, but nevertheless contrary to what the donor had intended. By placing such assistance under the supervision of the WFP, the donor could wash its hands of any direct involvement in the redirection of any aid designated for relief.[65]

Despite the usefulness of IGOs as relief channels, donor governments' recourse to them is marked by inconsistency and a degree of distrust. For example, no matter what the mandated roles of UNDRO, UNHCR or the WFP are, and no matter how developed their particular relief capabilities might be, a donor might deem it politically advantageous to bypass them. Conversely, when—as in the case of Afghanistan—an IGO can serve the particular interests of a major donor, that IGO may be inundated with resources well beyond its capacity to absorb them.

Donor governments also treat IGOs with a certain degree of distrust. This distrust is not necessarily a reflection upon an IGO's corporate character, but rather it is based upon a certain disdain for the diplomatic niceties and seemingly over-bureaucratized procedures that underpin their activities. Except in very few instances—for example UNICEF—IGOs are perceived as being too slow off the mark, too administratively top-heavy and too prone to make compromises with recipient governments to be truly effective vehicles for relief assistance.

To a very significant extent, this attitude is evidenced by the increased tendency of donor governments to 'earmark' relief contributions. 'Earmarking' is the procedure by which a donor designates the specific purposes towards which its contributions are to be applied. A government, for example, may earmark money to be used solely for the purchase of tents or medicines. Or it may offer specific commodities to be distributed to particular types of disaster victims. Be they funds or material assistance, the donor expects the IGO channel to comply with such restrictions and to report on how these contributions have been utilized in the field.

Earmarking is not inherently bad in theory. In practice, however, it poses severe problems. Invariably, earmarked contributions reflect what the donor government sees as appropriate assistance and not what the disaster victims necessarily need. Earmarked funds can lead to duplication of supplies or supplies that are just not needed. Earmarking also poses a dilemma for the IGO itself: not to accept a donor's contribution may alienate the donor, but to accept it may add to the administrative and distribution burdens of a relief operation. Furthermore, beyond the extra administrative demands that earmarking imposes upon IGO officials, earmarking also removes a considerable amount of assessment and control from an IGO's relief staff. In a very instructive discussion, a field representative from UNHCR described the consequences of earmarked funds for refugees in the Sudan in 1985 like this:

It is difficult for UNHCR to refuse or to say that we don't want your [donor governments'] contributions, and the choice is sometimes to accept earmarked contributions that probably we don't need. But if you're not going to get it in a form that [you] do need, you still tend to accept it. We were spending an enormous amount of time accounting for these contributions. So if you went to Wad Sharifi, which is a reception centre for 120,000 Eritreans on the outskirts of Kassala, you could actually look at two completely different programmes: one was the efforts by the Sudanese Commissioner for Refugees, the NGOs and UNHCR to manage a town of this size; the other was a mosaic of different components of what to any manager was the same problem, which was that the water supply here belonged to X, that the EEC had given all these tents, that those beans that were distributed came from someone who wanted us to keep track of them; there were Japanese blankets. Now this . . . trend in earmarking, if the money gets tied up like this at the beginning of an emergency, can be disastrous.[66]

Earmarking reflects to a very great extent donors' concern about the management and administrative capabilities of IGOs. Ironically, as one UNHCR official in Geneva remarked, 'The principle of earmarking is a way of controlling UNHCR but the real effect is to increase the bureaucracy, the constant writing of post-operation reports and audits.'[67] Yet, earmarking reflects more than donors' ambivalence about IGO capabilities and procedures. Even where IGOs do offer appropriate relief channels and their expertise is accepted, donors are wary that their contributions may be misinterpreted domestically and internationally. They do not wish to be seen contributing to any aspect of relief that might leave them exposed to criticism. They will want to be assured, for example, that their contributions have not been misappropriated by the Army in a disaster-stricken country or have not been siphoned off by corrupt officials. They will also still want to be able to tell their constituents about the kind of assistance that has been provided and the particular impact it has made.

Concerns about satisfying domestic constituents and accountability are two reasons why governments find non-voluntary organizations a convenient channel for relief assistance. 'A cynic would say that governments use voluntary organisations for their more sensitive aid efforts', remarked a member of Christian Aid, one of Britain's largest private agencies.[68] Yet, cynical or not, there are few within the non-governmental sector who are not aware that non-governmental organizations do indeed serve a useful purpose for governmental donors.

Most important NGOs in major donor countries represent some religious, ethnic or political constituency that goes beyond the immediate realm of the NGO *per se*. The pressures that such agencies can mobilize to persuade governments to respond to emergencies can often be very intense. When, for example, United States CARE sought to mount a food relief effort to assist Poland in the beginning of 1980, CARE 'started with its donor base in the Polish-American sector' and this began to attract the attention of those Congressmen who 'had large Polish-American constituencies.'[69] The increased ability of NGOs to mobilize this support has not been lost upon governments, and governments, in turn, recognize more and more the usefulness of employing NGOs as channels of assistance.

This usefulness, however, has to be seen as traditionally two separate elements that have only recently begun to merge. The first element is the domestic factor, namely governments' growing awareness that within donor countries voluntary agencies represent a force that has to be reckoned with. Well into the 1970s, government images of the voluntary sector reflected considerable contempt. Only too often government officials characterized voluntary agencies 'as bleeding hearts where each "volag" wanted to be the first and where problems arise with coordinating the junk that the public immediately unleashes from its medicine cabinets and closets.'[70] However, whatever the impression, the domestic impact of voluntary agencies was considerable and could not be ignored. As voluntary agencies became more professional in their lobbying, so governments had to recognize increasingly their presence and demands.

Oxfam's Michael Harris believed that the full acceptance of NGOs by government authorities had not really been gained until the beginning of the 1980s. What he called the 'first conscious change in attitudes' was not apparent until governments began to plan for the first International Conference on Assistance to Refugees in Africa in 1981.[71] In fairness to governments, this change in attitude reflected more than the lobbying capabilities of NGOs. The second factor, that of NGOs' growing capabilities in the world of development and relief, made governments more aware of NGOs' usefulness. Not only were NGOs emerging as pressure groups in their own right, but they were also demonstrating a level of professionalism that only too often seemed to be lacking in their IGO counterparts. Whereas the latter too often seemed to become immersed in diplomatic manoeuvring in New York, Geneva and the capitals of afflicted countries, the former were more often than not the first ones on the disaster scene. Their reports from the field were gaining credence for their accuracy, and their distribution, accounting and monitoring procedures were proving to be as effective, if not more so, than those of IGOs or recipient governments. They also had the right aura: they were seen to be unfettered by high administrative costs; they were dealing directly with the afflicted; and they were not so ostensibly embroiled in the political machinations of recipient governments.

The domestic impact of NGOs, combined with their growing professionalism, certainly makes them useful channels of relief assistance. Their use, like that of IGOs, again reflects an amalgam of humanitarian concerns and politics. As in the case of Ethiopia or Kampuchea, donors have to weigh up domestic pressure to help disaster victims under an 'unfriendly government' against the foreign policy implications of such assistance—the images of starving children versus the symbolism of approval or recognition that relief assistance from one government to another conveys. Here, the voluntary agency serves a useful function. By using a voluntary agency as a channel, a donor government avoids the political implications of bilateral assistance. Voluntary agencies generally present themselves as politically neutral and only concerned with humanitarianism. At least from the donor government's point of view, NGO assistance suggests no change in government policy, while at the same time reconciling the domestic pressures that governments face.

To some extent, even the device of channelling funds through an NGO cannot totally exclude political implications, and donor governments are the first to recognize this fact. When, in 1982, the West German agency Agro Action requested government assistance to support feeding programmes in Nicaragua, the request was turned down. The government did not want to be seen to support a country that was regarded as hostile by one of its main allies, the United States.[72]

On the other hand, the government on occasion might ask us [Agro Action] to do something in a particular area such as Angola. Because Angola does not accept the position of Berlin as described by the FGR's constitution, the government was unable to provide emergency assistance to Angola. However, at the same time, it wanted to make a gesture in order to build up better relations.[73]

These kinds of gestures keep doors open for donor governments. 'We have so many links [in a disaster-stricken country] that the government cannot be without us', commented a Christian Aid official. It is just this type of link that enhances the importance of NGOs for donor governments. Unwittingly, an NGO might serve as the eyes and ears of a government interested in keeping abreast of events in a country where access to officials is difficult.

The specific reasons why governments might resort to bilateral, multilateral or NGO relief channels do not imply that only one of these is used at any particular time. Normally, in most large-scale emergencies, all three are used. Yet, what is important to recognize are the different calculations that donor governments have to make in using each. Circumstances surrounding a disaster are rarely comparable from the perspective of governments. Each disaster has a unique context, quite apart from the immediate plight of disaster-afflicted people; and for this very reason, the ways in which the components of the international relief network are used by governments remain inherently unpredictable. (Refer to Appendix I for categories of donors.)

The Plight of Inter-governmental Organizations

Besides the more evident inter-governmental bodies within the United Nations, there are a variety of regional and economic groupings that play a part in disaster relief. Regionally, the European Community and the Organization of African Unity are two important examples. The former is important because of the increasing volume and level of assistance that it provides for relief; the latter's importance stems from the moral standards and the coherence it has given to one of the least recognized types of disaster, that of refugees.[74] The North Atlantic Treaty Organization also plays a limited disaster relief role when governments request certain types of logistics expertise for relief. There are also several regional bodies, such as the Pan-Caribbean Disaster Preparedness and Prevention Project, which have direct disaster responsibilities within specific regional confines. The Organization for Economic Cooperation and Development, comprising representatives from the world's most developed nations, also plays a marginal disaster-monitoring role through its Development Advisory Committee.

While all these different types of organization are part of the international relief network, the most consistent and universal remain those organizations within the United Nations. Like all inter-governmental organizations, those that comprise the United Nations family are essentially 'non-operational'. In other words, their responsibilities, broadly speaking, are not to distribute relief *per se*, but to ensure that those responsible for on-site operations, e.g., officials of recipient governments or voluntary agencies, have the resources they require. Their importance, however, very rarely rests on the actual amount of resources that they commit to most relief operations. Except in certain situations of extreme political complexity, for example Kampuchea/Thailand between 1980 and 1982, India/East Pakistan in 1971, the direct financial contributions of most IGOs to relief are relatively small when compared to bilateral aid. The importance of these IGOs more often than not rests upon factors less tangible than financial resources *per se*.

Perhaps the single most important aspect of an IGO in emergencies is that of access. In the vast majority of disaster-prone states, there are normally at least one or two United Nations agencies represented. Most likely there will be a representative of the United Nations Development Programme, and usually a mission from the United Nations Children's Fund, the Food and Agriculture Organization or the World Health Organization. These missions have established contacts within host governments and will, therefore, be known if and when an emergency arises.

Generally speaking, host governments regard IGO missions as relatively apolitical, 'relatively' being the operative word. Hosts' suspicions about the roles that IGOs play within a country and *vis-à-vis* donor governments can easily be aroused. This is particularly so for the United Nations High Commissioner for Refugees who is responsible for dealing with the highly sensitive issue of refugees and displaced persons. However, as a broad generalization, IGOs are regarded as less politically motivated than their bilateral counterparts.

Not only do IGOs have access to those government officials and departments within a host country, but they are also normally familiar with general infrastructure and resource conditions of the country. Either through specific projects, e.g., UNICEF vaccination programmes, or because of general responsibilities, e.g., UNDP's development advisory role, IGOs have some insights into the particular problems to be faced in mounting a relief operation.

Beyond the advantages of access, IGOs also offer a degree of relief expertise. The issue of expertise will be discussed more extensively below, but suffice it to say at this stage that most IGOs have either in-house experts or available consultants who can assess disasters and determine appropriate relief needs.

From a network-wide perspective, inter-governmental organizations also offer the advantage of focal points. Particularly where recipient governments may lack the administrative capability to deal with large volumes of aid coming from a variety of donors, the IGO can act as a recognized channel.

Yet, all the advantages that IGOs may offer in times of relief have to be measured against the difficulties that a disaster poses for them. They are frequently accused of being slow to respond in emergencies, of being more concerned with their own institutional interests than with the plight of the afflicted, and often too willing to comply with the dictates of donors. There is considerable truth in all of these criticisms, but they deserve to be seen in a wider context. The very structure of most IGOs, their uncertain mandates and the ways in which they are used by donors are factors that go a long way to explaining why the IGO is not as consistently effective a relief actor as some might wish.

In 1979 the international community began to know of the horrors caused by mass movements of people from Kampuchea to Thailand and the famine within Kampuchea itself. The United Nations Children's Fund was the first UN agency to become involved on both sides of the border. Since its mandate did not require it to seek the approval of member governments to intervene, it took the initiative. The then UN Secretary-General, Kurt Waldheim, therefore designated UNICEF the 'lead agency'. However, given the complexities of the operation and the probability that other United Nations agencies would become involved, Waldheim subsequently appointed Sir Robert Jackson as special relief coordinator to oversee the entire operation. Waldheim, however, soon to face the prospect of his re-election, felt that bringing other nationals into the operation would ultimately broaden his own support base; hence, he added yet another special coordinator, Ilter Turkman, a Turk who was UN Assistant Secretary-General, to serve alongside Jackson.

If the operation was to deal with feeding famine victims inside Kampuchea as well as refugees along the Thai border, the World Food Programme would have to become involved. However, for the WFP to become involved, it required the direct approval of the UN's Food and Agriculture Organization. But the highly centralized institution of the FAO was reluctant to authorize the emergency programme, for many member states—principally those from Africa—were vociferously complaining that there had already been an over-concentration on the problems of Asia at the expense of Africa.

And then, of course, there was the United Nations High Commissioner for Refugees who would have principal responsibility for the refugees. With the prospect of possibly the largest refugee influx since the East Pakistan crisis almost eight years before, UNHCR would be an obvious participant in the border relief operation. However, UNHCR, perhaps surprisingly, had been wary of becoming involved. According to the government in Bangkok, those on the borders were not refugees. They were 'economic migrants', and, strictly speaking, UNHCR did not have the mandate to assist those who were not refugees.

The United Nations Disaster Relief Office had been squeezed out of the affair. The scale was too vast and the animosity of its sister organizations too intense for UNDRO to serve any useful purpose. The other agencies maintained that UNDRO really had no relevant role to play, and UNDRO, attempting to mend fences with its more established counterparts, kept at a distance.

Bilateral donors were either providing direct assistance to Bangkok (and in the case of France and the Scandinavian countries to Phnom Penh) or to United Nations agencies with which they wished to work. Private voluntary agencies, as in the case of Oxfam, were introducing their own resources into Kampuchea, while numerous private agencies spent the millions of dollars donated by sympathetic members of the public to assist the border areas. Some voluntary agencies became the operational partners of UNICEF; others did everything they could to avoid such entangling alliances. Governments on occasion funded some private agencies directly and at other times 'earmarked' multi-agency funds to go to specific private agency relief programmes.

In observing the evolution of the massive relief operations on both sides of the border, it was difficult to say who was actually in charge. Governments were individually organizing their own bilateral aid programmes with either Bangkok or Phnom Penh. They were contributing massively to United Nations agencies, but frequently dictating—earmarking—how their individual contributions were to be used. Private voluntary agencies sought involvement in ways and in areas where they could best demonstrate their effectiveness to their own distant donors. Individually they established links with departments within the governments of recipient nations in order to promote their own particular programmes. It was, in the words of one senior United States official, 'pluralism run riot'.[75] The situation did not lend itself to any clearly coordinated effort. The United Nations coordinator in practical terms lacked the authority and the resources to constrain, let alone guide, the relief attempts of the multiplicity of participants who were descending upon the affected countries. He even had little control over the United Nations agencies that were becoming involved.

The FAO, after long delays, finally gave the WFP permission to provide emergency relief. UNICEF, the lead agency, found its own efforts constantly thwarted by recipient governments and constantly challenged by the UN High Commissioner for Refugees. And UNHCR, finally convinced that it had to become involved in the crisis, did so in ways that were regarded as 'prudent'. It distanced itself from any involvement that might be regarded as an infringement of its mandate and, in so doing, made only the most cursory effort to coordinate through UNICEF or the special relief coordinator.

In times of disaster, there are at least sixteen United Nations agencies which in one way or another can become involved in disaster relief activities. They range from the World Meteorological Organization and the World Health Organization to the International Labour Organization and the United Nations Development Programme. To this list, special offices such as the United Nations Office for Emergency Operations in Africa have been added recently to give special focus to acute problem areas.[76] For the most part, each of these agencies and special offices have significant degrees of autonomy, sustained not merely by their individual constitutions but also by support bases within the government departments of member states.

'To make the UN family truly effective', suggested a long-serving member of the Secretariat, 'one would have to tear it down and start again.' Yet, given this practical impossibility, he went on to suggest that there was an increasingly urgent need for member states to at least coordinate their own intra-governmental approaches to United Nations bodies. 'Every meeting of ECOSOC (the United Nations Economic and Social Council) seems to have 3000 different voices!'[77]

In part, the difficulty for United Nations agencies in responding in a consistent way to disasters stems from the inability of governments to deal with them in a consistent and coherent manner. This is ultimately reflected in the uncertain mandates of many United Nations agencies and indeed in the inconsistent uses of those agencies by governments. In turn, uncertain mandates and inconsistency influence the organizational behaviour of the agencies affect the ways in which the expertise of such agencies is employed, and ultimately generate conditions for intense inter-organizational rivalry within the United Nations family. As the United Nations family attempts to gear itself up for a major international relief effort, persistent and enduring problems mar its progress.

Uncertain Mandates

In one way or another, no United Nations agency really has adequate authority to intervene in the type of complex disasters that, increasingly, are faced by the international community. The cautious approach that UNHCR took towards the Kampuchean crisis is but one case in point. Confronted by growing numbers of people seeking food, shelter and security across international borders, the international community has been unwilling to create any effective international mechanism to relieve their plight. UNHCR must generally work within a framework that is no longer appropriate to meet the type of 'refugee problems' witnessed in South-east Asia, Africa, Latin America and elsewhere. Where a government refuses to accept that a mass of distressed migrants are, broadly speaking, refugees, UNHCR is severely handicapped. They can only be assisted when member states deem it convenient to provide an *ad hoc* and informal extension (namely 'the good offices' principle) of its mandate.

Throughout the United Nations system, one is confronted time and again with mandated authority inadequate to meet the crises of disaster victims. The World Food Programme is constrained in the provision of relief in at least three ways. To undertake emergency relief, it requires the authority of another United Nations agency (i.e., the FAO), one which on more than a few occasions has found itself at odds with the WFP. For actual relief supplies on any large scale, it depends upon the inclinations of donors represented on its Committee on Food Aid. And for any disaster of longer duration, for example refugees, its assistance is restricted to a maximum of two years. With such restrictions, WFP's attempts to plan in advance run aground on constitutional restrictions.[78] Even the United Nations Children's Fund, perhaps the most flexible of all the United Nations agencies, lacks a mandate to intervene in the very first stages of disasters.

The lack of effective mandates to deal with problems arising out of disasters reflects two fundamental issues: the first concerns the development of the United Nations family in general; the second involves the inherent tensions between state sovereignty and an effective international system. Only too often the answer to global or international problems is given by creating yet another inter-governmental organization. Over the past forty years, agencies have been heaped upon the system, often with little regard for overlap in responsibilities and certainly with only minimal concern for how the effort of one agency might affect the work of another. The sometimes lax or politically convenient imprecision of many agency mandates has compounded this higgledy-piggledy growth of inter-governmental organizations. Lack of clarity, overlapping responsibilities and a general disregard for the effect of a new agency on the IGO network as a whole have created an arena of ambiguity that increases inter-agency rivalry and complicates even the most basic attempts to coordinate.[79]

Given the ambiguity of their mandates, the agencies themselves are often uncertain how best to interpret their roles. More often than not, their objectives are determined not by their prescribed constitutions but rather by what they feel member states will tolerate. The components of the United Nations family have constantly to contend with the inherent conflict between states' interpretations of sovereignty and their own mandated authority. UNHCR will extend its 'good offices' to assist non-statutory refugees when it feels that governments will accept such non-mandated involvement. Yet, should governments show any sign that UNHCR might be overstepping the mark, the organization will retreat into the most conservative and prudent approach to fulfilling its responsibilities.

Inconsistent Use of United Nations Agencies

'There is a fundamental contradiction in the role of all UN agencies', remarked an official from the United States Agency for International Development. 'You can't tell governments whom you depend upon for your funds what to do.'[80] While, in part, this self-evident truth explains one aspect of the dilemma faced by United Nations agencies, it by no means encapsulates the more subtle interplay between governments and inter-governmental organizations. There are constant trade-offs between the two. Often governments do not wish to incur international opprobrium by failing to comply with an agency's request to assist afflicted peoples. In support of a particular objective, agencies have not been unwilling to play one political grouping against another: 'You've got to play the blocs, even within the Western bloc', suggested a former senior UNHCR official.[81] Conversely, inter-governmental organizations must also play the game: they, too, undertake activities which, in certain instances, have questionable legality or which at least circumvent the normal interpretation of their mandates.

Yet, generally speaking, it is not the issue of funding *per se*, nor the dubious trade-offs that most complicate the roles of inter-governmental organizations. Of far greater consequence is the inconsistency with which United Nations bodies in general are used by governments of member states. This inconsistency affects not only the ways in which inter-governmental organizations give priorities to their objectives, but also the resources at hand to deal with emergencies.

Even if the Secretary-General of the United Nations launches a major international appeal for an emergency, member states may well ignore his pleas. Jacques Beaumont, formerly in charge of emergency relief at UNICEF, recalled that:

ten days after a major international appeal was launched for the Lebanon there was no response. We in UNICEF decided not to approach anyone independently for funds, but nevertheless the US State Department just called to ask what we were doing about drugs for the Lebanon. The official at the State Department said that he didn't want to go through the Secretary General's special fund; he wanted the money to go through UNICEF.[82]

Member governments pick and choose how and when they wish to use inter-governmental organizations. In Honduras, the United States wanted UNHCR to undertake a repatriation programme to return refugees from El Salvador. When, in desperation, local UNHCR officials had to admit that none of the refugees were willing to be repatriated, the United States government refused to accept UNHCR's findings and turned to another IGO, namely the International Committee for Migration, to take on the task.

The World Food Programme, like all other United Nations agencies, feels compelled to respond to the dictates of its donors when at all possible. Despite the fact that WFP normally has very few personnel on the ground, food donors have increasingly besieged WFP with requests which it has neither the resources nor the manpower to meet. Monitoring of individual food donations by the EEC, Canada or Australia, purchasing of transport for relief operations inside Ethiopia are but two examples of undertakings imposed upon the WFP. Yet, from the organization's perspective, it cannot assume that such demands will continue. It cannot request increased funding nor seek to ensure an appropriate structure to enable it to undertake such tasks in the future when, in fact, it can never be sure that governments will continue to use it in those ways.

Whether they are concerned with technical issues or with those affecting broader policies, inter-governmental organizations, as mentioned earlier, live in a world made unpredictable by the inconsistent ways in which they are used. This fact has significant consequences for the very structures and behaviour of these organizations.

Organizational Behaviour

Uncertain mandates and the inconsistent use of international organizations go a long way to explain the over-centralized and ponderous decision-making structures that bedevil the vast majority of the United Nations agencies. These same factors also explain why only too often there is a wide gulf between the formal objectives of such organizations and their preoccupations with what might be termed 'organizational health'.

The greater the institutional insecurity, the less control it may have over its agenda and resource base, the greater will be the propensity to define organizational objectives in terms of the organization's survival. Organizational survival under such conditions is reflected in what one observer described as 'prudence'. Prudence, or caution, is reflected in certain basic organizational characteristics. There is a tendency to restrict activities to pre-established standard operating procedures, programmes and repertoires. Individual initiatives are frowned upon as being institutionally disruptive. Formalism marks the implementation of such pre-programmed operational activities, and employees respect relatively rigid lines of communication, with little cross-fertilization of ideas and information. Priorities are determined in terms of what the organization should be doing; means not ends provide the focal points for resolving problems.

The spectrum of United Nations agencies is broad. Some, such as UNICEF, with its wide network of voluntary support groups and more flexible mandate, is far less rigid than an organization such as UNHCR. For UNHCR, prudence pervades the whole of the organization's structure. Those within it view acceptable performance as complying with fixed routines more than testing initiatives. They become immersed in what might be described as 'lower task management', e.g. the compilation of reports and budgets, rather than the anticipation of new problems and new ways of dealing with them. Prudence and security demand that formal approval is given at each stage of the organization's hierarchy, and this process in turn means that all decisions of any consequence must filter up and be sanctioned by the central authority of the organization.

If one matches these organizational tendencies against the need for initiatives and flexibility so often demanded by disaster relief operations, there is little doubt that the rigidly hierarchical structures of the majority of United Nations agencies are unsuitable to deal with the plight of emergency victims. As one emergency officer for UNHCR admitted, United Nations agencies 'just lack the flexibility to deal with emergencies'.[83]

'Prudence', explained an old United Nations hand, 'is not as much a question of individual courage, etc., as much as it is perhaps due to the perception of individuals' roles from an organisational perspective. Prudence concerns the reluctance of individuals to push the organisation's response beyond what those within it feel will be accepted.'[84] UNHCR, in Kampuchea, turned its back on some of the most blatant violations of refugee rights because UNHCR officials felt that to protest would be regarded by headquarters as not in the interests of the organization.

All relief situations are redolent with ambiguity, and ambiguity is abhorrent to all organizations, particularly those that are predisposed to rely heavily on pre-programmed procedures and high degrees of formalism. The greater the ambiguity for rigidly hierarchical structures, the greater the tendency for those 'below' to depend upon instructions from the 'top'. Yet, where the top is uncertain about its own authority and not in control of resources, it resolves such ambiguity by guiding the organization towards a minimalist position: that which the organization can safely do. 'In an organisation such as UNHCR, one doesn't use a criterion of success or failure—merely what one can do; the more tangible aspects of such a minimum centre around donors' pressures being reflected from the organisation's headquarters.'[85]

The gulf between the ambiguity of organizational objectives and the preoccupation with institutional health are often bridged by focusing on the priorities implicit in money. Funding slices through ambiguity and provides a concrete basis upon which to determine priorities. It is not irrelevant that all too often those who have attempted to coordinate the efforts of inter-governmental agencies in emergencies speak of 'the power of the purse'. The availability of funds—the means—frequently determines the priority which emergencies—the ends—actually receive. Such attention to means, of course, also reflects organizational concerns with survival. The accumulation and expending of resources are concrete and identifiable standards of performance. They reflect both donor approval and organizational continuity.

However, when an emergency situation lacks ambiguity and when donors' reactions are judged to be sympathetic and host governments are cooperative, the relief machinery of the United Nations agencies can work in relative harmony.[86] Yet, in the world of disasters, ambiguity is generally the norm and the social and political complexities that they entail are never far from the surface. More often than not, those United Nations bodies involved in emergency relief cope with ambiguity and complexity by resorting to caution, by relying on well-established and rigid organizational routines and communication channels which ultimately ensure organizational health and define 'acceptable performance'.

The Expertise Dilemma

Like the over-bureaucratized structures of most inter-governmental organizations, the personnel policies of IGOs offer an easy target for criticism. Appointments based on criteria of quotas and patronage, lack of expertise, a general disinclination to abide by the standards of international civil servants, are all readily apparent failings of the inter-governmental world. Yet, these criticisms are too obvious. They ignore the complexities, the trade-offs that United Nations agencies have to face and they re-emphasize the inherent insecurities that are generated by uncertain mandates and the inconsistent behaviour of their inter-governmental constituents.

Even in instances where agencies such as UNICEF and UNHCR are not bound by the principle that recruitment be based on equitable geographic distribution, there are subtle and not so subtle pressures placed on agency administrators by governments to place their own nationals. It is interesting to note 'the consternation of US mission officials (in Geneva)' when UNHCR filled two headquarters appointments in 1980 directly without reference to the United States Office of Humanitarian Affairs. American officials, according to a United States' House of Representatives study, 'consider such appointments to be a form of patronage'; and the report went on to query why the American contingent on UNHCR's staff should represent only 11 per cent of the total when the United States contributes 'more than one-quarter of the UNHCR budget'.[87]

Staffing represents part of the trade-off that IGOs have to make to earn a modicum of flexibility and, more important, survival. Yet, personnel policies based on the sensitivities of national governments ultimately result in international administrations that, in the words of an early UNESCO report, 'n'est que la projection de l'administration nationale sur un plan élevé, avec des plus vastes proportions.'[88] Paradoxically, United Nations agencies justify these coteries of national interest by maintaining that national links ensure a direct IGO access to national negotiating tables. However, the reality is that 'officials are often considered representatives of the world community for purposes of bureaucratic bargaining at the national level, but these same persons in the daily activities of international institutions usually represent a particular national or ideological point of view.'[89]

Not only does this reality undercut the very concept of the role of the international civil servant, but it also means that on occasion even the most urgent issues such as disaster relief operations find their way into the maelstrom of contending national approaches and prejudices.[90] In a world in which a major disaster strikes on average three times a week, the inclination for those within the inter-governmental agencies to measure their responses in terms of what would be acceptable to their own individual governments is a complicating factor in the calculation of who receives assistance, when and where.

Patronage also leads to inappropriately trained officials assuming responsibilities for which they are ill prepared. While the level of understanding about approaches to disasters and disaster relief has gained in sophistication over the past decade, the level of expertise within the agencies to deal with disasters has not made a commensurate leap. In part this is due to the very conservative approaches that the agencies take to their own involvement in relief and in part it is due to their preoccupations with donor requests which only too often drown the expert in a sea of donor-orientated paperwork. In part it reflects the very real problem that agency personnel policies and the garnering of experts do not often coincide.

Despite these hazards, more and more specialists in disaster management are being introduced into different United Nations agencies. They are brought in either on a permanent or a temporary basis; yet, on whatever basis he serves, the expert must contend with certain inescapable realities. In theory, the expert's responsibilities should be focused on the plight of the disaster victim. The reality, however, is that he or she must constantly contend with two more pervasive pressures. Governments of the afflicted impose a variety of constraints on the expert: the government might, for example, view international intervention as undermining its own authority; and it may well, therefore, place limitations upon what the expert is allowed to initiate. A second pressure is that placed on the expert by his or her own agency. Field representatives of agencies must constantly balance the wishes of their headquarters in Rome, Geneva or New York with the wishes of the governments to which they are accredited. These tensions are passed on to the expert in a variety of ways, and tend to limit the effectiveness of the expert.

Field representatives may impress upon the expert the need for the latter to approach his or her task in a way that would not be embarrassing to the government. This tends to ensnare the expert in a way of thinking that reflects less the requirements of the disaster victim and more the requirements of the agency and the host government. Less subtly, the field representative may use his or her authority over relief allocations to control the expert, or he may force the expert to comply with management procedures that delay or frustrate the expert's task. These professional insecurities and unknowns exist for the disaster management expert because the agency with which he or she works abounds with these very same unknowns and insecurities, only on a larger scale. They affect not only the competence of the expert, but also the very relations that the agencies have with each other.

Inter-agency Relations

Uncertain mandates, the inconsistency with which agencies are used by governments and the hazards placed in the way of experts all spark off the mechanisms of agency self-protection. Some call it inter-agency rivalry. The more publicity a disaster receives, the greater the need for an agency to be seen to be involved. It would be wrong to conclude that inter-governmental organizations are not concerned about the distress of disaster victims; but, on the other hand, it would be right to conclude that organizational efforts on behalf of victims are undertaken with an eye to those organizations' support bases—principally governments.

What governments—donors or recipients—think about the efforts of inter-governmental bodies becomes a criterion in determining what organizations are inclined to do. Where governments are inclined to provide agencies with considerable financial support, the agencies see this as a cue to concentrate their own efforts. Where governments are not so inclined, the agencies' sense of priorities is commensurately affected. Not only does one have to be where the action is, one also has to be seen by supporters to be where the action is.

Thus, territorial claims in the world of relief become a major organizational preoccupation. The right to demonstrate one's authority and to justify one's organizational role represent a high stake in the game. The game, however, becomes a little more difficult when that right is unclear, when ambiguity blurs the boundaries of which agency should be doing what and where. The greater the overlap in mandated authority, the less clear-cut the roles of the relevant agencies, the greater is the propensity to fight for stakes. The more complex the disaster, the more ambiguity reigns.

In a situation in which victims of a natural disaster also become victims of man-made disasters, there is all too often a breakdown in the regulated responsibilities of the agencies. At what stage can UNHCR intervene, and if UNHCR does not feel that a particular situation falls within its own competence, does this leave the way open for another agency? Would the intervention of another agency set a precedent that would ultimately reduce the authority of UNHCR?

In the Kampuchean operation mentioned earlier, UNHCR was initially reluctant to become involved on the Thai border because 'economic migrants' did not fall within the competence of the organization. Technically, there was no international agency with the competence to respond to these distressed migrants until UNICEF entered the scene. UNICEF, normally restricted to assisting children and lactating mothers, justified its involvement by declaring that, in helping all such distressed peoples, it was 'preventing the creation of orphans'. UNHCR clearly began to realize soon after UNICEF's intervention that, despite the former's initially conservative interpretation of its mandate, UNICEF might well be encroaching on an area in which UNHCR itself should be involved. The clashes between the two in Thailand became legion, ultimately with UNHCR attempting 'to make a bid for the whole show'.[91] Relations between the two were marked by significant degrees of lack of cooperation, of independent initiatives and of a general unwillingness to harmonize efforts—all at the expense of the disaster-affected people.

Earlier in this discussion, the frequently mentioned influence of the 'power of the purse' was described as having an important value for the organization since it reflected a tangible criterion of acceptable performance. The resources available to fund relief operations are often difficult to find within the tight biennial budgets with which agencies are forced to live. 'It's only by finding small pots of money that they might be able to find disaster relief funds', stated a United Nations Assistant Secretary for Administration. Otherwise, they must depend almost entirely upon the voluntary contributions of member states for emergency funds.[92] Therefore, the purse is a cake to be fought over, for resources are a major factor in the security of an organization. Where there is money on the table, agencies show little restraint in gorging what they can. Each will seek to justify a greater portion by proposing operational initiatives which in a less competitive environment would be recognized as falling into the competence of another. The smaller the cake, normally the less the competition; but if the cake is large, then the energies of the agencies are bent on getting and justifying whatever they can grab.

In emergency operations, where funds may flow fast but time to plan is limited, the pressure to partake of the feast is particularly great. Appropriate needs and relevant and coordinated approaches give way to the kind of independent initiatives that will consume funds, and these pressures, in turn, tend to pit one agency against another. Such competition need not necessarily be the case. Very often it is not; but the organizational insecurities of the agencies only too often ultimately rebound on the very victims who await relief. (Refer to Appendix II for a list of United Nations specialized agencies.)

The Complex World of NGOs

The mass migration of peoples across the continent of Africa towards the end of the 1970s caused grave concerns for many within the international community, particularly those African countries that had opened their doors to these 'refugees'.[93] Not only were these migrations a sign of the parlous state of instability throughout many areas of Africa, but they also posed a potential threat to the stability of their host states. The refugee crisis demanded solutions, 'durable' solutions that would offer the millions of migrants some degree of self-sufficiency.

In 1981 the first International Conference on Assistance to Refugees in Africa (ICARA I) assembled to discuss the kinds of measures that should be taken to deal with the crisis. Potential donor governments, despite their ostensible concerns, were reluctant to make any significant increases in the aid they were already providing for general development programmes. The African host governments were wary of any solutions that might be reached at the expense of development programmes for their own indigenous peoples. In this kind of atmosphere, costs and cost-effectiveness were issues of more than minimal interest. For this reason, among others, donors looked towards non-governmental organizations to act as implementing partners in helping the refugees.

ICARA I, according to a former Oxfam Overseas Director, 'was a major breakthrough in the recognition of NGOs.'[94] For most of the three decades following World War II, donor governments were at best ambivalent about NGO 'do-gooders'. Now, however, NGOs throughout most of the developed world had become effective lobbyists. They had become increasingly adept at mobilizing public opinion, and they had also seemingly demonstrated an ability to deliver, distribute and account for aid more effectively and more cheaply than their governmental or inter-governmental counterparts.

The enthusiasm with which donors promoted the role of NGOs at ICARA was by no means shared by African host governments. They were suspicious that donors' increasing reliance on non-governmental organizations would directly or indirectly undermine host governments' authority and ability to control. IGOs responsible for ICARA, principally the United Nations High Commissioner for Refugees,[95] were more ambivalent about donors' reliance upon NGOs. IGOs, themselves, were not designed to undertake the grass-roots 'durable solution' projects that the refugee crisis required. However, they were used to acting as channels for international assistance and, like African host governments, saw the growing donor government–NGO partnership as a potential threat to their own authority and even institutional roles.

ICARA presented NGOs with tremendous opportunities. Never before had the chance of helping so many distressed peoples in such a relatively systematic way presented itself. The prospect of substantial resources from donor governments to assist refugees lay before them; involvement in solutions to ease the plight of millions would be the reward, a reward that, needless to say, would have further dividends in terms of even greater respectability and recognition.

Yet, the ostensible advantages of becoming the channel for a considerable portion of ICARA funding were not without their risks. Might the links forged between donor governments and NGOs by the resources of the former compromise the much-vaunted independence of the latter? Would the work of NGOs, no matter how well-intentioned, really challenge the authority of those governments that were hosting refugees throughout Africa? And to what extent could NGOs work independently of inter-governmental organizations who in so many instances supported NGO projects in which governments were not directly interested?[96]

The advantages that ICARA offered had to be reconciled with the risks that it posed. However, such dilemmas were, and are, not new; they are an inherent part of the complex world of non-governmental organizations.

Four NGO Dilemmas

After looking at the activities of a large number of United States NGOs, Tendler concludes that '. . . the only theme common to all of them may be the sameness of their claim that heterogeneity makes evaluation difficult.'[97] Yet, despite their obvious heterogeneity, most non-governmental organizations from the developed world working overseas share a common set of persistent dilemmas, four of which can be grouped under the following headings: (1) goal conflicts; (2) structural constraints; (3) scale; and (4) expertise.

1. *Goal conflicts.* Non-governmental organizations are, according to Morss, 'both religious and non-religious [organizations] whose primary goal has

traditionally been to alleviate human misery in developing countries.'[98] Such institutions span a vast array of types, motives, structures and sizes; and each, in one way or another, has goals that reflect institutional self-images. These goals may range from 'promoting the love of Christ through action' to 'liberating the oppressed through direct community participation.' Yet, whatever the objectives that reflect institutional *raisons d'être*, one consistent goal-related self-image is that of 'independence'. The vast majority of non-governmental organizations adamantly espouse this fundamental article of faith: they are free from the influence of any other organization that might interfere with their avowed aspirations. It is an article of faith inherent in the self-image of an NGO that it would seem that little could challenge it. And yet, in the day-to-day operations of an NGO, this fundamental precept is constantly put to the test—and often found wanting. It is not that the NGO easily abandons this particular principle, but rather that the principle clashes with other aspects of its self-image. For an NGO that professes to seek to assist the afflicted, the opportunity to provide assistance is at the core of its purpose. But what sacrifices to its independence might an NGO have to consider in the pursuit of its goal of relieving suffering?

If a donor government provides a significant amount of food for an NGO to relieve the suffering of a famine-affected people, can that NGO truly maintain that its independence is not potentially compromised? To that question, most NGOs would reply that they might take the food, but that it would in no way affect their independence. In reality the process that might erode the principle of 'independence' is more subtle than that. Take, for example, the case of World Vision in Ethiopia in 1985.

By the early part of 1985, the problem faced by the relief operation in Ethiopia was less one of food *per se* and more one of logistics. The United States Agency for International Development, to enhance the delivery capabilities of World Vision, offered to provide that NGO with over one hundred trucks for its operations in the north of the country. It was an 'irresistible offer', but it took World Vision three months to finally accept it. The NGO was fully aware that the kind of assistance that USAID had offered would create a 'priority bind', allowing the donor 'to structure the operations of the agency'.[99]

The conflict for most developed NGOs in their dealings with donor governments is not that the latter uses resources to bribe or directly control NGOs: the issue is more subtle than that. Through its resources, a donor government wittingly or unwittingly seduces its NGO counterpart. By contributing large amounts of assistance to an NGO's operations, the NGO becomes used not only to relying upon the resources of governments, but also comes to appreciate the effect of low overheads that these available resources ensure.[100] The non-governmental agency may be able to justify its acceptance of such resources because a greater volume of resources allows it even greater scope to relieve suffering. At the same time, however, there is the ever-present danger that the agency will get used to a donor's generosity. This has a distorting effect, a lure that in one way or another will make the agency more prone to see relief through the eyes of those who have created a relationship of resource alliance.

The independence so fundamental to an NGO's self-image is closely linked to another article of faith, that of 'working directly with people rather than with governments'.[101] Yet, this seemingly worthwhile objective is also not without its dilemmas. If disaster-prone peoples are to be assured of help in time of emergency, clearly there is a need to strengthen the capabilities of governments of such states to respond. And yet, by claiming to work directly with the people, in a none too subtle way an NGO frequently finds itself bypassing the only semblance of a permanent structure that has the potential capacity to be always on hand to deal with disasters. It is far better to find some way of integrating one's activities with the government of the afflicted than to seek to evade all the 'bureaucratic and corrupt practices'[102] of such governments.

Of course, the choice is a difficult one. Faced with the suffering of the disaster-stricken, there is the ever-present temptation to avoid anything that hampers the relief process. Yet, only too often, that temptation not only bypasses but undercuts the attempts of well-intentioned government officials who are as concerned about their own people as are foreign representatives of NGOs. In 1983, in southern Sudan, the consequence of NGOs' determination to 'work directly with people rather than with governments' led NGOs—perhaps unintentionally—to immobilize the efforts of the Sudanese Commission for Refugees and to alienate local officials who had made extensive provision for the Ugandan refugees streaming into the country. NGOs' lack of sensitivity about the efforts being made by government departments, their determination to work directly with the people, introduced a high level of conflict in a situation where cooperation could and should have been the order of the day.[103] The dilemmas which self-images create for non-governmental organizations are not easily reconciled. They are made all the more complex by structural constraints that in one way or another are common to those that comprise the non-governmental sector.

2. *Structural constraints.* Heterogeneity is a term that describes not only the goals but also the structures of those organizations that lie within the non-governmental sector. Be it size, constituencies, or operational procedures, the most consistent structural feature of the NGO sector is the diversity of its components. And yet, no matter how different one NGO structure might be from another, they are forced to face institutional constraints that clearly have a common thread. These structural constraints are in no small part a consequence of the relationship between an NGO and its support base.

One major article of faith described by Tendler is an NGO's 'willingness to be flexible and experimental'.[104] NGOs are probably on the whole more flexible and more willing to experiment than their governmental or IGO counterparts. However, as the dilemmas posed for NGOs by the International Conference on Assistance to Refugees in Africa demonstrated, their ability to experiment and innovate is constrained by the resources that NGOs receive from their support bases. Whether these support bases are governmental or the public at large, an NGO—when compared to governmental agencies or IGOs—has no consistent assurance that resources to undertake its activities will always be available. While under most circumstances their governmental or inter-governmental counterparts can assume a general level of predictable funding, the NGO, by comparison, cannot. Its resources to conduct a relief operation, let alone those needed to sustain its normal activities, are frequently dependent upon a sensitivity to what can only be described as 'the market-place'.

The forces of the market-place lend a degree of institutional instability to the activities of NGOs, which are rendered so by persistent concerns about what kinds of activities will be acceptable to those who fund its activities. An Oxfam official commented that, in mid-1984, he had grave doubts about his organization's ability to 'sell' the Ethiopian famine to the British public. His perception of public reaction led him to conclude that sufficient relief resources could only be raised if one brought the Ethiopian issue into the wider context of an African emergency. In so doing, he readily admitted, the severe plight of Ethiopia became clouded by the less focused and more ambiguous general African appeal.[105]

There are disasters to which the public at large—a vital constituency for non-governmental organizations—are more sympathetic than others. It is easier for an American non-governmental organization to elicit sympathy and funds for disaster-afflicted children in Latin America than for typhoon victims in Vietnam. No matter how obvious this may be, the fact remains that an NGO's ability to relieve suffering is often less dependent upon the needs of the afflicted than on the kind of response it feels a particular disaster can generate. The consequence for the NGO engaged in relief activities is fundamental. Its goal of alleviating misery is dependent upon the extent to which it can mobilize support. Where such support is difficult to raise, then the NGO is faced with the difficult choice of possibly alienating its support bases or limiting its involvement in an unpopular cause.

The market forces to which NGOs must be sensitive lead to basic issues about the ways in which they must conduct their relief efforts. There is always latent tension in any major relief operation between an agency's staff in the field and staff at headquarters. The tension reflects a fundamental structural problem in the operations of an NGO. Broadly speaking, an NGO's staff in the field is concerned with undertaking relief activities. Those at headquarters are anxious to ensure adequate support for those in the field. This seemingly harmonious division of labour, however, has to contend with often conflicting needs. Headquarters are concerned with issues of visibility: is the agency being seen by those who might support its activities? Has another agency gained more publicity than its own in demonstrating its work? These are not irrelevant considerations; for without the appropriate level of publicity and visibility, there is the ever-nagging possibility that an agency's work in the field will be cut short by lack of resources.

The pressures that such concerns impose on the operations of an NGO are several. Many in the field complain of the unnecessary demands placed upon them by headquarters for publicity material, photographs, dramatic stories and the like. These demands, though generally regarded as necessary by field workers, are nevertheless diversions from the priority of providing assistance. During operations in western Sudan in 1986, relief workers complained that headquarters were only concerned with the publicity and financial reporting procedures of the field staff. The relief activities seemed to be a secondary consideration.[106]

Whether or not this perception reflects reality is difficult to determine, but that it is a real perception is clearly and consistently the case. There can be little doubt that an NGO needs the visibility that only reports and pictures from the field can provide. Furthermore, as the ICARA conferences made very clear, the reputation of NGOs in no small part rests on their purportedly accurate accounting and monitoring capabilities. Hence, headquarters view such accounting tasks as extremely important while those in the field often resent the amount of time needed to fulfil such institutional requirements.

These kinds of structural tensions unfold an explanation for one of the most prevalent problems that hamper effective relief, namely, preoccupations with 'turf'. Time and again, the promotional and administrative prerequisites of the organization affect the ways in which an NGO structures its relief operation. While everyone involved in the relief process may wish to be seen to be involved with the most severely affected, the rush for prime sites can have an extremely disruptive impact.

These prime sites, or turf, are sought after because they increase prospects of visibility and are frequently chosen because they facilitate administrative tasks. The unseemly rush of NGOs into the famine-stricken region of Ethiopia's Sidamo region in August 1984 serves as an appropriate example. When news of the famine broke, agencies flooded into the region, and set up operations with little regard for what other agencies were doing or for who else was there. Most of them established themselves along the main routes, routes that were not only accessible to relief transport but to journalists as well. Though certainly well-intentioned, the actions of the agencies resulted in activities that were generally chaotic and in certain instances even harmful.

The chaos that resulted from the rush of agencies into Sidamo needs little explanation. A dozen agencies—determined to plant their banners in a new area of tragedy, each eager to demonstrate its particular relief capability and each clinging to its bit of turf—could not but lead to disjointed and competitive responses. However, more unfortunate was the fact that the sites selected by the agencies in many instances compounded the problems of the famine victims. By stationing themselves along the roadside, the agencies were forcing many people to leave their villages in the hinterland to find help. The journey to the relief stations for those already suffering from malnutrition merely intensified their problem; for though they were able to receive assistance when they finally got to the roadside relief camps, the trek itself forced many to expend an inordinate amount of energy. And, in many instances, the relief aid received there was substantially consumed on the victims' journey home.

The Sidamo experience reflects to a significant extent the pressures that non-governmental organizations face in responding to relief. Along the main road leading to Kassala in the Sudan, Radda Barnen, the distinguished Save the Children Fund of Sweden, found itself unable to assist in any major way the thousands of refugees who had fled from Ethiopia. While the conditions of the refugees were desperate, there was little that Radda Barnen could do. 'It lacked the resources to respond', observed an agency official. 'You can't do much if you don't have the funds.'[107]

For so many NGOs involved in the Ethiopian relief operation, the disaster was a financial bonanza. The resources for most agencies in the developed world increased significantly. Many agencies in the United States and United Kingdom doubled their annual income during 1984.[108] Structurally, however, these times of plenty can impose serious strains on a non-governmental organization. Donors' responses to NGO appeals can frequently be unpredictable, at times falling far short of expectations and at times well surpassing anything that an NGO might have anticipated. In instances such as the Ethiopian or Kampuchean crises, NGOs often found themselves with more resources than they could handle. They were generally obliged to dispense the funds and materials that flowed into them, but they lacked the manpower, both at headquarters and in the field, to dispense such bounty effectively. The greater the available resources, the more headquarters became preoccupied with monitoring and accounting functions, and consequently the greater was the pressure upon small field staffs to focus upon tasks which the latter regarded as of secondary importance.

In a relief operation, an NGO might find that pressures resulting from such a wealth of resources lead it to shift the focus of its distribution patterns. Less attention is devoted to determining the particular needs of the afflicted, and greater emphasis is placed on ways of dispensing resources at hand. The means, in other words, determine the ends; the availability of resources structures the operation rather than the operation determining the requirements that agencies seek to fulfil.

3. *Scale.* 'If private voluntary agencies [NGOs] grow too big', remarked an official from World Vision, 'they will just become big, bureaucratic machines like IGOs.'[109] Traditionally, NGOs have viewed their roles in terms of working directly with people on small-scale projects at grass-roots level. These generally avowed intentions, however, again pose dilemmas for the NAGO, dilemmas that spill over into the world of disaster relief. NGOs are generally used to working on a small scale, be it in development or relief. The village-based project in rural areas or the community-based project in urban areas directly affects a limited number of people only, and these are normally in defined groupings, for example village farmers, handicapped children, some lactating mothers in an urban slum. When a disaster strikes, the scope of an NGO poses practical problems.

In a very practical sense, those who support an NGO in a particular country often assume that the very presence of an NGO in that country means that it is well placed to intervene. However, an NGO is very often working in isolated areas far away from the impact of a disaster. It is by no means always on hand, and to become involved means that fundamental decisions have to be made. One such fundamental decision is whether or not to divert its resources and man-power to the site of a disaster. In such instances the very advantages that the international community attributes to the non-governmental sector often become disadvantages. The limited expenditure on manpower, the low over-heads, and the small-scale grass-roots projects—all facets of an NGO that have been so highly esteemed by the international community—mean that a switch away from development to relief imposes tremendous strains on an NGO. Sometimes agencies, faced with these kinds of decision, accept that the diversion of resources and manpower in times of disaster will have little overall impact on relief, and, therefore, 'ignore' the disaster. This was the case in early 1984 when the Oxfam field director in Ethiopia accepted that he 'was too preoccupied in development work and saw the famine as just too vast' to focus upon the disaster befalling the country.[110]

Yet, when the decision to intervene in a disaster is made, an NGO's scale can still often present problems. The question is 'what basic role to play?' Oxfam's Marcus Thompson recognized this issue when dealing with Oxfam's response to the Ethiopian crisis: 'Does an agency try to take an overview of the situation or just do its own little thing?' he wondered. If the former, then an agency may well find itself confronted with a level of demand and a need for an organiza-tional structure that go well beyond any single agency's capacity. If the latter, the advantage is that an agency will know what it is good at doing, but that may not be entirely appropriate for the crisis at hand.[111]

In the Horn of Africa crisis, many private agencies had experience with 'supplementary feeding'. In other words, they were good at identifying vulner-able groups and providing the small quantities of high-protein substances that might save the lives of those, e.g. children, who were most threatened by malnutrition. However, as these agencies became involved in supplementary feeding programmes, it became abundantly clear that 'we were supplementing nothing. There were no basic rations [for the disaster afflicted] to supplement.'[112] For the agencies, the lack of basic rations presented them with a very fundamental problem. Most lacked the resources and the manpower to become involved in providing large amounts of grain, oil and dried, skimmed milk for basic rations. They were not used to the monitoring and distribution processes that the provision of basic rations would require. Nor were they particularly eager to merge their own relief capabilities into an overall relief effort that would lose the distinctive quality of their own work. As Thompson noted, by August 1984: 'there were masses of private voluntary organisations [in Ethiopia] doing supplementary feeding programmes. They felt most comfortable with this'.[113]

For an agency to expand the scale of its operation, on the other hand, presents very real problems: 'The temptation to feed people, to grow as an agency is always there.'[114] Yet, the decision will invariably introduce basic institutional issues concerning the consequences of such growth. To grow incrementally, or, in other words, to adjust one's capacities by working with the same field and headquarters staff, will tax the structure to the extreme. However, to gear up for a major adjustment in scale may well mean that, once the immediate crisis is over, there may well be insufficient funding available to sustain that growth. The dilemma of scale presents a difficult set of choices for private voluntary agencies surviving for the most part on the goodwill of an unpredictable public. To a very significant extent, it is a problem that is inextricably linked with the dilemma of 'expertise'.

4. *Expertise.* In the early days of non-governmental organizations, many in the governmental and inter-governmental sectors viewed the well-intentioned efforts of those in the private sector as amateurish. Now, in the 1980s, the reputations of major non-governmental organizations are noted for their professionalism. The medical, nutritional, agricultural and hydrological expertise of many NGOs rank as high as any in the world of development and relief. Yet, while their expertise has grown both in practice and repute, it also presents NGOs with institutional dilemmas that can skew their responses to emergencies.

Most private agencies are known by potential support bases for particular kinds of activities. They are regarded as particularly adept, for example, at dealing with the problems of children or agriculture; they may have a reputation for health care work or clean water projects. Whatever their areas of expertise, NGOs have a vested interest in seeing issues—be they development projects or disaster relief—in terms of what they are good at doing. Institutionally, expertise forms part of their reason for being; promotionally, this expertise is the key to fostering the public resources upon which they depend.

In and of itself, specialization, to the extent that it exists within the private sector, is not inherently bad. As suggested earlier, growing awareness about relevant capabilities of organizations within the international relief network has added a modicum of coherence to an otherwise all too disparate band of relief actors.[115] Yet, paradoxically, the very expertise of agencies can create confusion and distort even the ostensible goals of an agency in dealing with relief.

The big battle among the NGOs in Ethiopia in 1984 was between the nutritionists and the medical people, as one agency representative observed.[116] The former were convinced that priority intervention should be given to the kind of feeding programmes that would deal with the requirements of particularly vulnerable groups, while the latter argued that disease emerging as a direct consequence of malnutrition should be the first issue to be addressed. The question of priority was important because, in a relief operation where logistic support was poor, who and what had first use of off-loading and trucking facilities was only too often a question of life or death.

Underlying the dispute was the issue of institutional perspective: the way in which an agency determined need depended to a very significant extent on the institutional referrants of individual organizations.[117] The expertise that may distinguish one organization from another can add increased uncertainty in an already chaotic disaster situation. Those, for example, in government departments of an afflicted country may be confused by conflicting reports emanating from the field. NGO officials at headquarters may reinforce the uncertainty by pressing donors to supply relief based on the isolated views of their field staff; or conversely, headquarters staff may determine relief requirements through their own institutional perspective, based for the most part on what they know their institutions can most effectively provide . . . in some cases despite what their field officers feel should be recommended or what governments of the afflicted may deem to be appropriate.[118]

Perhaps, in an even more fundamental way, the very expertise of an agency can distort a further 'article of faith' which, according to Tendler, is common to all NGOs, namely, the emphasis on participation of the poor in decision-making.[119] Cuny, Harrell-Bond and others have recognized the failure of those seeking to provide relief to include the disaster-afflicted in the very relief process that is designed to relieve their suffering.[120] In one sense, this imposition of aid reflects what have earlier been described as the conceptual misunderstandings that pervade the very nature of disaster relief. The imposition of aid has distorting effects. People stricken by a disaster generally know what they need in terms of immediate needs and post-disaster rehabilitation. Outside intervention is most effective when it is used to facilitate the process by which the needs of the affected are met. This process can only be set in motion when decision-making is a shared activity. However, this process must surmount the constraints imposed by the very expertise that relief institutions bring to a disaster.

On one level, an NGO that specializes in a particular form of assistance has a vested interest in promoting that expertise. It reflects not only what that agency is good at doing, but also forms a basis upon which it can launch its appeals. Furthermore, those whom it sends into the field will most likely be experts in the agency's specialization, and, hence, may well see disaster problems and solutions in terms of that agency's perspective. Hence, victims' participation in decision-making quickly becomes excluded from, or is at least limited in, the process because institutional requirements and perspectives have already closed off certain options. The fact that this is so often the case is not a dilemma for NGOs alone; but, given the high value that they place on victims' involvement in relief decisions, the dilemma stands out acutely. It is but further evidence of the complex world in which NGOs must operate.

The Media's Seach for a Handle

'The wider issues raised by some disasters may, perhaps, make them too important to be treated "responsibly" ', suggests Peter David of *The Economist*.

There can be little doubt that, over the past fifteen years, the media has become the 'fourth estate' of the international relief network. It is the media in all its forms—press, television, radio—that is so often both mobilizer and severest critic of the relief process.

Many people throughout private and governmental relief agencies acknowledge that the first indications that a disaster has occurred have come from the media. They are sensitive to this reporting since the media's accounts—whether accurate or not—play a critical role in structuring the relief response. It is the media that is often the key to raising funds; it is television primarily, but also newspapers, journals and radio that promote one cause, abandon another, and in so doing determine priorities. It is also the media, through its relentless search for a handle on a disaster story, that exposes the purported strengths and failings of the relief process, and consequently affects the institutional interests of those with direct or indirect roles in the international relief network. The power of the media to affect the response of the international relief network cannot be over-emphasized; and, given such direct influence, one must ask how effective a 'relief actor' this fourth estate is.

A Moral Dilemma

A doctor who assisted patients after the Chernobyl nuclear disaster in the Soviet Union in 1986 recently commented that he saw a persistent conflict of interest between his own professional responsibilities and those of the media. Reporters pressed him to describe the condition of his patients, but, as he reminded them, 'How tolerable would it be for you, if a member of your own family was seriously ill in hospital, for me to give information to the world about that person's state of health?'[121] The issue posed the very simple dilemma that exists between the public's right to know and the individual's right to privacy.

The issue, for that doctor, introduced an additional professional dilemma as well. In a situation such as that at Chernobyl, replete with uncertainties and unknowns, to what extent does a professional scientist make prognostications about an issue that may possibly affect the lives of people for several decades? The press wants 'facts', clarity, certainty and not ambiguity; but the professional all too often can only offer guarded alternatives. Instant analyses might sell newspapers, but they also cast unnecessary anxieties over the lives of many thousands for years to come. Guarded alternatives, however, do not make good stories. Furthermore, for that doctor and others like him to be allowed to continue his work in the Soviet Union, he would necessarily have to be attuned to the sensitivities of the government. To 'grandstand' over Soviet failures or to give the impression that the Soviet nuclear industry has shortened the lives of many hundreds of thousands would quite possibly mean that he and his colleagues would in the future be denied the opportunity of continuing to help.

In the West, one has become used to a press that thrives on confrontation and exposés; yet, it is a style that raises the issue of what role the media should play. If a plane crashes, is the fact that the vast majority of planes do not crash or that one plane did crash 'news'? Should the media seek to pacify and comfort, to put news into a broader perspective for the general public, or should it focus on the 'exceptions' that, once raised, may cause undue levels of anxiety? Having posed the question, one should not begin the answer from the premise that the freedom of media expression be limited. However, in the context of disasters, the responsibility of the press constantly poses moral dilemmas for both the reporter and his or her sources. The complexities of these dilemmas can be seen from the very ways in which 'what is a story' is determined, from the hazards associated with the sources needed to make a story, and from the very business of getting a story to be seen and heard.

The Story

'Reporters, in dealing with disasters, fly on auto-pilot. They always ask the same questions: how many died; what went wrong; who's to blame; will it happen again?' Yet, at the same time, the reporter is also aware that, to keep the story alive, he or she must break away from the automatic questions and find a new angle. The reporter must get a new handle on the story, or, like the gas explosion disaster in Cameroon's Lake Nios, the interest of the public will soon die.[122]

The need to invent a new handle very often forces the media to transform the context of the story. The Union Carbide chemical disaster at Bhopal in India opened up the issue of the moral obligations of multinational corporations working in developing countries; the East Pakistan cyclone disaster of 1970 became increasingly focused on the 'indifference' of West Pakistan towards its eastern half; the Ethiopian famine story was transformed into one concerned with the inherent failings of state-controlled agriculture.[123] These kinds of handles are certainly worthy news approaches: they serve the public interest, but they expose certain general failings of the news process as well. As in the case of Cameroon, if there is no handle to hang the story on, the story's fate is short-lived. This does not mean that no disaster has occurred or that people are not continuing to suffer, but, without some angle that will grip a large audience, the natural inclination of both reporter and editor is to let the story die.

This natural and obvious fate would have little consequence if it were not for the fact that the media often determine the priorities that the international relief network gives to a disaster. The key to fundraising, to the mobilization of resources and to the attention given to any single disaster is the media's clarion. The Thai/Kampuchean border operations were swamped with assistance once the press found a handle. Until the BBC's Jonathan Dimbleby 'discovered' the Ethiopian famine of 1973, few were willing to 'blow the whistle'. A little more than a decade later, another Ethiopian famine found itself ignored until a British Independent Television News team brought the Korem story on to Western television screens in October 1984.

But what happens if a handle is not found? For a story to be 'big' in terms of audience appeal, the inherited journalistic wisdom is that, for a story to count, a disaster has to be huge and pictures have to be dramatic. When reporters first got a hint of a potential disaster in Ethiopia in mid-1983, many were disappointed that they could not do more to publicize the situation, but 'there were no acute cases of starvation to film, so it wasn't news'.[124] And even if a disaster is news, its presentation may be framed in such a way as to lose the impact of the disaster itself. The handle is all-important. Thus, despite an extensive tour of Korem's relief operations given to one journalist in early 1984 by a representative of the Save the Children Fund, the journalist's story focused mainly on the political involvement of the United States and the guerrilla war.[125]

In theory, what the media regards as news should have little impact on the operations of the relief network. It should not be the reporter's responsibility to guide international response, but in the peculiar nexus of the Western press, pressure groups, public opinion, IGOs, NGOs and governments, the durability of the story is too often what counts in making the relief network act. The influence of the media in this sense naturally conflicts with the need for a reporter to find a handle. If there is no handle, then a possible story recedes into the store of those hundreds of annual disasters that were deemed not to have audience appeal. Indeed, the handle itself may so distort the picture of a disaster that an appropriate relief response becomes an additional victim of the disaster. 'The general public's impression of disasters is formed not by relief agencies, but by journalists, who are rarely experts in this area, but who are often called upon to interpret quickly both the event and the relief efforts for the rest of the world', complains the environmental agency, Earthscan.[126] When, in 1970, reporters saw cases of cholera after the East Pakistan cyclone disaster, newspapers around the world told of a major cholera epidemic about to add to the misery of the cyclone's survivors. Medicines poured into the country (including weight-reducing pills, birth control pills and aspirins!), and thousands of Bengalis were vaccinated against cholera; but, as Sommer and Mosley subsequently concluded, there never had been any evidence of increased levels of cholera.[127]

The media's hue and cry about homelessness after a disaster can instigate a deluge of tents and blankets, which may not be at all a priority for people living in tropical climates. The perennial handle of 'corruption' can lead donors to justify 'earmarking' of relief items and funds that may in fact kill appropriate or coordinated relief. The way in which the media focus on 'a good famine story' might make it difficult for relief agencies to persuade donors to give essential items, e.g. medicines, rather than food.[128] Yet, for the media, the story is what matters. Without a handle there is no story. How to get the handle becomes the crucial issue. This is by no means to suggest that the press is necessarily unconcerned with the plight of the afflicted. However, even the most caring reporter knows that in a world grown used to or even tired of disaster sagas, the only way to get a story run is to find a different angle.

Sources

'Some reporters feared touching their notebooks if they accidentally dropped them on the dirt', wrote the *Washington Post*'s Blaine Harden from Ethiopia in 1985. 'No one ate or dared think about food in the camps. In hotels back in Addis Ababa where Western famine-watchers . . . stayed, we dined together over discussions of the advisability of repeated shampoos to get germs out of our hair.'[129] Few reporters are experts in disasters. Such expertise is not part of their profession. Their own knowledge about disaster assessment or causation is normally quite limited, and their familiarity with areas in which a disaster may have occurred often equally so. They depend on the specialist, the expert, to get the facts about disasters.

Contacts, however, have views that derive from particular contexts. Field representatives from non-governmental organizations may well seek to push the work of their own agencies into the limelight. It is a natural reaction of those who depend on mobilizing the public's goodwill. The information that these NGO contacts provide is normally given with no attempt to distort or deceive, but a field representative nevertheless sees a disaster or a disaster relief operation in terms of what his or her organization feels it should be doing. Government authorities also see a disaster in terms of more abiding interests. They may wish not to panic a local population, or they may wish not to be seen to be ignoring or to be exaggerating a particular disaster.

Similarly, contacts in inter-governmental organizations dispense information in ways that also reflect particular institutional interests and perspectives. In Cameroon, in 1986, the United Nations Disaster Relief Office sought to get its interpretation of the volcanic gas disaster rapidly before the eyes of the world, but UNDRO's haste for visibility inevitably led to serious inaccuracies.[130] In the same way, in early 1986, the inter-governmental agencies fed the media with dire warnings of disaster about the food situation in the Sudan, since no one dared to be seen to be minimizing the potential disaster, as had happened in Ethiopia through mid-1984.

Yet, the experts do not always provide the handle that reporters need to make their stories. Like the doctor at Chernobyl, specialists are frequently aware of the complexities and uncertainties that arise in a disaster. Their own ambivalence may provide few stories. In search of a story, the reporter must frequently depend upon groups with fringe interests in a disaster, but with specific interests in viewing a disaster from a wider context. They may promote values and beliefs that are clear, if not didactic, and these views—in the absence of any other hard 'facts'—are promoted to an importance that may well not be deserved.[131]

News reporting engenders a feedback loop in which contacts structure the story, and in turn find themselves 'structured' by the story. The handle that keeps a story alive establishes the boundaries within which the relief process must operate. If the media determines that the relief network has been slow in providing temporary housing, housing then becomes a priority. The fact that housing is an issue stems in part from the observations of often untrained analysts, namely, the reporters themselves, and from contacts who may or may not have vested interests in imposing their own assessments on the relief process. Yet, once the story takes hold, the relief operation is only too often locked into an approach and set of commitments that, if left to more careful scrutiny, might never have been promoted. The more didactic the assessment, the greater is the possibility that such views will become news. The more original the story's handle, the greater that story's chance of survival in the helter-skelter of competing stories.

Competition

A handle on a story is one thing, getting that story to a wide audience is another. The media is subject to the same free market forces as most competitive industries. A disaster story may be good; it may have a handle; but if it cannot compete with other items regarded as newsworthy, it is relegated to obscurity. Michael Buerk recalled how people from the United States National Broadcasting Company had said to him that interest arising out of his film on famine in Korem would 'only last a week. The American public will soon get bored with that sort of stuff'.[132]

Rivalries within the media industry to get a story before the public are intense. Peter Gill of ITV recalled that 'rivalry between Britain's two main television channels played a big part in public awareness of food emergencies in Africa. For a period in 1980, for instance, two journalists based in East Africa, Brian Barron of the BBC and David Smith of ITN, regularly outdid each other in the discovery of fresh horrors in northern Uganda.'[133] The problem for both the media and the public who consume this reporting is not the rivalries per se, but what is done in the light of those rivalries to structure the relief that may or may not follow. Starving children generally fuel the consciences of donors, but famine relief normally involves far more complicated assistance than that involved in supplying the nutritional requirements of that particularly vulnerable group. Yet, the race to the story needs a handle, and the handle may obscure some of the most important aspects of a situation and exaggerate the less important.

How can a disaster story win a place in the competition for coverage, given all the other possibilities that an editor must consider? In the midst of an American election, would 'a few starving kids' really elicit much interest, wondered Visinews' Mohamed Amin in 1984.[134] When television reporter Michael Buerk first went to Korem, he was filmed holding a starving child who subsequently died. Even then the story was not given priority on the news: 'it came mid-bulletin between the French Prime Minister resigning and Israeli involvement in the Lebanon.'[135]

To a significant extent, the media finds itself damned if it does, and damned if it doesn't. Reporters know full well that without an angle that will grasp the attention of the public, they will not have a story. The reporter also knows, however, that to attempt to base a story on the uncertainties and ambiguities that are the hallmarks of so many disasters, the warnings that so often mobilize the diverse components of the international relief network may never be sounded.

Notes

1. Chap. 2, note 1.
2. This is the theme of the Swedish Red Cross's *Prevention is Better Than Cure*, Stockholm, May 1984.
3. Churchman, C., *The Systems Approach*, New York, Dell Publishing Co., 1968, p.29.
4. Pettman, R., *Human Behaviour and World Politics: A transdisciplinary introduction*, London, Macmillan, 1975, p.133.
5. Interview with Sir Robert Jackson, United Nations, New York, 26 September 1983.
6. Interview with Dr A. Mackie, USAID, Addis Ababa, 10 October 1984.
7. The reasons for the distortion of information will be more fully discussed in the following chapter. See, for example, discussion on 'the information-loading cycle' in Inter-organizational Relations, Chapter 5.
8. See comment by then United States Secretary of State, Kissinger, to the proposal to internationalize disaster relief assistance, p.81.
9. Chapter 2, pp. 62-3.
10. Interview with Thom Kersteins, Secretary-General, CEBEMO, The Hague, 29 May 1984.
11. Interview with an official from USAID, Washington, DC, 16 September 1983.
12. Interview with Zia Rizvi, Independent Commission on International Humanitarian Issues and former assistant to the UN High Commissioner for Refugees, Geneva, 23 March 1984.
13. Interview with Penny Jenden, Band Aid, London, 5 June 1986.
14. Interview with Sven Kilde, Norwegian Red Cross, Oslo, 4 June 1984.
15. These figures come from information provided by the United States Office of Foreign Disaster Assistance, USAID.
16. As Brown points out, the:

    distinction between disaster relief 'recipients' and 'donors' is both unfortunate and artificial. A staff member of the United States Agency for International Development estimates that 'local' assistance from 1965 to 1976 was almost twice that of all the international disaster assistance provided. Somehow, the local and national sense of community and the kaleidoscopic international response must merge into an effort of mutual cooperation to alleviate human suffering. [Brown, B., *Disaster Preparedness and The United Nations: Advance planning for disaster relief*, New York, Pergamon Press, 1979, p.15.]

17. The difficulty of distinguishing between the wretchedness of poorer peoples and actual disaster victims in so many countries was a theme brought up in many interviews, for example the interview with Sven Lampall, League of Red Cross Societies, Geneva, 21 March 1984, and that with Faruk Berkol, former UNDRO Coordinator, Geneva, 21 March 1984.

18. This unfortunate fact can be seen in the relatively few changes in tables on disaster plans and preparedness compiled by UNDRO. An assessment of the state of disaster preparedness in disaster-prone countries was prepared by this author in 'The Disaster Monitor', *Third World Affairs 1987*, London, Third World Foundation, 1987, pp.266–74.

19. 'The opposition leader, Khaleda Zia, criticized the relief operation for cyclone victims as inadequate. She told reporters she had visited several islands last week and saw scores of starving people without shelter.' *The Guardian*, London, 18 June 1985.

20. Interview with Faruk Berkol, Geneva, 21 March 1984.

21. Interview with Sven Lampall, Geneva, 21 March 1984.

22. In early 1985, after a large influx of refugees had poured into Sudan's Kassala province from Ethiopia, Sudanese officials were anxious not to announce the outbreak of a measles epidemic in the refugee camps. They were concerned that if word of such epidemics got out, the local populations would turn not only against the refugees, but against themselves as well. Equally important to them, they knew that they did not have the resources to deal with the spread of an epidemic if it did occur, a fact they also were loathe to make known.

23. Interview with Gunilla Drysellius, Radda Barnen (Swedish Save the Children Fund), Stockholm, 8 June 1984.

24. This kind of problem was witnessed by the author in refugee relief camps in Luuq in Somalia in late November 1984, where local relief officials were under enormous pressure to account for rations that could not be accounted for in the way that outside officials were demanding. David Kemball-Cook and Rob Stephenson deal with such matters in their excellent discussion in *Aspects of Logistics in The Somalia Refugee Relief Operation*, London, International Disaster Institute, June 1983, F10.

25. The suspicions of the Ethiopian government were not abated by the supposed involvement of a CIA official in Ethiopia in fomenting opposition in Addis Ababa against the Marxist regime during 1983. According to press reports, Vernon Walters, a United States ambassador-at-large in 1984, undertook a special mission to Addis Ababa to negotiate the agent's release with the Ethiopian leader, Menguistu Haile-Mariam. See, for example, Joe Pichirallo's report in the *Washington Post*, 25 April 1986.

26. This fear is by no means restricted to the involvements of Western voluntary agencies. Pakistan officials dealing with Afghan refugees on occasion complained about the fundamentalist Islamic doctrines that went hand-in-hand with aid being dispensed by members of the Saudi Arabian Red Crescent Society in Peshawar in northern Pakistan in 1986 and 1987.

27. Interview with Julius Holt, London School of Tropical Medicine and Hygiene, London, 6 September 1983.

28. This was clearly evidenced by the way in which the Indian Government took charge of the East Pakistan refugee relief operation throughout 1971. However, it is a consistent theme, and was stressed in discussions with Indian officials from governmental and non-governmental organizations; for example, Ajit Bhomik, Secretary-General, Indian Red Cross; M.N. Chanda, Executive Officer, St. John Ambulance; S.K. Basu, Joint Secretary, Ministry of Supply and Rehabilitation; and T.N. Kaul, formerly Indian Foreign Secretary. Kaul's comment in a 15 March 1983 conversation with the author is interesting in this context. He stated that:

I, for one, would be very hesitant to let intergovernmental organisations be distributing agencies . . . Unfortunately, international governmental personnel do not really know how to deal with disasters. The Government of India has always been hesitant to let outsiders [in] . . . International agencies should try to send as few people as possible. Too many people from the outside tend to create suspicion: 'why do they want to send them? don't they trust us?' are the kinds of issues which foreign involvement begins to generate.

29. Perhaps one of the most interesting political features to arise out of the 1971 East Pakistan refugee crisis was India's firm determination not to request assistance but to suggest that the crisis was an issue of international morality and would have to be resolved by international commitments through the good offices of India. In an interview with L.K. Jha, former Indian Ambassador to the United States, on 18 March 1983, he confirmed that 'I was never asked [by the Indian Government] to ask for help. The help which was offered was conveyed through the US ambassador in Delhi.' This was the position which Swaran Singh maintained in a subsequent interview with the author two days later.

30. Interview with Maurice Williams, former Deputy Administrator, USAID, and subsequently Director of the World Food Council, United Nations, New York, 29 September 1983.

31. Interview with Joseph Sisco, Washington, DC, 12 September 1983.

32. Interview with Edward Heath, former British Prime Minister, London, 27 June 1985.

33. Interview with Stephen Tripp, Washington, DC, 15 September 1983.

34. It is interesting to note in this context that Maurice Williams, cited above, who maintained that relief is above the battle, was one of the prime spokesmen for the White House's attempt to publicize American relief assistance programmes. As Tripp saw it, 'Williams would call AID information and press people. He wanted to get all this out. It was not just a casual affair; it was intended. I said all the time that what we were doing is showing up the government. If you're going to be magnanimous, you better be magnanimous in the right sort of way.'

35. United States State Department Archives, Sengler to Farland, Confidential Telex, 19 November 1970.

36. Telephone interview with Archer Blood, former United States Consul-General in Dacca, East Pakistan, Washington, DC, 20 September 1983.

37. Interview with J. Blankenberg, Emergency and Humanitarian Aid Section, Development Cooperation Department, Dutch Ministry of Foreign Affairs, The Hague, 29 May 1984. Blankenberg was referring to the minister to whom he reported.

38. Interview with Peter Ekelund, Disaster Section, Swedish International Development Authority, Stockholm, 8 June 1984.

39. Interview with Eric Bjovueby, Humanitarian Assistance Section, Norwegian Ministry of Foreign Affairs, Oslo, 5 June 1984.

40. Interview with P. Van Ballegooy, ICCO, Zeist, 30 May 1984.

41. It is a point that was made during interviews with officials in the Emergency Services Section of the EEC Commission, 22 and 23 May 1984.

42. Not only do religious-based organizations carry electoral weight but, in many Western European countries, for example West Germany and the Netherlands, these organizations have regular and formally agreed access to television and radio broadcasting time for disaster relief appeals.

43. Out of a total of $3,321,994,087 United States government assistance made available for foreign disasters between 1964 and 1985, $1,924,517,410 was provided through PL480.

44. Interview with an official from the Multilateral Assistance Section, World Food Programme, Rome, 5 July 1984.

45. See note 38.

46. Interview with M. Meeng, Special Program Section, Department of Development Cooperation, Dutch Ministry of Foreign Affairs, The Hague, 29 May 1983.

47. Interview with Dr Martin Howell, Director, Office of US Foreign Disaster Assistance, Washington, DC, 13 September 1983.

48. In Sweden, for example, any assistance requiring more than SK 3 million requires a Cabinet decision; in West Germany, amounts exceeding DM 500,000 need the approval of the Minister of Finance; in Britain, the amount that the Disaster Unit

may distribute without further authorization was limited in the early 1980s to £10,000 in cash or £100,000 in supplies.

49. Interview with Nils Dahl, Natural Disasters Section, Norwegian Ministry of Development Cooperation, Oslo, 5 June 1984.

50. Interview with M. Van Bosse, The Hague, 29 May 1984.

51. Interview with M. Anstee, UN Department of Technical Cooperation for Development, New York, 23 September 1983.

52. In all governments interviewed for this study, refugees were handled within departments directly under the responsibility of foreign affairs ministries.

53. See note 37.

54. Alfred White, then USAID's Acting Assistant Administrator, suggested this trend when, in November 1980, he commented to this writer that:

the key issue in a bureaucratic sense is whether the Disaster Unit [USAID's Office of Foreign Disaster Assistance] is regarded as too soft to be truly effective when a disaster strikes which demands special or increased allocation of funds. The issue is whether or not the country desk officer, given a serious disaster, is really better to deal with the matter.

55. As one American official noted:

If Ethiopia were a friendly country, McPherson [USAID's Administrator who in 1983 took direct responsibility for the US response to Ethiopian famine relief requests] wouldn't be there [directly involved]. The significant factor is Jeane Kirkpatrick and Jesse Helms. Every time you say 'Ethiopia', they foam at the mouth. McPherson had to take this issue over. [Interview with USAID official, Washington, DC, 16 September 1983.]

56. See note 54.

57. Even the International Committee of the Red Cross, an organization highly sensitive to the political concerns of governments, accepted that:

our groups are mainly the most vulnerable, women and children. In every relief operation of this nature, in proportion to what we are doing, one cannot exclude the possibility of feeding combatants. Ultimately any women or child over the age of fifteen could possible be a combatant. [Interview with official from the ICRC, Geneva, 20 March 1984.]

58. This was a hope that certain officials within the British Foreign and Commonwealth Office (FCO) also harboured, according to interviews with FCO officials in August 1984.

59. 'State/AID Response to General Accounting Office's Draft to the Congress: "Need to Build an International Disaster Relief Agency" ', Appendix I, Comptroller-General of the United States, *Need For an International Disaster Relief Agency*, Washington, DC, GAO, 1976, p.19.

60. Interview with officials from the Disaster Unit, British Overseas Development Administration, London, 7 July 1981.

61. See note 38.

62. Interview with Michel Barton, UNHCR, Geneva, 21 March 1984.

63. This reflects the opinions of those interviewed within USAID, Washington, DC, during the second and third weeks of September 1983. McPherson was under enormous pressure from certain United States Congressional sectors—principally Congressman Howard Wolpe's Sub-Committee on Africa—to respond more favourably to Ethiopian food and transport requirements (Wolpe *et al.* to McPherson, 1 June 1983; McPherson to Wolpe, 13 July 1983). At the same time, McPherson was confronted with strong opposition to Ethiopian assistance by members of the National Security Council (NSC). Reputedly one of the strongest opponents of assistance to Ethiopia, was NSC staffer, Fred Wettering, who eventually left to take up a position with the CIA (Jack Anderson, *Washington Post*, 17 January 1985). The figures that McPherson gave the Congressional Committee in July 1983, perhaps to satisfy Wolpe's criticism of USAID, were seemingly distorted, reflecting a sensitive balancing act by McPherson to avoid having the administration ask for more funds (Internal Memorandum: 'McPherson Response to 1 June Congressional Letter on US Response to Ethiopian Food Crisis', Sub-Committee on Africa, 14 July 1983).

64. Interview with Lillemore Lind, Desk Officer for Bilateral Aid for Kenya and Ethiopia, Swedish International Development Authority, Stockholm, 6 June 1984.

65. Interview with an official from the World Food Programme, Rome, 5 July 1984.
66. Recorded discussion of a meeting with an official from the Office of the United Nations High Commissioner for Refugees, Oxford, 19 March 1986.
67. Notes from an interview with Fabrizio Gentiloni-Silveri, UNHCR, Geneva, 22 March 1984.
68. Interview with John Montagu, Christian Aid, London, 7 July 1981.
69. Interview with Fred Divine, Deputy Executive Director, CARE, New York, 14 December 1981.
70. See note 54.
71. Interview with Michael Harris, former Overseas Director, Oxfam, Robertsbridge, 21 June 1985.
72. Interview with Erwin Langer and Wolfgang Nierwettberg, Special Programs Division, German Agro Action, Bonn, 25 May 1984.
73. Ibid.
74. Goodwin-Gill comments that, in contrast to the 1951 Convention on Refugees which gives UNHCR its authority:

    the 1969 OAU Convention declares the principle of 'non-refoulement' [no refugee should be returned to a country where he or she is likely to face persecution or danger to life or freedom] strongly and without exception. No formal concession is made to overriding considerations of national security, although in cases of difficulty 'in continuing to grant asylum' appeal may be made directly to other member states and through the OAU. [Goodwin-Gill, G., *The Refugee in International Law*, Clarendon Press, Oxford, 1983, p.96.]

    This is but one example of the moral standard set by the OAU Convention.
75. Interview with Victor Palmieri, former United States Assistant Secretary of State, Bureau for Refugee Programs, New York, 23 September 1983.
76. The Office for Emergency Operations in Africa (OEOA) was set up by the Secretary-General of the United Nations at the end of 1984 to harmonize the efforts of the international community in responding to the African famine. The OEOA, having accomplished what it had been created to do, closed down operations by the beginning of December 1986.
77. Interview with Diego Cordovez, United Nations Under Secretary-General for Special Political Affairs, New York, 16 December 1981.
78. For a useful discussion on this problem, see Karadawi, A., 'Constraints on Assistance to Refugees: Some observations from the Sudan', *World Development*, **11**, No.6, 1983, pp.537–47.
79. Perhaps the most blatant example in this regard was the creation of UNDRO. Fifteen years after its creation, the mandate of that organization is still riddled with ambiguity.
80. Interview with Hunter Farnham, Office for Refugees, Emergencies, Disasters and Food Aid in Africa, United States Agency for International Development, Washington, DC, 15 September 1983.
81. Interview with Zia Rizvi, Independent Commission on International Humanitarian Issues, Geneva, 23 March 1984.
82. Interview with Jacques Beaumont, Emergency Relief Officer, United Nations Children's Fund, New York, 27 September 1984.
83. Interview with Philip Sargisson, Chief of the Emergency Unit, Office of the United Nations High Commissioner for Refugees, Geneva, 20 March 1984.
84. See note 81.
85. Ibid.
86. The United Nations' joint assessment mission in Chad in 1983 was regarded as very much of a success in terms of inter-organizational cooperation.
87. 'Reports on Refugee Aid', Committee on Foreign Affairs, United States House of Representatives, Washington, DC, United States Government Printing Office, 1981, p.33.
88. The 1951 UNESCO report as quoted in Weiss, T., *International Bureaucracy: An analysis of the operation of functional and global international secretariats*, Lexington,

Mass., Lexington Books, p.55.

89. Ibid., p.59.

90. One Norwegian official of a United Nations agency complained at the end of an interview in 1984 of 'reverse racism' in UNHCR. While these points have not been corroborated with any other source, this writer's notes that follow reflect at least one middle-level official's view of 'national approaches and prejudices':

He [the UN official] spoke of the horrors which were faced by his compatriots, particularly the UNHCR Res Rep in Luanda who was a Swede. The Swedish representative was blatantly discriminated against by black members of UNHCR in Geneva. They held him responsible for 120 Zairean deaths in refugee camps despite the fact that the Angolan Minister of Foreign Affairs said that was impossible. He [the Res Rep] was told to find out what happened to $1.5 million which had not been spent, and—after considerable wastage of staff time—was informed that he should have known that the matter was a pure mistake. When he wanted to go on home leave, he was not provided with any support staff. On the other hand, despite the resistance of the Angolan government, UNHCR imposed a man from Cape Verde as the next Res Rep who was regarded as having been a Portuguese spy prior to Angolan independence. The Res Rep whose credentials were never accepted by the Ministry of Foreign Affairs left after a year; however, during the year, he had accumulated approximately $1000/month telephone bills to Geneva, etc. This reflected the discrimination of the 'brotherhood' in Geneva.

91. Interview with John Saunders, former Assistant Secretary-General of the United Nations, Brighton, 17 December 1985.

92. Interview with George Davidson, New York, 22 September 1983.

93. By 1980, there were approximately 2,936,000 refugees in Africa, mainly gathered in some of that continent's poorest countries, for example Tanzania (154,000 Burundi), Cameroon (100,000 Chadians), Somalia, Sudan, Djibouti (1,954,000 Ethiopians), Uganda, Angola (69,000 Zaireans), Uganda, Burundi, Tanzania, Zaire (175,000 Rwandans), Zaire, Zambia (178,000 Angolans). United States Committee for Refugees, 1980 World Refugee Survey, as cited by Newland, K., Refugees: The new international politics of displacement, World Watch Paper 43, Washington, DC, World Watch Institute, March 1981, p.11. While refugees were moving into these host countries, the World Bank had announced in 1981 that many of those same countries were 'vulnerable to financial collapse'. They pointed in particular to Sudan, Tanzania, Zaire, Uganda and Zambia.

94. Ibid.

95. The ICARA Steering Committee is composed of senior representatives of the UN, the OAU, UNDP and UNHCR.

96. African governments were very concerned that ICARA-based projects would be funded by donors diverting assistance away from indigenous development projects.

97. Tendler, J., Turning Private Voluntary Organizations Into Development Agencies: Questions for evaluation, USAID Program Evaluation Paper No. 12, Washington, DC, USAID, April 1982, p.1.

98. Morss, E., 'Greater Coordination of NGOs in Refugee Work', paper prepared for a study on refugees for the Independent Commission on International Humanitarian Issues, 1985, p.5.

99. Interview with an official from World Vision of Great Britain, Northampton, 2 October 1986.

100. Ibid.

101. Tendler, op. cit.

102. Accusations by NGOs of bureaucratic and corrupt practices can frequently be a mask to cover what Harrell-Bond rightly labels 'battles for sovereignty' between local government officials and NGOs. See Harrell-Bond, B., Imposing Aid: Emergency assistance to refugees, Oxford, Oxford University Press, 1986, p.69.

103. Ibid., pp.64–102.

104. Tendler, op. cit.

105. This was a point brought out during a meeting organized by the Refugee Studies Programme, Queen Elizabeth House, Oxford, 26 April 1986, in which Oxfam officials took part.

106. Discussions with volunteers returning from relief operations in December 1986.
107. Interview with Nick Winer, Oxfam Field Director, Khartoum, 29 October 1984.
108. According to Michael Brophy, Director of the Charities Aid Foundation in Britain, Africa's crisis in 1984 saw an increase in donations to international agencies of a 'staggering 163 per cent'. 'Band Aid attracts £56 million to head charity table', *The Guardian*, 13 August 1986.
109. See note 99.
110. Interview with Hugh Goyder, Oxfam, Addis Ababa, 13 October 1984.
111. See note 105.
112. Interview with John Seaman, Medical Officer, Save the Children Fund, Mogadishu, 17 October 1984.
113. See note 105.
114. See note 99.
115. Chapter 3, pp. 70–1.
116. See note 110.
117. See Chapter 5, Organizational Behaviour.
118. Certain agencies during the 1984 Ethiopian crisis, for example the Save the Children Fund, were unhappy about the levels of rations and the distribution system of the American Relief Services. CRS officials in Ethiopia were aware of the problems that their approaches were having, but maintained that these approaches were imposed on them by the source of their assistance (e.g. USAID), and headquarters felt that USAID's criteria had to be met.
119. Tendler, op. cit., p.97.
120. This is a fundamental lesson to be learnt in the relief process, yet it is one that is ignored all too often when external actors seek to impose aid, whether in developed or developing societies. In an examination of flood warning systems in the United States and in Bangladesh, Schware and Lippoldt note that, 'little effort has apparently been directed toward examining whether such disaster forecast, prediction, and warning systems will be of use to the ultimate users, especially the populations most "at risk", such as those located in villages.' Schware, R., 'An Examination of Community Flood Warning Systems: Are we providing the right assistance?', *Disasters: The International Journal of Disaster Studies and Practice*, 6, No.3, p.195.
121. This comment was made by Prof. Robert Gale, University of California, Los Angeles, during discussions at a conference on the Chernobyl nuclear disaster, sponsored by the Annenberg Schools of Communication, Washington, DC, 9–10 October 1986.
122. David, P., 'The Responsibilities of the Press', a paper prepared for a conference on the Chernobyl Nuclear disaster sponsored by the Annenberg Schools of Communication, Washington, DC, 9–10 October 1986.
123. State-controlled agriculture did indeed become one of the whipping boys for the media once the initial story of Ethiopia's famine began to wear thin. However, resettlement, fuelled by the accusations of the French relief agency, Médecins Sans Frontières, that hundreds of thousands were dying because of resettlement policies, became a dominant media story at the beginning of 1986. Resettlement was the new handle, despite the fact that the old story, namely, starvation, was continuing to affect significant sections of Ethiopia's population.
124. Gill, P., *A Year in The Death of Africa: Politics, bureaucracy and the famine*, London, Paladin, 1986, p.92.
125. Philo, G., 'Hungry for Catastrophe', *The Guardian*, cited in a description of Philo's 'From Buerk to Band Aid', London, Television Trust, 1986.
126. As quoted in Gill, op. cit., p.94.
127. Sommer, A. and Mosley, W., 'The Cyclone: Medical Assessment and Determination of Relief and Rehabilitation Needs', in Chen, L. (ed.), *Disaster in Bangladesh: Health crises in a developing nation*, New York, Oxford University Press, 1973, p.131. Pakistan authorities felt in part compelled to undertake a massive cholera vaccination programme because of their concern that not to take such action would lead to

further condemnation by the press, both domestic and international.

128. Interview with an official from the United States Office for Emergency Operations in Africa, 15 October 1986. One of the reasons for establishing the OEOA was to ensure that priority and appropriate needs were directed to afflicted populations. However, as one official complained, even the efforts of the OEOA in certain instances could not change the types of assistance being provided because the media had predisposed donors to focus solely on food aid.

129. Harden, B., 'Notes of a Famine-Watcher', the *Washington Post*, 17 March 1985.

130. UNDRO initially maintained (25 August) that there were 10,000 people in the affected area; the following day it reported that there were 20,000 people in the area; and, by 28 August, it reduced that figure to 5,000. This kind of rush for statistics can wreak havoc with a relief operation, and in the case of the Cameroon disaster it did, as emergency distribution centres overflowed, with five times the quantity of tents, blankets, food and drugs required to care for the survivors.

131. These kinds of problems are discussed in Friedman, S. *et al.* (eds), *Scientists and Journalists: Reporting science as news*, New York, The Free Press, 1985.

132. Buerk is quoted in Harrison, P. and Palmer, R., *News Out of Africa*, London, Hilary Shipman, 1986.

133. Gill, op. cit., p.92.

134. Philo, op. cit.

135. Ibid.

4 The Network in Action: Priority Formulation and Perceptual Variables

When the first signs of famine in Ethiopia began to be recognized in 1983, there were at least fifty-one other major disasters occurring at the same time. While 2 million Ethiopians were reported in that year to be suffering from the consequences of drought, 5,580,000 Argentinians were reported to be flood victims, 20 million Brazilians were categorized as victims of drought, 5 million in India had been affected by cyclones, 700,000 refugees sought relief assistance in Somalia, and a further 700,000 Ghanaians were registered as displaced and destitute.[1] The sheer number of disaster-stricken people around the world must raise the obvious question of how do various components of the international relief network choose when and in what disaster to intervene. And when components of this disparate and pluralist network do decide to respond, how do they do it? What factors influence the assistance that they provide and, furthermore, how do the individual relief components view their roles in the context of an overall relief effort?

These questions go to the heart of what we shall call the processes of the international relief network. Clearly, in formulating their responses, each component views any single disaster from its own individual perspective; yet, no matter how diverse and pluralist the international relief network, all within it are subject to certain common pressures and hazards, influences and constraints that affect their activities as a whole. The next two chapters will explore these factors under four general headings: (1) politics and the priority formulation process: (2) perceptions and persuasive communications; (3) organizational behaviour; and (4) inter-organizational relations. Each of these considerations is fundamental for understanding the dynamics of the relief process, and each has to be seen in the broader context of what in Chapter 1 were called the criteria of effective relief.

In discussing the criteria for effective relief, we suggested six inter-related categories that would improve the management of disasters. The impact of disaster agents could be more effectively mitigated through preventative and preparedness measures that, technologically, are increasingly within mankind's grasp. An issue as fundamental as any, namely that of assessment, has been approached on more and more occasions with increasing sophistication. Assessors and monitors have at their disposal ever more sensitive guidelines to determine disaster impacts and relief needs. Indeed, as information technology progresses and is increasingly utilized in developing countries, the ability to update vital statistics and transmit information about changing relief requirements is rapidly growing.[2]

With more effective assessment procedures, clearly the ability to provide more appropriate relief should increase commensurately. The dumping of useless medicines, inappropriate foodstuffs and all kinds of irrelevant paraphernalia onto the scene of a disaster need not occur, since enhanced assessment procedures afford greater precision. Related to appropriate relief input is the crucial question of timely intervention. Experience over the past decade and a half has made relief officials more sensitive to the very basic problems that arise by responding too slowly or too quickly or for too long. And fundamental to all these first five criteria is that of coordination.

Coordination—that buzz word that has circulated the relief network for the past fifteen years—has been discussed in several ways, as Chapter 2 sought to suggest. Yet, the potential for effective coordination, under whatever guise or mode, has certainly been enhanced by the increased number of communication networks operated by a number of institutions and by advances in communications technology itself. Like all the other relief criteria, coordination is an aspiration that in its most perfect sense can never be achieved, but it is increasingly evident that one can come closer to better forms of cooperation. That these criteria for effective relief are so infrequently met is explained in many respects by the process factors that determine how, when and where the international relief network intervenes. The four process factors to be considered are by no means unique to international intervention in disasters; to the contrary, they are inherent in all human endeavours. Yet, what makes these factors of particular relevance is the way in which disasters dramatize them.

Politics and the Priority Formulation Process

Politics as a process

A distinguished Indian civil servant, P.N. Haksar, once commented that in international relations 'there is no system which can move in a humanitarian rather than a political fashion. There are two streams in society: emotions of conscience and the state system. The first is prevented by the second.'[3] Haksar's reflection returns us to a crucial issue briefly considered in Chapter 3 (pp.70 ff.) namely, the extent to which politics becomes a critical determinant in international responses to disasters. Time and again, 'politics' is blamed for the ways in which responses to disasters are made. It was 'power politics playing its usual role', according to Oxfam's Michael Harris, that explained the failure of the international community to respond to the plight of Ethiopia in 1984.[4] 'If politics is not the decisive factor in determining who gets what and when in disasters,' contended D'Souza, 'then how do you explain why the Gambia received $11.5 million worth of aid in a matter of a few weeks during [UN Secretary-General] Waldheim's attempt to get re-elected, or why the Afghan refugees are awash with assistance, or why the US Congress in a matter of days appropriated $50 million for the Italian relief operation? It is all political.'[5] For Sir Robert Jackson, who acted as the United Nations Secretary-General's Special Representative in several major disasters from 1972 to 1983, the Kampuchean relief operation demonstrated 'deep superpower politics'. And, in a telling vignette, Jackson quotes Waldheim as saying that 'four years ago (1974) I believed that humanitarian relief was above politics. Now I know that humanitarian relief is politics.'[6]

Of course, in seeking to determine the impact of politics upon the relief process, it would be worth asking what one means by the term. If one begins with the assumption that politics is a process principally concerned with the allocation of values and resources, then one must ask how such allocations are determined.[7] One predominant view of politics is implicit in Haksar's comment, namely, that states, in the Palmerstonian sense, are devoid of sentiment and have no friends. States only have interests. State behaviour and, hence, the allocative process in international relations, is assumed to be motivated by the pursuit of 'national interest'. While Morgenthau—the founder of the modern school of political realism—accepts that 'political reality is replete with contingencies and systematic irrationalities', he and his many adherents maintain that state actions reflect a persistent drive to enhance or preserve power and prestige.[8] It is a view assumed by Morris Davis when he wrote in *Civil Wars and International Relief* that 'real or potential donor nations habitually put their perceived national interests over humanitarian concerns.'[9]

This predominant and enduring view, or 'realist paradigm', assumes both a rational and holistic conception of state behaviour. Statecraft is holistic in that it reflects a persistent and relatively consistent consensus—as reflected by the actions of states—about the objectives of the state. State activities are deemed to be rational because policy options are continually assessed in terms of those choices that will maximize and ensure power.[10] However, these assumptions about politics are open to challenge if one looks at the processes by which those in authority within the state make decisions. True, there are certain precepts that form consistent themes in state policies.[11] Later we shall refer to these as 'norms'. Nevertheless, one would be mistaken to assume that such themes serve as predictable standards upon which individual decisions are made. An alternative way of understanding state behaviour and resource allocation is to view politics as a process.

Both within and outside government there exist groups constantly promoting and competing for particular values and resources. The values and resources that each seeks to garner are not necessarily devoid of 'emotions of conscience', but the ways in which they must be sought are inherently 'political' for, in the final analysis, politics is about the strategies and tactics, the trade-offs and linkages employed to promote what contending groups regard as priorities. Ultimately, priorities are determined by those decision-makers with allocative authority. However, as there are many different types of allocative issues, so, too, are there many levels of allocative decision-makers, each with its own agenda determined by decisional roles and guidelines and each affected by the impact of contending interests. Yet, this should not leave one with the impression that allocative decisions are necessarily handled in a predictable or orderly way, or that they progress up a hierarchical ladder on top of which is an ultimate decisional authority. This view ignores the intense interactive dynamics throughout the decisional process.

Allocative policies emerge from many quarters. Some may be triggered by senior decision-makers, may descend or move laterally to other levels but never be acted upon. Some issues that would normally be handled by lower-level decision-makers may find their way into the upper reaches of policy-making. Other issues that might well deserve the attention of senior-level decision-makers may never emerge past lower levels, with the consequence that significant policy initiatives may be occurring without the awareness of those who should know.

If these allocative dynamics suggest a political process out of control, then the image is too strong. If, on the other hand, the image portrayed is one in which frequently unpredictable and incomplete agendas are placed before decision-makers and are in a constant state of flux, then the picture seems to reflect more readily the realities of political processes. In that sense, the political process is a cascade of conflicting pressures colliding at various junctures with seemingly endless inputs and outputs. The unpredictability of the process also bears a resemblance to Prigogine's view of change in the physical sciences. His concept of chemical organization might serve as a useful analogue for the dynamics affecting 'political agendas':

all systems contain subsystems, which are continually 'fluctuating'. At times, a single fluctuation or a combination of them may become so powerful, as a result of positive feedback, that it shatters the preexisting organisation. At this revolutionary moment . . . it is impossible to determine in advance which direction change will take.[12]

One way of viewing political process from this perspective is to assess the impact of roles, norms and contending interests as they affect allocative functions. The determinants of allocative functions are as follows:

1. Roles. Lloyd Jensen has written that 'one might anticipate that the higher in the role hierarchy a decision is made, the more likely it is that broader and longer-range interests will be reflected.'[13] Yet, as he and many others have demonstrated, the assumption is flawed.[14] As one moves up the hierarchy, one by no means finds a broadening of perspectives, but rather just differing perspectives reflecting different kinds of roles. In the much-quoted phrase found in Allison, 'where one sits is where one stands'; or, in other words, 'the diverse demands upon each [political] player shape his priorities, perceptions and issues. For larger classes of issues—for example, budgets and procurement decisions—the stance of a particular player can be predicated with high reliability from information about his seat.'[15]

All those directly involved in the allocative process (for example Parliamentarians, dictators, members of executive and legislative branches of governments) take office with certain assumptions about their responsibilities or roles. An individual's role is affected by a combination of 'role clarity' and 'role consensus', the former referring to a person's perception of what type of behaviour is expected and the latter concerning the degree to which others agree to that type of behaviour.[16]

It is essential for the decision-maker to maintain role consensus. Maintaining role consensus normally depends upon balancing a variety of competing interests, each seeking allocative decisions. There are constant tensions in any individual's role, and most policy choices present the decision-maker with imperfect options. These imperfect options are made more acute by the fact that the roles of others are equally as complex, and each must find some way of accommodating or reducing the threat posed by others. The former British Prime Minister, Harold Wilson, suggested as much during the furore over Britain's failure to provide relief for starving Biafra in 1968.

The head of the government, [he wrote in his memoirs] has to face these problems not singly or single-mindedly, but simultaneously, against the background of a hundred other issues, economic, financial and political. The headlines, however sensationalised or selective, fail to measure even the tip of the iceberg in the sea of democratic government, where the heaviest and most lethal pressures are below the surface, sometimes concentrated within the heart of the individual.[17]

The cumulative impact of roles on the political process can be demonstrated by viewing episodes in the American response to the 1983 'Andean creeping disaster'.[18] Ostensibly, the political element of a proposal to assist El Nino-affected nations was uncomplicated. There was proven need, and the five relevant bureaux (namely the Office of Foreign Disaster Assistance, USAID's Program and Policy Coordination division, its Latin American Bureau, the State Department desk and the Food for Peace programme) were all convinced that action to assist should be taken. However, funds were not available, and the Congress would have to be approached for additional allocations.

The head of AID's Office for Program and Policy Coordination was responsible for seeking Congressional authorization for additional allocations. Yet, he could only do so by first convincing the Office for Management and Budget (OMB), the Executive's watchdog for governmental expenditures, that further funds were required. His OMB counterpart was convinced there was a problem, but said that he did not want AID to approach Congress because of end-of-year fiscal problems 'which would probably negate AID efforts'. OMB's reactions presented an immediate role conflict for the PPC official. On the one hand, he had to be sure that USAID had to be and had to be seen to be fiscally responsible. On the other, however, it was his responsibility to find funds. The latter role was affected by his colleagues from the four other bureaux; the former was being emphasized by OMB.

For the PPC official, one way of resolving the conflict between his two roles was to seek means to 're-obligate funds' from what were called 'failed projects' for purposes of emergency relief. Re-obligation meant that unspent funds initially designated for development projects in those Andean countries now suffering from drought would be allocated to emergency relief. This seemingly straightforward matter, however, was complicated by the fact that all unspent American federal allocations had to be returned to the American Treasury. 'Re-obligation' was contrary to the most fundamental budgetary principles of the American government.

Both end-of-year fiscal problems and the constitutional hazards of 're-obligation' meant that OMB for one was unwilling to support the 're-obligation' solution that the PPC official saw as a means of resolving his own role conflict. OMB suggested instead ways in which USAID could 'rejuggle' other AID funds without risking the problems implicit in re-obligation. However, to follow the rejuggling recommendations of OMB would mean that uncommitted funds in other AID divisions might be threatened, and the PPC therefore felt unable to draw from these for the Andean emergency. Role consensus in this instance meant that the PPC could not be seen to be undermining allocations within other AID departments.

The only solution remaining to the PPC was to seek Congressional approval for AID's proposed re-obligation scheme. This would mean incurring the wrath of OMB by bypassing it, and going directly to Congress—'by the back door'—to persuade Congress to provide a legal basis for re-obligated funds.

To maintain role consensus, the PPC chose to put its responsibilities of 'budgetary scepticism' aside and pursue funding in ways that the OMB clearly found unorthodox. USAID's lawyers worked 'in the back corridors' with various Congressional staffs to find a re-obligation formula. Finally, four months after the five bureaux had agreed to contribute to the Andean disaster, Congress had approved PL98/63, allowing AID to re-obligate failed project funds for purposes of disaster relief.

Of course, re-obligation authorization in this instance did not lead automatically to assistance, for the impact of roles was felt once again as various agencies sought to determine how these re-obligated funds were to be allocated. 'Who should do what', in the words of one PPC official, became a fundamental management issue. 'Food for Peace wants to know whether ports can handle food'; the Office of Foreign Disaster Assistance felt that the operation should come within its own purview while the Latin American Bureau regarded the disaster as falling outside OFDA's competence. All these stances reflected the particular roles to which the individual decision-makers were committed. Where one sits determines where one stands; and in the case of the Andean creeping disaster, it took two further months to reconcile these contending roles before the bulk of relief aid began to flow to the disaster-stricken people.[19]

2. *'Norms'*. Joseph Sisco, a former Assistant Secretary of State under President Richard Nixon, once remarked that 'no bureaucracy resists policy changes. What happens is that administrations rely upon the specifics of policy which in turn provide for continuity.'[20] Policy, however, is not merely handed down from a political apex to bureaucracies below. There is what Sisco has called an 'inherent tension' between policy-makers and implementers. Roles constrain the degree to which radical changes can be made, and both roles and policy change are conducted within a framework of overall contextual consensus. This contextual consensus refers to the 'norms'—the political *Zeitgeist*—in which policy is formulated. Where roles reflect institutional standards of behaviour, norms (as we are defining them) suggest the general boundaries that limit the context in which all policy-makers operate. Thus, in extremis, whatever the conflict in roles between policy-makers in Western defence and foreign affairs ministries, no one would view capitulation to Soviet power as an acceptable option. There are, in other words, certain norms that are taken as given in the policy-making context. However, it is within these norms that the tensions between roles are felt.

The problem for policy-makers is often that even 'norms' are not necessarily clear. While capitulation to the Soviet Union may be an extreme example of an unambiguous norm, assisting a Communist country in a disaster may not be. In this kind of situation, ambiguous norms and roles may come into conflict. American provision of relief assistance to Angola is a case in point. Officials in USAID's Office of Refugees, Emergencies, Disasters and Food Aid in Africa were faced during the latter part of 1982 and early 1983 with the portent of serious food shortages in Angola and Mozambique. Both countries were regarded as 'communist' and, hence, not of immediate interest to the United States. This certainly was the position taken by members of the National Security Council (NSC), which has responsibilities to advise the President on foreign policy matters. The Kirkpatrick-Helmes lobby[21] was making every effort to ensure that American assistance of any kind would not reach nations that were not aligned with American interests, a norm that pervaded many senior-level policy positions within the administration.

However, for middle-level policy makers within the Agency for International Development, the Kirkpatrick-Helmes norms were far more ambiguous than they were, for example, for certain NSC staff members.[22] There was genuine disagreement about the way in which this rigid posturing would scuttle any American efforts at some form of dialogue in southern Africa—a view shared with State Department desk officers—and there was also a genuine concern that the United States could not continue to ignore the mounting consequences of food shortages in Angola and Mozambique in particular. There were, therefore, serious tensions between the policy norms of the administration and the roles of middle-grade officials within the Agency.

Faced with these tensions, the officials within USAID decided to avoid a direct confrontation with senior-level officials and resorted to alternative assistance channels. Allocations for assistance to the two countries were funnelled through inter-governmental organizations, principally UNICEF, and emergency assistance continued to be so directed for well over a year, despite the established norms that circumscribed the policy postures of those in the White House.[23]

The consequence of tensions between policy norms and roles is by no means unique to the United States. A consistent theme of officials in the eight 'donor nations' interviewed for this study reflected the complexities of fulfilling role obligations that were consistent with policy milieux. The officer in charge of West Germany's Section 301 which deals with humanitarian assistance, for example, spoke of the difficulty of ascertaining a policy norm when emergency assistance may at any one time involve three different ministerial interpretations of policy: namely the Ministry of Foreign Affairs, the Ministry of the Interior and the Ministry of Economic Cooperation.[24]

For a senior official within the Dutch Ministry of Foreign Affairs, there were also rarely consistent policy norms that determined the fate of a disaster response. More often than not, the norm was a direct result of the interpretation of which department within which ministry was handling the matter;[25] and for that official's counterpart in the Emergency Relief and Humanitarian Assistance Unit within the Foreign Ministry, policy was a function of the way in which 'I will decide how to route it [the request for disaster assistance]'.[26]

In the dilemmas created between norms and roles, the key factor so often is clarity. An issue that fits starkly into the context of policy norms more often than not coheres easily with appropriate roles. The greater the ambiguity inherent in an issue, the greater the possibility that policy formulation will reflect strains between norms and decisional roles. The consequence of such tensions intensifies the potential for unpredictable and disjointed allocative decisions.

3. Interest groups. Clarity, for the purpose of this discussion concerning the policy process, has far less to do with accuracy of information and far more with explicitness. Explicit information is that which clarifies both roles and norms. If there is any single all-embracing function of interest groups, it is that of promoting clarity. It is important to emphasize that one is not talking of accuracy but rather of removing ambiguity. The purpose of any single interest group—be it directly within the decisional structure or outside it—is to urge upon those with allocative functions the urgency and priority of its own particular interest. This is accomplished in a number of ways. Parliamentarians are urged by outside groups to press ministers; junior as well as senior officials lobby legislators; middle-level officials may use outside groups to influence more senior policy echelons. The methods used by interest groups are numerous, but the purpose is the same: to ensure that issues reflecting particular interests gain priority consideration, and, in so doing, gain the clarity that is needed to mobilize roles without creating conflicts within accepted norms. Take, for example, the effect of the actions of a variety of American interest groups in the case of assistance to Ethiopia in early 1983. The policy norm was that Ethiopia was a 'problem for the Soviets to handle'. This, according to the chargé d'affaires in Ethiopia at the time, was reflected in the position adopted by State Department's Africa desk at the time.[27]

Nevertheless, several long corridors away, USAID officials had by late 1982 established an inter-agency task force on Ethiopia and the Sudan (IGETSU) to monitor the effects of the famine. Ironically, at the same time that IGETSU began to undertake its activities, AID's programme assistance for Catholic Relief Services' (CRS) activities in Ethiopia was severely cut. CRS, eventually joined by Bread for the World and Lutheran World Services, used this cut as a reason to begin lobbying sympathetic Congressmen to restore CRS's programme assistance and to increase general assistance allocations to Ethiopia.

One of these Congressmen was Howard Wolpe, Chairman of the House Sub-Committee on Africa, who had been pressed by the then Ethiopian chargé d'affaires in Washington, Tesfaye Demeke, to visit Ethiopia, in part to witness the famine for himself. Wolpe's increasing interest in Ethiopia made his office a natural conduit for back-channelled information from officials from AID's IGETSU, who were becoming convinced by mid-1983 that larger amounts of assistance would be required than was being acknowledged by the State Department. By 1 June 1983, the informal coalition being formed between Wolpe, his Committee members and middle-level officials from USAID was aided by an unusual event. The Association for Ethiopian Jews, partly because of fears of the drought's effect on the Falashas,[28] 'undertook an enormous mailing campaign to the Congress which led to considerable pressure on the [Reagan] Administration.'[29] McPherson, USAID's Administrator, came under heavy fire to explain why American assistance to Ethiopia was being cut back at a time of growing need.

By 13 July 1983, McPherson wrote to Wolpe that 'the American people have always wanted the US to respond to disasters without regard to politics . . . Ethiopia is no exception.'[30] What in effect McPherson was admitting was that he had not anticipated the ferment of the 'sub-systems' within and outside the administration to press for restoration of assistance to Ethiopia. In effect, he was caught off guard by the tensions being created between the roles of his own officials and the policy norms of the Reagan administration. Nor, for that matter, could he, or did he, anticipate the clarity that a variety of disparate interest groups—the Association for Ethiopian Jews, the Congressional Sub-Committee on Africa, Catholic Relief Services, USAID's Africa emergency office—gave to that specific issue.

Yet, the situation in which McPherson found himself was not an unusual example of the policy process. The waterfall effect of diverse interests establishing agendas, modifying them, mobilizing various roles and pushing at the bounds of established norms represents *the* political process. It suggests why the political result is often disjointed, inconsistent and unpredictable. If inconsistency, disjointedness and unpredictability are often the hallmarks of the policy process, then one must ask how issues involving disasters and disaster relief enter into allocative decision-making. How, in other words, do disasters gain access to the 'priority formulation process'? To some extent, we have already suggested certain types of pressures that influence the fate of disaster decisions. Yet, there are particular characteristics of disasters that one should consider as one attempts to understand the dynamics of the international relief network in action.

Disasters and Priority Formulation

The additional complexities affecting the ways in which disasters gain access to the priority formulation process are fourfold: (1) limited constituencies; (2) information loading; (3) *ad hoc* coalitions; and (4) contending interests. In total they suggest not only why some disasters gain priority attention and others do not, but also why particular types of relief response actually emerge.

1. *Limited Constituencies*. In Chapter 1 we discussed the ways in which disaster phenomena were perceived. In that discussion, we suggested that disasters were

viewed essentially as aberrations—events distinct and isolated from what is usually regarded as 'normal life'.[31] To a very significant extent, this view of disasters rebounds upon the political process, which affects the attention that disasters are given.

The constituencies that take an interest in issues concerning disasters and disaster relief are limited. Institutionally, they lack bargaining power and are isolated from issues in which the struggle for more enduring interests takes place. This point has importance—as we shall see in a later section in the next chapter—both in terms of organizational behaviour and for our immediate discussion on political processes.[32]

Whether it be in the United States Office of Foreign Disaster Assistance, in West Germany's Section 301, in Sweden's Emergency Office within SIDA or in Britain's Disaster Unit, what might logically be regarded as key rungs in the disaster response ladder—namely those cells with defined relief responsibilities—are more often than not out of the mainstream of allocative action. They all have a limited amount of funds at their disposal; but when it comes to a major disaster requiring substantial assistance, they only too often take a back seat in the formulation of priorities.

This introduces four points that suggest why disaster issues must initially rely on very limited constituencies. The first of these arises from the fact that disasters are perceived or, for the most part, treated as isolated and distinct phenomena. The disasters and those with formal responsibilities to deal with them are essentially cut off from any enduring interests that would allow for consistent bargaining power. Links with those interest groups, both within and outside governments, involved in development or with agricultural policies, for example, are for the most part tenuous. These limited constituencies have no permanent interest groups to build upon, nor do they have sufficient allocative authority to give them a stake in the allocative game. There are, of course, exceptions to this general rule. Every disaster unit has its stories of 'ambulance chasers', seeking to sell their fish, boats or tents to disaster agencies. However, they are relatively minor when compared with the more enduring interest groups such as those found in development, where agricultural inputs, turnkey industries and the like, constantly interact with those that have far greater resources at hand.

Secondly, since disaster units generally lack sufficient resources to make any significant impact on most major disasters that occur, resources depend upon those agencies, departments or organizations that do have resources. This in turn means that disaster responses often depend on institutions, eg. agricultural ministries, that might have adequate supplies but that also have other priorities than disasters. This brings us back to that recurring refrain—where one sits is where one stands. The approach one takes to an issue depends upon the pressures being exerted in terms of roles and norms. While officials within the United States Department of Agriculture or its Canadian counterpart may be aware of a disaster, their responses are determined by the costs and benefits to their respective institutions in the light of issues extraneous to the disaster, e.g. legislators' pressures to offload certain types of surplus commodity.

The third point that naturally leads from the second is that of linkage. The size of a constituency focusing on any particular disaster depends on the types of link that different groups make between a disaster and issues with which they are immediately concerned. Morton Halperin, a former senior official on the US National Security Council, once remarked that disasters rarely grab the attention of presidents. 'They lack the time or inclination to concern themselves with such issues. A president might link a particular policy with a particular disaster, but the bottom-line is that the president is just too busy to focus upon anything but the larger strategic issues.'[33] Former OFDA Coordinator, Stephen Tripp, came to the same conclusion. The reason why President Richard Nixon took cognizance of the 1970 East Pakistan cyclone disaster was that Pakistan was a key component in his China policy, and at the time of the disaster, Nixon was focusing considerable attention on Pakistan.[34] For the same kind of reason, Jordan received $5 million worth of relief assistance in the wake of the 1971 Jordanian–Palestinian conflict—(despite the fact that Tripp had believed that only one-tenth of that amount was needed)—because the White House at that particular time was concentrating on improving American–Jordanian relations.[35]

Finally, the disaster relief constituency within the political spectrum is limited because the attention that sustains relief issues within the political process is short-lived. Disasters are not only regarded as aberrant and isolated phenomena, they are also assumed to be of short duration. They are viewed, in the words of one Swedish NGO representative, as 'unwarranted interferences in the normal course of affairs'.[36]

Beyond instant demonstrations of sympathy and the kudos that may be derived from such demonstrations, prolonged involvements in disasters are constantly challenged by the pressures arising out of more enduring issues. 'Normal priorities' constantly push their way into the agendas of decision-makers, agendas that constantly fluctuate in the face of shifting pressures. When one USAID official spoke of the fear of being 'mousetrapped' by disaster relief into long-term commitments, he was acknowledging two types of concern. The first was the more obvious anxiety about a recipient assuming that emergency assistance implied more than just short-term involvement. The second, however, reflects the fact that any form of prolonged commitment would divert resources and attention away from those interests that ensured his role consensus. There are, in other words, few within the political process who have vested interests in the world of disaster relief.

2. *Information Loading.* Between May 1985 and April 1986, there were at least eighty major disasters that led to assistance being received from the international community.[37] Information about these disasters enters into the priority formulation process in a variety of ways, ways that are rarely consistent or predictable. A field worker from an NGO may alert his or her headquarters to a disaster onset, or an ambassador from a potential donor country may be informed by a host government official that a serious disaster has occurred, or someone in a government agency in some distant capital may have read about a disaster in a newspaper or heard about it on a radio or television broadcast. Given the vagaries with which disaster information enters the system, a response depends on the routes through which the information is channelled. As that information progresses through the channels, it becomes 'loaded' with matters that are frequently extraneous to the plight of the disaster victims themselves, but which are a natural outcome of the way in which information is processed. Information loading becomes a fundamental factor in the inter-relationship between roles, norms and contending interests in the priority formulation process. The more incomplete and ambiguous the informational input, the more that information is moulded by recipients according to their own referents. These referents are a

function of perceptions and institutional behaviour but, for our purposes here, they will be described as a function of roles and norms.

In a political process in which disaster issues find a limited constituency with limited allocative authority, the roles and norms of those in the mainstream of allocative responsibilities become crucial determinants in weighing the importance of any single disaster. They must, however, be persuaded or must recognize that a particular disaster issue falls within their competence or sphere of interest. For an officer on the Ethiopia/Somalia desk in the British Foreign and Commonwealth Office in August 1984, the FCO's responsibility was to ensure that aid to Ethiopia was consistent with certain fundamental objectives, i.e. compensation for nationalized British property. This objective was reinforced by what she referred to as 'the general political philosophy of the new Thatcher government'.[38] For her and her colleagues, information about an impending food crisis in Ethiopia was weighed in terms of their ability to achieve their role responsibilities and to remain consistent with the ethos of the administration. Her colleagues at the Overseas Development Administration (ODA) had different ways of assessing the information they were receiving from Ethiopia. They accepted that the impact of the drought was becoming increasingly severe in Ethiopia, but given ODA's particular concern with the Sudan, ODA officials responded to the information in terms of the drought's impact on movements of peoples from northern Ethiopia into the Sudan.[39]

Information is screened out of the process, or else accepted, all depending on the extent to which it is consistent with roles and norms. If and when it is accepted, information is processed in terms of how it is seen as fitting into the particular roles of those who process it. Thus, for example, in 1985 the United States Department of Defence would only accept USAID's proposal for airlift operations in Ethiopia if American military aircraft could be used.[40] In 1971, according to a White House official, reports of millions of refugees crossing into India from East Pakistan were given scant attention. The White House was only concerned about presenting Pakistan as a stable regime.[41] Two miles away, at the United States Department of State, senior officials, despite the fact that they had no direct responsibility for refugees, took the position that the refugee influx represented one of the most serious threats to South Asian regional stability since Indian independence. These State Department officials pushed for assistance for the refugees, contrary to the wishes of the White House, since they felt that India, not Pakistan, was the critical component in South Asian security.[42]

These differences are examples of the ways in which information becomes 'loaded' by the roles and norms that decision-makers assume. The way in which such differences are reconciled or accommodated depends in part on the impact of the ad hoc coalitions formed by interest groups.

3. *Ad Hoc Coalitions.* Earlier, we suggested that the function of interest groups is to add clarity to issues in which ambiguity arises between roles and norms. The term clarity has little to do with accuracy, and far more to do with reducing ambiguity—for our purposes an important distinction.

According to the FCO official cited above, the FCO's stance on Ethiopian assistance began to come under review when 'enormous pressure from MPs and masses of letters were created by the Jewish lobby concerned with the Falashas.'[43] Of course, in the study of politics, there is nothing new in suggesting the impact of pressure groups on the political process. Every minister, government official and legislator is more than amply attuned to the influences of special interests.

However, what is important to bear in mind in the study of disasters in the context of political processes is that—as opposed to many forms of representation both within and outside governments—disasters and disaster relief do not have their own permanent lobbyists. The type of response that a disaster receives all too often depends on the *ad hoc* coalitions that may adopt a particular disaster issue at any one time. The limited constituencies that may be more predictably at the forefront in promoting the cause of disaster relief, those within the non-governmental sector or disaster relief cells in governments or IGOs, normally rely on coalition partners—e.g., those with no specific relief mandates—who have their own particular interests to join in pushing the priority of a particular disaster issue.

These latter members of *ad hoc* coalitions may participate for a myriad of reasons. In Sweden one MP said, with a certain degree of embarrassment, that he was on occasion prodded by the housing industry to ensure that the Swedish government responded to a disaster . . . with Swedish housing materials.[44] There is also the apocryphal agriculture minister who feels compelled by his role to ensure that a disaster operation is supported with his nation's wheat, a role priority that may take precedence over policy norms. There is also the middle-level diplomatic official who, as Halperin has noted, pushes such issues because of a particular interest or concern in a particular geographical area. The *ad hoc* coalitions that are formed to push a particular disaster relief decision to the fore are not necessarily self-serving in their interests. The 'mutual interests' that prompt individual components of such coalitions should not be confused with a lack of 'emotions of conscience'. Yet, in the political process, disasters are in many respects orphans, depending all too often on being adopted by those with role and norm perspectives that have no ostensible responsibility for responding.

Although the force of these *ad hoc* coalitions may push a particular issue to those levels where allocative decisions may be made, the disaster issue for the most part sustains its priority hold with considerable precariousness. Since *ad hoc* coalitions normally comprise those with limited responsibilities for disasters, the tendency is for coalitions to rapidly dissipate owing to changing individual agendas that reflect pressures more consistent with expected role performance. Hence, even if a Prime Minister becomes part of or the object of an *ad hoc* coalition seeking to intervene in a disaster, his or her attention is short-term at best. As former British Prime Minister, Edward Heath, recalled, 'Matters of disaster relief may arise during Cabinet discussions, but if they do, it is because they are part of a general foreign policy discussion determined by those within the Foreign Office who prepare the Foreign Minister's brief.'[45] The attention span given to a disaster is brief.

4. *Trade-offs and linkages.* We have suggested so far that, within the political process, most disaster responses are affected by the fact that disaster relief—as a priority issue—is sustained by a limited constituency, a constituency that for the most part lacks the interest base and, hence, allocative authority to push disaster issues to the forefront of the priority process. More often than not, the priority status that any single disaster issue gains in the allocative process depends upon *ad hoc* coalitions. These coalitions, however, comprise components that do not necessarily have direct disaster relief responsibilities. They respond to a disaster

because of the ways in which a disaster issue affects their ability to fulfil roles and maintain role consensus, and their perceptions of the relevance of their roles generally depend on how they receive information. The information that they receive, as described earlier, may well be loaded, owing to the ways in which disaster information is presented, and may be further loaded by the manner in which that information has been interpreted by individual components.

What all this suggests is that disasters, as an issue within the political process, very often depend on factors that are extraneous to the issue itself. Response to a disaster frequently depends on trade-offs and linkages among an array of differing roles to gain access to the priority formulation process. Without the prospect for such trade-offs and linkages, those with allocative authority may never actually focus on the disaster. Yet, the effect of trade-offs and linkages may, on the other hand, distort the response that is eventually made.

By trade-offs, we mean the compromises that have to be made within the formulation of policy that will allow any single component within the allocative process to perceive a vested interest. For example, the head of the Natural Disasters Section of the Norwegian Ministry of Development Cooperation commented that 'there are enormous surpluses of dried fish and salted fish, and we're under certain pressures to use them. I've had chairmen of the Fisheries Committee in Parliament calling me on the phone to get me to use such surpluses for relief.'[46] Such pressures are often hard to resist—even though the disaster-afflicted may be unaccustomed to dried or salted fish—since that parliamentarian's influence may help in mobilizing greater support for the disaster relief operation.

One of the problems that hampered USAID's attempt to support transport assistance to the Ethiopian relief operation in 1984 was the fear that American automobile manufacturers would object to American dollars being used to purchase spare parts and trucks for foreign vehicles.[47] The possibility of a trade-off for those with influence within the allocative process was indeed limited on this particular issue. Giving assistance to non-governmental organizations is indeed regarded as a convenient trade-off within the political process by many officials in Europe with responsibilities for disaster relief, since, in the words of one Dutchman, 'it allows us to satisfy the religious-based domestic constituencies which they represent.'[48]

Trade-offs, both large and small, are a normal part of the political process. For disaster issues, however, where those with responsibilities for disasters have limited bases from which to bargain, the potential for bargaining is more often than not in the hands of those who have their own particular views on what might or might not be gained from some form of involvement in disaster relief. The trade-offs, in other words, are all too often out of the direct control of those who have direct responsibilities for relief. Yet trade-offs must be found, if the pressure from those who can directly influence the allocative process is to be mobilized.

Halperin, in describing the ways in which disasters gain the attention of senior decision-makers in the United States, suggested that 'disasters get the attention of junior officials. Who really cares becomes a matter of a quirk. What turns junior people on to particular issues?'[49] His point is not that senior officials are necessarily indifferent to the plight of the afflicted, but rather that—as mentioned above—the roles they seek to fulfil isolate their attention to particular kinds of issues. Only when these issues might be linked with a particular disaster does the possibility increase that a disaster will gain their priority attention. The role of the junior official, with a 'quirk' about a particular disaster, is to find that linkage.

However, as the earlier cited examples of Nixon's response to the East Pakistan cyclone and the Jordanian–Palestinian conflict suggest, the President was sensitive to these disasters because they were both linked to particular aspects of policy upon which he had been focusing at the time. The issue for the junior official, as he attempts to promote a particular relief response up the decisional ladder, frequently depends on finding ways to link the response with other policy priorities.

Yet, disaster initiatives are by no means always the result of the ways in which junior officials link such initiatives with the prevailing concerns of senior policy-makers. Senior policy-makers can indeed make their own links! A member of SIDA's emergency unit explained that Swedish disaster relief to Bolivia was prompted by the Swedish Cabinet, which wished to demonstrate solidarity with another socialist government. Similarly, Swedish assistance to Vietnamese hurricane victims around the same time was prompted by a strong desire on the part of a majority of Sweden's Parliament to expand contacts with the Vietnamese government.[50]

The head of Norway's Natural Disaster Section in the Ministry of Development Cooperation referred to the same kind of linkage in discussing relief aid contributions to Benin:

When the Minister of Industry for Benin was coming to Norway, our minister [of Development Cooperation] asked if there was anything we could do for that country. We telexed the United Nations Disaster Relief Office that we had $50,000, and UNDRO replied that they were looking for funds to cover an operation involving $27,000 for the salary of a specialist, and we sent the money to UNDRO for Benin.[51]

These links and trade-offs are by no means unusual phenomena in the policy formulation process. The particular kind of trade-off and link that may push one issue to the fore and leave others behind adds to the unpredictability of political results. In the realm of disaster relief initiatives, the unpredictable consequence of trade-offs and linkages means that criteria of needs, types of intervention and the choice of afflicted population to receive assistance all too frequently become hostages to matters extraneous to the plight of afflicted peoples. However unfortunate this conclusion, it does nevertheless reflect the workings of politics. Of course, to a very significant extent, the resort to linkages and trade-offs largely depends on the clarity—both in terms of roles and norms—that surrounds any single issue. This, too, is a factor inherent in the political process.

While disaster issues are subject to the same process factors, as perceived aberrants they lack the support of more permanent interest groups that would give them greater access to those with allocative responsibility. Disaster relief is too often dependent upon limited constituencies, and only when such constituencies are supported by *ad hoc* coalitions does relief begin to move up the rung of the priority formulation process. Being highly susceptible to 'loading', disaster issues frequently engender tensions between roles and norms, ultimately making the recourse to linkages and trade-offs the only way in which to move a disaster initiative up the priority queue. In the final analysis, it is not that the political process is necessarily devoid of 'emotions of conscience'; rather, it is that conscience cannot be separated from the ways in which roles, norms and interest groups interact to determine priorities.

Though treated in isolation, the politics and the priority formulation process cannot be divorced from perceptual variables, organizational behaviour and inter-organizational relations. And yet, at the same time, such considerations offer their own particular insights into the functioning of the international relief network. For our purposes, each is interrelated, but each at the same time deserves special consideration.

Perceptual Variables and Persuasive Communications

One may recall the media's stark and salient images of the camp in Korem, in Ethiopia's Wellop province, or of those deserted villages surrounding Cameroon's Lake Nios in August 1986. One may reflect on the devastated towns surrounding Colombia's awakened volcano, Nevada del Ruiz, in November 1985, or remember the pictures of thousands of starving Chadian refugees who made their way to the borders of the Sudan, in October 1984. Clarity—implicit and explicit—marked those images of horror and despair. To the outside observer, there could be little doubt that a disaster had occurred and that its impact was self-evident. Perhaps few who were exposed to these images would have any question about what was required to relieve the plight of the disaster-afflicted. Yet, the clarity and certainty that so often underpin disaster images are belied by what the participants view as 'reality'. For those who deal with the direct consequences of disasters, ambiguity reigns supreme; uncertainty is the norm. The very impact of a disaster, as well as the requirements for appropriate relief, are frequently shrouded in mystery for days and even weeks after the event has taken place. And often at the heart of the ambiguity and uncertainty lie complex perceptual and communications variables.

'Knowing does not start by registering and processing the raw information provided by man's sensory system', writes Rolando Garcia in his discussion on famine. 'It is not the case that sensation is simply registered and then processed.'[52] To the contrary, the variables that influence the ways in which human beings process information are indeed far more complex. Human beings are predisposed to interpret information based on belief systems, values and attitudes that may have little to do with the 'facts' in question. The factors that might lead them to change their attitudes have little to do with simply 'registering and processing raw information'. What, then, are the factors that influence the ways in which 'we see,' the ways in which we change our minds, and the ways that lead us to accept communications from one source but not from another? Let us look at some of these under three headings: (1) predispositions; (2) attitude change; (3) persuasive communications.

Predispositions

Morren, in his analysis of Botswana Bushmens' disaster-coping mechanisms, comments, 'When is a drought not a drought?', or more properly speaking, 'When is a problem perceived as drought, not a drought?' The Bushmen case shows the ambiguity of the question. They respond as though there were a drought when, 'in our common understanding of that term, drought is not the problem.'[53]

Inherent in Morren's comment is the fact that human beings are predisposed to respond to their surroundings in ways that reflect particular socio-cultural, environmental and experiential considerations that may differ from one society to another. It is a point that has been made in Turnbull's well-known study of a Pygmy's first reactions to the world outside his native forest:

He (Kenge) saw the buffalo, still grazing lazily several miles away, far down below. He turned to me [Colin Turnbull] and said, 'What insects are those?' At first I hardly understood; then I realised that, in the forest, the range of vision is so limited that there is no great need to make an automatic allowance for distance when judging size.[54]

A person will view and interpret an event largely in terms of what he or she has been led to expect. Hence, the more familiar a particular phenomenon, the more quickly it will be recognized, and even rare occurrences, given the force of previous experience, may lead one to mistake them for the usual.[55] Furthermore, information that is consistent with expectations is rated by observers as more accurate and indeed is remembered better than information that is inconsistent with the expectations of observers.[56] Even if a particularly unusual object or event is recognized as unusual, there is a tendency to explain it in terms of one's own previous experience, environment and expectations. Kenge, the Pygmy, for example, was convinced that the buffalos he saw were insects. Yet, when he finally accepted that they were not, he still refused to believe that they were buffaloes, since they were twice the size of forest buffaloes and 'we would not be standing out in the open if they were.'[57]

One's predispositions in seeing events can clearly be influenced by explicit instructions and contexts. A large body of psychological literature demonstrates how different information, namely specific instructions, about a similar situation leads to different assessments of the situation. Reactions towards an individual described as 'cold' differ markedly from subjects' reactions towards the same individual when described as 'warm'.[58] Context, as Jervis points out, significantly influences perceptual predisposition, not only by framing the object under focus but also by triggering 'evoked sets'. If people are shown an ambiguous figure that could either be a cat or a bird, those who have been shown pictures of birds will interpret the ambiguous figure as a bird, whereas those who have been looking at cats will view the ambiguous figure as a cat.[59] In other words, what one sees—particularly when confronted with an ambiguous situation—will depend on the framework in which that situation has been introduced.

What one sees and what one believes are closely inter-related. Perceptions as well as confirmation of information are intertwined in the 'belief system' of the observer. A belief system provides internal referents that stem from values that may have many different sources. Upbringing, environment, experiences all lead one to adopt certain criteria for determining what is good or bad, what is true or false, appropriate or not. The more ambiguous or ill-defined an event or information, the more readily an observer seeks an explanation from internal referents derived from values inherent in that person's belief system.

The tenacity with which people seek to maintain their own beliefs in the face of blatantly contradictory evidence has been demonstrated by Kulik in his study of subjects' analyses of introversion and extroversion. In assessing the interaction between perceptions of behaviour, beliefs about others and beliefs about social situations, Kulik concluded that:

Taken together, these results suggest that our beliefs about others are unlikely to maintain or change as a simple function of impartially tallying each instant of consistent and inconsistent behaviour (cf. Rothbart, 1981); rather, our images of others persevere in part because consistent behaviours are accepted largely at face value as dispositionally caused and therefore as corroboration for the original beliefs, whereas the potential belief-altering implications of inconsistent behaviours are negated by liberal perception of situational causality.[60]

Attitude Change

Despite the relative consistency of one's belief system and the accumulative factors of experience and environment that influence perceptual predispositions, one's beliefs and attitudes do change. Attitudes are not fixed and impenetrable barriers to new information about events or objects. Yet, how and when they change are important considerations.

Cognitive consistency. Psychologists who espouse the view that human beings seek to maintain 'cognitive consistency' see that attitudes and beliefs only change when overwhelming evidence forces individuals to adjust their attitudes and beliefs. The human inclination to resist fundamental changes in the way an individual interprets events or objects is deeply held. The individual attempts to protect the consistency of his or her views by using even new information in such a way as to sustain initial attitudes or beliefs. Until dissonance—contradictory evidence—reaches such an intensity that it can no longer be ignored or rationalized, the individual will not alter opinions or accept information that is outside his or her conceptual framework.

Individuals protect their cognitive consistency in a variety of ways. People might attack the source of new information; they might disregard it because it diverges too far from the views of those towards whom the recipient feels greater affinity; they might discount the information by attacking the methodology that led to it. In whatever ways an individual may fend off dissonant inputs, the conclusion is that human beings do not readily adjust their views, their beliefs or perceptual predispositions without overwhelming evidence to the contrary. Cognitive consistency theorists see that the individual resists attitude change until his or her rationalization process is expended.

Attribution theory. Psychologists increasingly suggest that cognitive consistency behaviour is more readily apparent when people deal with issues deemed 'highly emotional' in terms of personal values. However, there are other forces at play where individuals confront information that is less threatening to deeply-held beliefs. Among these are 'attributional factors', and they are reflected in the ways that individuals seek to interpret the world around them. Fundamental to attribution theories is the belief that the individual assumes and actively seeks causation by attributing behaviour according to a combination of environmental and personal factors.[61] Broadly speaking, the theory assumes that if an actor is perceived to have had a choice of actions, then the actor's behaviour is seen as intentional; and hence the observer makes inferences about the dispositions (personal characteristics) of the actor. Otherwise, situational factors are deemed to be the cause of the behaviour.

There is in effect a pattern in the ways that individuals attribute causality. To explain one's own actions, one tends to refer to situational factors that influenced the need to undertake a particular course of action. To explain the actions of others, one is inclined to attribute causation to the personal characteristics or disposition of those whom one is observing.[62] Hence, an individual may explain his own examination cheating in terms of lack of funds for textbooks, parental pressures, etc., but regard the cheating of others as due to their untrustworthy dispositions. However, there is a propensity to ascribe one's own success to one's personal characteristics, and the success of others to factors in the situation!

While attribution theories may suggest that human beings are active and rational in their attempts to deal with new information and the world around them, the process by which attributions are made need not necessarily lead to accurate conclusions. On the contrary, individuals' attributions reflect propensities to skew information according to fixed beliefs about people and contexts that are not dissimilar to the potential distortions one sees arising from cognitive consistency mechanisms. Physical features and artefacts (for example sunglasses), as well as non-verbal cues, all in one way or another affect the attributions one makes about others.[63]

Similarly, individuals are influenced by the contexts of situations, so that the setting in which an event takes place may indeed influence the way one explains the event—rightly or wrongly. 'Vividness', either in terms of a particular person or situation, provides an excellent example of the way in which a specific cue may lead to a distortion of causal explanations. In 1973 thousands of children died in the Sahel because of factors associated with the drought. The explanation for such deaths was given as being due to 'natural causes'. Three years later, as described earlier, there was a drought in Britain. But 'nobody would have thought it "natural" for thousands of British children to die because of the drought'.[64] Vividness and contexts determine the attributions one makes.

When combined with the kinds of cues that determine the ways in which people view situations and other people, the general pattern of attributional explanations suggests once again that accuracy of perception and information processing is by no means a certainty. The propensity to misconstrue or to be over-influenced by irrelevant cues may lead to distortions and misconceptions every bit as unpredictable as those that arise from the more static attempts to maintain cognitive consistency.

Schema theory. 'Research in cognitive psychology', writes Larsen, 'has demonstrated that human beings frequently make important decisions and judgements on the basis of sparse information, haphazardly combined. People simply do not have the time or capacity to follow more elaborate, systematic or thorough decision-making procedures.'[65] Schema theory suggests that people in coping with new information seek to short-cut the 'cost' of dealing with such inputs by categorizing and labelling. Both are determined by the store of memory which an individual has about subjects, situations, events and people.

To explain the stimuli to which a person is subjected, that person will rely on 'schemas' or 'prototypes'. He or she will seek to match input with previous experiences stored in his or her memory. The individual will categorize or label new inputs by bringing the latter into already-established categories. Snap judgements, stereotyping and 'tell-tale' actions are all indicative of the ways in which the individual procedes to bypass the difficulties of dealing with new and complex inputs. The process of categorizing and labelling, therefore, obviously depends on the kind of schema stored in a person's memory that is available to be matched with new information.

Larsen, based on the work of Abelson and Nisbett and Ross, refers to three consequences of such matching. The first is the tendency to create 'episodic' scripts in which seemingly similar experiences or incidents will form a more general categorical script. Secondly, there is the tendency to create 'metaphors', so that a person 'tries to match what he is experiencing to a preconceived schema describing analogous situations in the past.' Finally, there is the type of schema 'that often influences judgements about others—the "persona". Personae are cognitive structures representing the personality characteristics and typical behaviour of certain "stock characters".'[66]

As with all short cuts, there is an inherent danger in over-simplifying events or individuals under focus. There is the ever-present problem that, in our efforts to come to some judgement, the wrong analogies are used, the store of available categories is inappropriate and the propensity to stereotype is increased. Here, too, as with cognitive consistency and attribution theories, schema theory leaves one with the prospect that changes in attitude or dealing with ostensibly 'observable facts' are vulnerable to a wide range of misperceptions, miscueing and stereotyping.

Persuasive Communications

In disasters requiring assistance from an international community which represents a very wide range of socio-cultural, ethnic, linguistic, and institutional norms, the transmission of information that affects predispositions, perceptions and attitudes poses many difficulties. For this very reason, it is worth bearing in mind at least a few of the factors that make communications 'persuasive'. Some writers break the persuasive communication process down into source, message and recipient variables. There are no simple answers to making communications persuasive, as McGuire's recent review of the persuasion and attitude-change literature demonstrates. He classifies attitude change theories within a matrix of sixteen major approaches, each of which would implicate different factors in persuasion. He also refers to a twelve-stage process of accepting a persuasive communication. While social psychologists have identified a plethora of variables and issues, certain major factors stand out with regard to the belief process.

It is a commonplace to suggest that the source of a communication—the level of credibility attributed to the sender—is a critical determinant in the acceptability of information. Credibility is a function both of the perceived informational value being transmitted and the reliability of the sender. Persuasiveness, however, does not necessarily depend on both factors being of equal weight. Race, social status, attractiveness and expertise unrelated to the specific message influence the credibility given to the message.

The persuasive impact of information increases when 'general knowledgeability cues' of the sender, such as a high level of education, social status and professional attainment, are perceived by the recipient.[67] This is particularly the case when a low level of involvement allows the receiver to accept or reject the conclusion on the basis of source competence without having to study the arguments. However, these general knowledgeability cues may backfire when the sources appear personally involved in the issue and thus less objective. Trustworthiness may therefore be influenced by the sources' disinterestedness in the outcome, lack of interest in persuading, or when sources appear to argue against their own self-interests, or against the obvious preferences of their audiences.

There is an obvious relationship between 'source similarity' and persuasiveness. Where senders and receivers are ideologically similar, abstract evaluations have a greater chance of acceptance; where they are demographically similar (e.g. ethnically), there is a greater likelihood of behavioural compliance. 'In more traditional and contentious societies', argues Davis, 'demographic tends to catch up with ideological similarity'. However, according, to Yabrudi and Diab, even in a country as polarized as Lebanon, ideology remains more important than denominational similarity.

Obviously, the persuasiveness of a communication will also be influenced by sources' perceived power and influence, or ability to punish recipients' failures to act. However, a message can be persuasive when the source seeks to 'dominate through weakness', attempting to elicit compliance through sympathy. The way in which messages are structured also clearly affects persuasiveness. 'The threatening negative appeals may produce more bureaucratic compliance (Weinmann, 1982a), higher immediate intention to comply, and more reported compliance, but positive appeals may yield better recall of the recommendations and more actual compliance weeks later (Evans et al., 1970; K.H. Beck, 1979). Positive appeals promote coping with the danger while negative appeals promote coping with the affect (Monat & Lazarus, 1977, Leventhal & Nerenz, 1983)'.

Kelman distinguished between compliance, identification and internalization. The first depends on the source's power and the ability to maintain surveillance; the second depends on the desire to maintain a particular role relationship with the persuader; the last depends on the perception of the source's credibility, that is, both trustworthiness and expertise. Only this last implies a long-term persuasion, in the absence of the source of the message, and it is affected by whether the new information fits in with other values and beliefs. Clearly, all these processes or any two might be operating in any persuasion attempt; futhermore, the source's power may bring about compliance which may itself, according to dissonance theorists, bring about attitude change.

Persuasiveness, in other words, is often a function of a variety of imprecise, double-edged and subjective variables. Recipients' perceptions of the sender's competence, authority and potential power to enforce compliance are important factors. So, too, are the similarities between source and recipient, the former's perceived self-interest and the very structure of the message being conveyed.

From this brief survey of perceptual and persuasive communications variables, one might well assume that disasters and disaster relief situations can compound the difficulties of assessing and transmitting 'facts'. In situations where chaos appears to abound and in which assistance may depend on a wide range of diverse actors, there is an increased probability that distortion of information and misperceptions will intensify. The ways in which this can and does too often occur might be better understood by looking at perceptual and communication dynamics in three phases of an emergency:

- Has a disaster occurred?
- Assessing the disaster.
- Responding to a disaster.

Has a Disaster Occurred? Even when disaster warnings or information are clearly communicated, recipients may tend to interpret that information based on their predisposition towards the source. An officer on duty at USAID's Office for Foreign Disaster Assistance early in 1980 received news over his telex that a hurricane disaster had occurred in a particular country that he labelled a 'beggar country': 'You know the kind that always tries to get everything it can when an event of this kind happens.' The officer was not unsympathetic to the potential plight of the victims, but he was reluctant, given his particular perception of the disaster-stricken nation, 'to over-respond'. He approached the situation with a degree of reticence that he would not have reserved for countries that he felt 'do not always cry wolf'.[68] He was predisposed towards a typology of actors, viewing nations along a spectrum of those who 'cry wolf' and those 'who try to hide the event'.

Predispositions are clearly influenced by the context in which information is given. In evidence before the House of Commons Foreign Affairs Committee in 1984, the Overseas Director of the Save the Children Fund (SCF) explained that 'it is very difficult for people to believe there is a famine unless they see the outward signs of it. People mistrust evidence if they do not see beggars or emaciated children . . . It is very difficult to persuade people that there is really an enormous problem sitting there.'[69]

As SCF accepted, part of the problem the organization faced in trying to persuade both the World Food Programme and the British government that a famine loomed in Ethiopia was due to the context in which SCF conveyed the warning. Officials at the British embassy in Addis Ababa and the World Food Programme (WFP) indicated the SCF had a 'vested interest' in 'promoting disasters', and that, while there might be famine indicators, SCF might also be exaggerating the likelihood of famine for its own purposes. Furthermore, the officials viewed SCF and certainly several of those associated with that agency as being 'a bit pro-Ethiopian'.[70]

'Evoked sets', those issues and concerns that are at the forefront of an observer's mind, also influence ways in which objects or events are perceived. Officials in UNHCR's Geneva headquarters in late 1984 were reeling from donors' criticisms of their seemingly lax approach to verifying numbers of refugees in the Horn of Africa. These criticisms so dominated the minds of many senior officials that when UNHCR's Sudan representative urgently warned of hundreds of thousands of Tigrayans crossing into Sudan, UNHCR tended to ignore the communications. It was not, as UNHCR's eventual response was to indicate, that headquarters did not want to act. Rather, the organization interpreted the problem in terms of registration and did not focus on the problem as an emergency influx.[71]

The propensity to discount or exaggerate information about a disaster is an ever-present hazard in the relief process. Even the strong probability that the Nevada del Ruiz volcano would erupt within hours did not lead local Colombian officials to undertake emergency procedures, since they were predisposed to interpret the warnings as 'uncertain' and they did not want to subject the population to evacuation in the inclement weather![72]

The propensity to resist dissonant information and the response to such information when dissonance becomes overwhelming is reflected in the reactions of one official to the build-up of famine in Ethiopia. Throughout 1983 and 1984 many donor country representatives tended to ignore the urgent pleas of Ethiopia's Relief and Rehabilitation Commission (RRC) concerning the impending food crisis. The reaction of the United States Counsellor in Addis Ababa had been that the Ethiopians were 'crying wolf' and that, in reality, the country always faced a chronic food shortage. He viewed the Ethiopian regime with tremendous hostility, and maintained that one could not trust documents produced by the RRC. He attacked the methodology of the RRC's Early Warning System which had issued the famine warnings, and consistently preferred the evaluations of the World Food Programme that reflected lower food requirements. When the acute famine proved the RRC to be only too accurate, he subsequently insisted that the RRC had actually minimized the extent of the famine, that the number of potential victims was even greater than the RRC had indicated.[73] The intense distrust that led that particular individual to minimize the famine warnings now explained, after a significant change of attitude, why he believed that the figures the RRC had presented were too low.

The attributional analysis of information processing is exemplified in another case from Ethiopia. During the early months of 1984, private voluntary agencies had begun to receive warnings that a serious famine had broken out in the southern province of Sidamo. The warnings, however, were being discounted because the agencies assumed that, if there really were a problem, the Ethiopian Relief and Rehabilitation Commission would have notified them. The agencies had given high marks to the RRC for its Early Warning System, and felt it important to acknowledge the credibility of the RRC.

For several critical weeks, relief agencies tended to ignore the warnings filtering through to them from two RRC officials in Sidamo since RRC headquarters had not initially supported the Sidamo officials' claims. Once the agencies finally realized that a serious famine did exist, they explained their initial reactions in two ways. The agencies themselves attributed their initial failure to the conditions presented in southern Sidamo. Famine in that kind of region was difficult to anticipate. The area was 'rather diffuse and nomadic populations made analysis difficult'. On the other hand, they attributed the failure of the RRC to respond to the Sidamo situation in terms of the weaknesses of the RRC's Early Warning System and to the lack of training and poor reporting system found at RRC headquarters.[74]

In the wake of information about a disaster, officials with relief responsibilities often feel under pressure to react. Their reactions may ultimately tend to play down or exaggerate the situation but, in either case, they feel compelled to make a decision. The cost calculation of analysing the incoming information may be short-cut by intuitive categorizing. Unconsciously, they may label the event or the source of information according to their own predetermined schemas.

When, in 1972, thirty nights of ground frost occurred in the highlands of Papua New Guinea, observers noted that considerable damage to natural vegetation and to food gardens ensued. 'The immediate reaction of local expatriate observers was to interpret this "extreme geophysical event" as being of "disaster" proportions. Following representations to the central government, a massive famine relief programme was mounted.'[75] Yet, the decision to mount an urgent relief programme had little to do with the conditions of the local population. The judgement was based on the reactions of those who had seen the destruction of food gardens in West Africa during the Nigerian–Biafran civil war. They assumed that damage to the food gardens of subsistence agricultural-ists would naturally lead to famine. They did not take into account the coping mechanisms of the local people, but responded to what they perceived as a crisis based on their 'schema' of disasters from an irrelevant crisis.[76]

Predispositions and factors affecting attitude change are closely linked to what are perceived as persuasive communications. In the unfolding Kampuchean relief efforts throughout 1979–80, 'many believed that US Ambassador to Thailand Abramowitz was exploiting the humanitarian crisis for the purposes of America's anti-Vietnamese policy'.[77] The positive initiatives that the United States ambassador took to relieve the suffering of Khmer peoples on the Thai border were initially viewed with distrust by various international organizations. They could not believe that the 'source'—the American ambassador—would ever undertake activities that, no matter how indirectly, might be seen to be supporting the Vietnamese-backed Heng Samrin regime.

The problem of message–source interaction also goes some way to explain why the warnings by the Sudanese Commission for Refugees of a refugee influx from Tigray and Eritrea were being ignored in August and September 1984 by various inter-governmental and non-governmental organizations. Outside observers from these organizations often spoke disparagingly of the Commission's capabilities. The Commission was considered to lack a professional infrastructure and was also seen as having a vested interest in exaggerating the numbers of refugees who might enter the Sudan. The Commission's credibility was low at a time when several IGOs and NGOs were becoming increasingly concerned about potential famine affecting indigenous Sudanese in the west of the country. Despite the Commission for Refugees' clear—and eventually proven—concerns, the international community continued to regard the Commission's figures as highly inflated.[78]

Assessing the Disaster. Even when a disaster has been recognized, its assessment is by no means free of the perceptual and communications variables that may tend to skew information. Once again, 'fact' is dependent upon a range of predispositional and communication factors that may exaggerate, minimize or misconstrue the needs of the afflicted. Well before the international community accepted the seriousness of the Ethiopian famine, USAID officials were aware that famine existed in that country. However, as one expert saw the situation, 'there is a standard deficit of one million tons of food every year. This is a situation in which emergency assistance becomes a chronic emergency situation.'[79] That expert did not doubt that there existed a serious food shortage, but he was predisposed to view the 'emergency' merely as a consistent food shortage that always plagued Ethiopia.

In February 1976, a group of agencies within the Christian Relief and Development Association were informed that a 'measles outbreak in some of the relief camps (in the Ogaden) is inflicting heavy loss of life among the children.'[80] There were indeed some indications of measles in two camps, i.e. Segeg and Dehun, but the epidemic proportions announced at the CRDA meeting reflect the result of observers' evoked sets on disaster assessment rather than a careful assessment of facts. Aware that there might be measles, observers assumed that the number of free grave cloths distributed within a short period for burial in these camps was due to a measles epidemic. Granted, there were cases of measles. However, the reason why so many grave cloths were being distributed had nothing to do with a sharp rise in infant mortality. It was merely due to the distribution procedures being followed by local camp officials. 'Large numbers of graves were not found',[81] but an awareness that measles might be a problem, combined with the periodic distribution of grave cloths by local officials, led outside observers to assume the worst.

When a team of assessors was sent by the Food and Agriculture Organization and the World Food Programme to determine, among other things, the delivery capacity of the Ethiopian port of Assab, the team interpreted its instructions as to evaluate port capacity in terms of its demonstrated record. Yet, this perception skewed the team's findings, since recent records primarily involved deliveries to Eritrea and Tigray where civil war had made deliveries particularly difficult. The team's conclusion disregarded the potential capacity of the port to provide for deliveries in areas not affected by civil strife, and because its attention was highly focused on recent records it severely understated the amount of relief Assab could handle.[82]

The consequence of highly focused attention and the dynamics of cognitive processes are reflected in the serious emergency that began to unfold in Bangladesh in 1978. There, significant numbers of Burmese refugees had settled along the Bangladesh border, and foreign agencies began the difficult task of providing the refugees with food. Despite the efforts of the World Food Programme and its NGO operational partners, infant mortality in the camps increased dramatically. The WFP and the government of Bangladesh began to round on the NGOs for failing to distribute the food rations effectively. However, the obsession with food distribution had blinded those involved in the relief efforts to the real cause of rising infant mortality, namely, lack of adequate sanitation. Sanitation, not food, was the problem; but not until the fixation on food and distribution had been exhausted did one begin to seek alternative explanations.[83]

The reasons that the Oxfam field director gave for his slow response to the famine in Ethiopia in 1984 also demonstrate a mixture of highly focused attention and attributional explanations at play. In evaluating his reactions, Hugh Goyder maintained that he was too preoccupied with Oxfam's development projects to focus on the emerging crisis; furthermore, in retrospect, he suggested that he felt the famine would be just too vast in scale for Oxfam to play any significant role. He attributed his failure to be more aggressive in his famine warnings to his 'believing, back in May 1984, that WFP or FAO knew something about Ethiopia's food aid needs'. He suggested that his assumption about those organizations' assessment competence led him to explain away his own misgivings about the impending crisis. In attributing expertise to WFP and the FAO, he was able to concentrate on Oxfam's development projects, despite clear warnings that a crisis was imminent.[84]

The poisonous gases that spread rapidly from Cameroon's Lake Nios to surrounding villages in August 1986 quickly led the United Nations Disaster Relief Organization to warn that 26,000 people were in imminent danger of asphyxiation. The number provided by UNDRO was large and dramatic, but it was not accurate. Given the pressure of time, officials monitoring the disaster short-circuited more accurate assessment procedures by assuming that the gas would be carried to population centres well beyond the actual range that such gases could reach. They assessed the impact of Lake Nios by using analogies with hazard impacts affecting more densely populated areas. Their reliance on inappropriate schemas ultimately led to a response that was inappropriate for the disaster at hand.

Responding to a Disaster. It is instructive to return to the 'famine that never was' in Papua New Guinea in 1972; for, having decided that there was an imminent threat of disaster owing to ground frost, relief officials organized a massive effort that ultimately undermined local and regional autonomy and created unnecessary institutional dependencies.[85] In providing feeding programmes that lasted up to eight months, feeding up to 150,000 people, the expatriate relief officials—no doubt sincere in their beliefs that they were fending off imminent mass starvation—completely ignored the coping mechanisms of the local population. 'All the available evidence indicates that they [the local people] knew quite well

how to deal with a familiar hazard; it was the third in living memory . . .
Essentially, their normal response is characterized by a high degree of flexibility
with an escalating set of strategies according to the gravity of the hazard.'[86] Yet,
the perceptions of those initiating the relief effort led them to see a food crisis
where none existed. In so doing, their subsequent activities blocked the migratory pattern that was central to the indigenous coping mechanism, created
dependence in the local people on handouts, and undermined the very confidence of the people for whom massive assistance had been intended.

Only too often, the predispositions of outside relief officials are imposed on the
disaster-afflicted with little understanding of the consequence of their intervention. One person involved in planning and policies for the United States Catholic
Relief Services complained that those within her organization 'kept referring to
malnourished Ethiopians in relief camps as 'refugees'. This totally inappropriate
term 'colours the way you look at the relief camps', she commented. One CRS
director wanted 'to plan on how you're going to use at least 50% of $30 million
for schools', and other CRS officials were anxious to begin reafforestation
projects and undertake other activities suitable to rehabilitation. The only
fundamental problem with these proposals was that they were suitable for
'refugees' who might be faced with prolonged periods away from their land, but
they were not suitable solutions to the problems of famine victims who, once
nutritionally restored, wanted to return to their farms and villages.

This 'refugee mentality' permeated many of the approaches the CRS took
towards the problems of the famine victims. Where emphasis should have been
put on ways of easing the victims' return home, the relief effort was structured in
such a way that there was an inducement to stay as camp residents. 'The refugee
mentality was so imbued in the minds of CRS officials that even in the CRS
evaluation of its Ethiopian operations the word, "refugee", kept appearing
throughout the document.'[87]

Throughout relief responses in the Third World, agencies from developed
nations often interpose remedies that are not appropriate for disaster-afflicted
populations. In the Thai–Kampuchean operation in the early 1980s, doctors flew
children to American hospitals to perform highly sophisticated operations.
During this same period, children in the Karamoja were being fed by three
different agencies at the same time. In the north of Ethiopia, three years later,
one major agency was giving children more food than they could ever have
expected even during the best harvest conditions. All this assistance would seem
to be praiseworthy, if it were not for the damage that it ultimately inflicts on
recipients. The imposition of Western standards of medical attention and
nutrition creates expectations that cannot be sustained once the relief workers
depart from the scene of a disaster. Sophisticated levels of assistance would be
more than acceptable were the international community to make the commitment that would enable disaster-stricken peoples to maintain that standard.
However, without this commitment, relief remains only too often a reflection of
the brief interjection of standards and values imposed by donors. In large part, it
is a reflection of the perceptual schema that donors bring to a disaster site. They
view the afflicted in terms of their own perceptions of how things should be.
They rarely seek the opinion of the afflicted themselves, and more often than not
rely on their own cultural biases or on the opinions of those whom they deem to
be 'experts'.

In the relief world, as Cuny has complained, there are few real experts.[88]
Disaster relief, maintains the WFP's Trevor Page, is 'the last bastion of

unprofessionalism.'[89] And yet, 'expert opinion' is sought in dealing with relief. The question, therefore, must be: who are the experts? When it comes to the persuasiveness of communications during relief operations, the expert is that individual who shares certain common cultural links with the donor. He or she may know very little about the logistics of disasters, for example, but they may be regarded as an expert because of the amount of time that he or she has spent in the country. Rather than consult with a national of the country, the relief community would prefer to consult with an outsider who, granted, might be familiar with the country, but whose main qualifications are only too often that he or she shares a common bond with foreign relief workers.

In the Sudan in 1985, UNHCR sought experts from Geneva to help in its relief efforts. UNHCR's Resident Representative had hoped that he might find volunteers from the Kampuchean relief operation. When asked why Sudanese would not be able to fill these slots, the UNHCR representative maintained that it might be difficult to ask Sudanese to work in a highly sensitive area affecting their own country. When then asked why Africans in surrounding countries were not sought, he maintained that they might not have the proven expertise. The fact that there were indeed many African people from nations surrounding Sudan who had considerable experience in helping refugee populations was a point that was gently ignored.[90] The propensity to view the expert in terms of his or her own socio-cultural ties with donors is not necessarily a conscious phenomenon. It is one, however, that does permeate through the selection of experts in disaster relief situations. It reflects an important aspect of what makes communications persuasive, and it also suggests why time and again one finds that responses to disasters mirror the values and assessments of outsiders rather than those of the people directly affected by disasters. The perceptual and communication complexities that affect the ways in which disasters are recognized, assessed and handled are intertwined with the dynamics of organizational behaviour.

Notes

1. These figures were supplied by the Office of US Foreign Disaster Assistance.
2. See, for example, Committee on Emergency Management, National Research Council, *The Role of Science and Technology in Emergency Management*, Washington, DC, National Academy Press, 1982.
3. Interview with P.N. Haksar, former Principal Secretary to the Prime Minister of India, 1971–3, New Delhi, 16 March 1983.
4. Interview with Michael Harris, former Oxfam Overseas Director, Robertsbridge, 21 June 1985.
5. Interview with Frances D'Souza, Director, International Disaster Institute, London, 30 September 1982.
6. Interview with Sir Robert Jackson, United Nations, New York, 21 November 1980.
7. Easton, D., *A Systems Analysis of Political Life*, New York, Wiley, 1965.
8. Morgenthau, H.J., *Politics Among Nations*, 5th edn, New York, Alfred A. Knopf, 1973, p.8.
9. Davis, M., (ed.), *Civil Wars and The Politics of International Relief: Africa, South Asia and the Caribbean*, New York, Praeger, 1975, p.91.
10. For a description as well as a critique of the 'realist paradigm', see: Vasquez, J., *The Power of Power Politics: A critique*, London, Frances Pinter Publishers, 1983.
11. This may be due in part to the ways in which those in one nation view those in others; see, for example, Buchanan, W. & Cantril H., *How Nations See Each Other*, Urbana,

University of Illinois Press, 1953, pp.51–2. It might reflect the kinds of educational and professional orientation of particular societies, as suggested by H. Kissinger in 'Domestic Structure and Foreign Policy', in Rosenau, J. (ed.), *International Politics And Foreign Policy*, New York, Free Press, 1969. The consistency of precepts might also reflect a tradition of dealing with problems in certain kinds of ways. A. Bozeman suggests this when comparing African attitudes towards conflict with those of American or European cultures, in *Conflict in Africa*, Princeton, Princeton University Press, 1976.

12. Prigogine, I. & Stengers, I., *Order Out of Chaos: Man's New Dialogue With Nature*, London, Flamingo, 1984, p.xv.

13. Jensen, L., *Explaining Foreign Policy*, Englewood, Prentice-Hall Inc., 1982, p.37.

14. Ibid., and see, for example, Fisher, G., *Public Diplomacy and the Behavioural Sciences*, Bloomington, Indiana University Press, 1972, p.66.

15. Allison, G., *Essence of Decision: Explaining the Cuban Missile Crisis*, Boston, Little, Brown & Co., 1971, p.176.

16. Bauer, R. & Gergen, K., *The Study of Policy Formation*, New York, Free Press, 1968, p.228.

17. Wilson, H., *The Labour Government, 1964-1970: A Personal Record*, London, Weidenfeld & Nicolson and Michael Joseph, 1971, p.559.

18. This narrative is based upon interviews with members of United States Congressional staffs and various officials within USAID and the US State Department during the second and third week of September 1983.

19. Interview with Len Rogers, Office of Program and Policy Coordination, USAID, Washington, DC, 14 September 1983.

20. Interview with Joseph Sisco, former Assistant Secretary of State for Near Eastern and South Asian Affairs, Washington, DC, 12 September 1983. Of Sisco, Henry Kissinger commented that he was:

enormously inventive, with a talent for the stratagems that are the lifeblood of Middle East diplomacy . . . He was adroit in the ways of Washington and quickly established a personal relationship with me, perceiving that in the Nixon Administration Presidential authority would be the ultimate arbiter . . . After I became Secretary of State I made him Under-Secretary of State for Political Affairs, the highest career policymaking position in the Department.

[Kissinger, H., *White House Years*, Boston, Little, Brown & Co., 1979, p.349.]

21. Interview with officials from USAID, Washington, DC, second and third weeks of September 1983.

22. Ibid.

23. Ibid.

24. Interview with Dr Ekkehard Hallensleben, Section 301, Humanitarian Assistance, Ministry of Foreign Affairs, Federal Republic of Germany, Bonn, 24 May 1984.

25. Interview with J. Van Bosse, Head of North Africa Desk, Dutch Ministry of Foreign Affairs, The Hague, 29 May 1984.

26. Interview with J.F.L. Blankenberg, Department for Development Cooperation, Dutch Ministry of Foreign Affairs, The Hague, 29 May 1984.

27. Interview with David Korn, former US Chargé d'Affaires, 1982-5, US Embassy in Addis Ababa, London, 22 January 1986.

28. The Falashas are a small peasant community in north-western Ethiopia that practises a unique form of Judaism.

29. Interview with Alison Rosenberg, Staff of the Republican Majority, US Senate Foreign Relations Committee, Washington, DC, 16 September 1983.

30. Letter from M. Peter McPherson to the Hon. Howard Wolpe, 13 July 1983.

31. See Chapter 1, 4 ff.

32. See 'Organizational Behaviour' in Chapter 5.

33. Interview with Morton Halperin, former staff member of the National Security Council during the Nixon Administration and author of *Bureaucratic Politics And Foreign Policy* (Washington, DC, The Brookings Institution, 1974), Washington, DC, 14 September 1983. Maurice Williams, who as Deputy Administrator of

USAID, had been the 'President's relief coordinator six times', told this writer that:

Presidents do get involved where there are sensitive political issues. Sometimes the president is concerned, sometimes he isn't. I was called by the President to deal with the Managua earthquake because the President was afraid that because of the corruption, the Left might take over. Disasters get all wrapped up in politics. With the Sahel operation, the operation reflected the emergence of black Americans increasingly becoming a political force. There is a question of visibility in matters of relief efforts . . . Each case is quite specific in a political and country context. [Interview with Maurice Williams, New York, 29 September 1983.]

34. Interview with Stephen Tripp, former Coordinator, Office for US Foreign Disaster Assistance, Washington, DC, 15 September 1983. This was also a position suggested by Joseph Farland, former United States Ambassador to Pakistan during the 1970 cyclone and 1971 refugee crises. (Interview with Joseph Farland, Washington, DC, 18 September 1983.)
35. Ibid.
36. Interview with official from the Swedish Red Cross, Stockholm, 6 June 1984.
37. This figure derives from statistics provided by UNDRO and the Office of US Foreign Disaster Assistance.
38. Interview with official from Ethiopian/Somali Desk, Foreign and Commonwealth Office, London, 21 August 1984.
39. Interview with official from the Overseas Development Administration, Foreign and Commonwealth Office, Khartoum, 31 November 1984.
40. Interview with John Kelly, US Agency for International Development, Washington, DC, April 1985.
41. Interview with Hal Saunders, former staff member of the National Security Council under the Nixon Administration, Washington, DC, September 1983.
42. Interview with Christopher Van Hollen, former US Deputy Assistant Secretary of State for Near Eastern and South Asian Affairs from 1969 to 1972, Washington, DC, 19 November 1980. For an intriguing analysis of the 'White House versus Bureaucracy', see Van Hollen, C., 'The Tilt Policy Revisited: Nixon–Kissinger Geopolitics and South Asia', *Asian Survey*, **20**, No.4, April 1980, pp.339–61.
43. See note 38.
44. The comment arose in an interview with Peter Ekelund, Disaster Section, Swedish International Development Association, Stockholm, 8 June 1984.
45. Interview with Edward Heath, former British Prime Minister, London, 27 June 1985.
46. Interview with Nils Dahl, Natural Disasters Section, Norwegian Ministry of Development Cooperation, Oslo, 5 June 1984.
47. Interview with Dr Martin Howell, Director, Office of US Foreign Disaster Assistance, Washington, DC, 13 September 1983.
48. See note 26.
49. See note 33.
50. See note 44.
51. Interviews with officials from the Norwegian Ministry of Development Cooperation and Ministry of Foreign Affairs, Oslo, 5 June 1984.
52. Garcia, R., *Drought and Man, Vol.1: Nature Pleads Not Guilty*, Oxford, Pergamon, 1981, p.7.
53. Morren, G., 'The Bushmen and the British: problems of the identification of drought and responses to drought', in Hewitt, K. (ed.), *Interpretations of Calamity*, Boston, Allen & Unwin, 1983, p.51.
54. Turnbull, C., *The Forest People*, New York, Simon & Schuster, 1961, pp.252–3, as quoted in Jervis, R., *Perceptions and Misperceptions in International Politics*, Princeton, Princeton University Press, 1976, p.149.
55. Jervis, op. cit., p.147.
56. Berman, J., Kenny, D., Read, S., 'Processing Inconsistent Social Information', *Journal of Personality and Social Psychology*, **45**, No.6, December 1983, p.1211.

57. Turnbull, op. cit.
58. Kelley, H., 'The Warm–Cold Variable in First Impressions of Persons', *Journal of Personality*, **18**, 1950, pp.431-9.
59. Jervis, op. cit., p.151.
60. Kulik, J., 'Confirming Attribution and the Perception of Social Beliefs', *Journal of Personality and Social Psychology*, **44**, No.6, 1983, pp.1171-81.
61. Jones, E., Kanouse, D., Kelly, A., Nisbett, R., Valins, S. & Weiner, B. (eds), *Attribution: Perceiving the causes of behaviour*, Morristown, General Learning Press, 1972.
62. Jones, E. & Nisbett, R., *The Actor and the Observer: Divergent perceptions of the causes of behaviour*, Morristown, General Learning Press, 1971.
63. See, for example, discussion by Deaux, K., and Wrightsman, L., in Chapter 11 *Social Psychology in the 1980s*, 4th edn., Monterey, Calif., Brooks/Cole Publishing Co., 1984.
64. Garcia, op. cit., p.9.
65. Larsen, D., *Origins of Containment a Psychological Explanation*, Princeton, Princeton University Press, 1985, p.50.
66. Ibid., p.55.
67. The following discussion on persuasive communications follows W.J. McGuire's analysis in 'Attitudes and Attitude Change', in Lindzey, G. & Aronson, E. (eds), *Handbook of Social Psychology*, **2**, 1985, pp.233-346. Reference to all the sources cited can be found here.
68. Interview with George Beauchamp, Operations Officer, Office of US Foreign Disaster Assistance, Washington, DC, 19 November 1980.
69. Examination of Witnesses, 21 November 1984, House of Commons, Second Report from the Foreign Affairs Committee, Session 1984-1985, *Famine in Africa*, London, HMSO, 24 April 1985, p.12.
70. Interview with official from the British Embassy in Addis Ababa, 13 October 1984.
71. This point was raised in a closed meeting with UNHCR officials at Queen Elizabeth House, University of Oxford, 19 March 1986.
72. Office of the United Nations Disaster Relief Coordinator, UNDRO News, Geneva, November/December 1985, p.4.
73. Interview with an official at the US Embassy in Addis Ababa, 6 October 1984.
74. Interview with H. Olafsson, Norwegian Church Aid, and other representatives of NGOs during October 1984.
75. Waddell, E., 'Coping with frosts, governments and disaster experts: some reflections based on a New Guinea experience and a perusal of the literature', in Hewitt, op. cit., p.33.
76. Ibid., pp.35-6.
77. Shawcross, W., *The Quality of Mercy: Cambodia, holocaust and modern conscience*, London, André Deutsch, 1984, p.183.
78. This comment is based on conversations with officials in Khartoum from the International Committee of the Red Cross, UNHCR and Oxfam during early November 1984.
79. Interview with official from USAID, Washington, DC, 15 September 1983.
80. Minutes of the 101st General Meeting of the Christian Relief and Development Association, Addis Ababa, 2 February 1976.
81. Minutes of the 103rd General Meeting of the Christian Relief and Development Association, Addis Ababa, 1 March 1976.
82. Interviews with H. Dall, FAO representative, Addis Ababa, 12 October 1984 and Kenneth King, UNDP Resident Representative, Addis Ababa, 12 October 1984.
83. The interpretation of this event is this writer's own; the information about the situation came from an interview with A. Aurora, in charge of Bangladesh/Nepal and Afghanistan, World Food Programme, Rome, 5 July 1984.
84. Gill, P., *A Year in The Death of Africa: Politics, bureaucracy and the famine*, London, Paladin, 1986, p.31.

85. Waddell, op. cit.
86. Waddell, op. cit., p.35.
87. Interview with Isabelle Bivings, Catholic Relief Services, Addis Ababa, 15 November 1986.
88. Cuny is quoted as saying that 'anyone can call himself a disaster expert, and no one will challenge him or hold him accountable if things go wrong. It's all on-the-job training here and that means waste and errors. No one wants to see that the management capacity is missing.' ('African Relief Efforts Hit for Lack of "Pros" '. The *Washington Post*, 14 July 1985.)
89. Overheard by this writer in a conversation between Desmond Taylor, WFP representative in Addis Ababa, and Trevor Page, Addis Ababa, 3 October 1984.
90. See note 71.

5 The Network in Action: Organizational Behaviour and Inter-organizational Dynamics

Organizational Behaviour

> During the Indochina crisis, too often the bureaucrats at the [UNHCR] head office reacted slowly to urgent requests from the boondocks of Asia.

> Behind the organisational flaws [in the US State Department and White House in dealing with the Sahelian drought operation] . . . was an unresolved dilemma between the demands of urgency and speed in the delivery of relief and the need for some monitoring and accountability.

> It has been argued—with justification—that most information produced by international relief organisations about their work is designed to enhance the agencies' reputations, to satisfy past funding sources, and to elicit future support.

> The tendency for the same organisations—the ICRC, UN agencies, CRS, Oxfam and so on—to participate in one civil war after another also means they keep bringing their own predilections, predispositions, and internalised experiences with them.[1]

Warnings missed, relief delayed, insensitivity to victims, inappropriate relief —all these are accusations all too often justifiably laid at the doorstep of the major organizations—governmental, inter-governmental, non-governmental—which have the capacity to respond to disasters. For many observers, the organization, with its preoccupation with institutional survival and mechanistic approaches to complex problems, must bear much of the odium of callousness and inefficiency that mark the international relief network in action. And yet the problems that such organizations must face in responding to disasters should be balanced against their successes and, more important for this section, should be considered in the light of the problems inherent in what we shall call 'organizational behaviour'.

Inside the Organization

'An organisation is a collection of interacting and interdependent individuals who work toward common goals and whose relationships are determined according to a certain structure.'[2] Most organizations are designed to deal with various types of complex problems on a continuous basis, and in order to deal with complex problems, organizations employ specialists with particular problem-solving expertise. The work of specialists has to cohere with the overall objectives of the organization; and to ensure harmony and coordination, there is a variety of supervisory rungs created to do just that. The overall structure of an organization is, therefore, fundamentally hierarchical in which authority over more and more specialist sub-components increases as one moves from the base to the apex of the organizational pyramid.

The organization's perspective—the way in which it views and seeks to achieve tasks—is in one way or another determined by four considerations: (1) goal definition; (2) personnel; (3) uncertainty control; and (4) complexity.

Goal definition. Organizations are designed to achieve a particular set of goals. Yet, no matter how clear the formal goals of an organization may be, all organizations have 'unofficial objectives' that may or may not overlap with their official responsibilities. These unofficial objectives can be viewed as the organization's concern with its own 'health'—its survival and growth.

The link between formal agendas and unofficial objectives is twofold. Firstly, an organization—deemed to be expert in dealing with a certain set of problems, e.g. development, disaster relief—proceeds from the assumption that its very 'health' is a basic requisite to fulfil its formal goals. Hence, the pursuit of resources, manpower and finances is as fundamental to fulfilling its role as the formal goals themselves. Secondly, an organization is very much a collection of individuals. Individuals commit themselves and their security to an organization in the assumption that the organization can satisfy their needs. When the ostensible goals of an organization appear to depart from the needs of individuals, then unofficial objectives tend to dominate the activities of individuals within the organization. The result is reflected in various protective measures by employees, for example over-compliance with rules, rigid formalism, limited exchange of information among sub-divisions within the organization.

Of course, the architects of an organization's formal objectives may purposely or inadvertently have failed to make these objectives clear.[3] Hence, there is a propensity within organizations to determine 'internally' the ways in which the goals of the organization are to be interpreted or defined. The referents that determine the extent to which formal goals are defined from within depend both upon what the organization assumes it can do, based on available resources and manpower, and the clarity of the objectives it has been designed to achieve.

Personnel. Organizational perspective determines and is determined by its personnel. To deal with complex problems on a continuous basis, an organization employs a variety of specialists. Specialists are brought into the organization to handle a wide range of matters, from clerical and administrative to programme formulation and policy supervision. The specialist views the organization's goals essentially from the task that he or she has been assigned. When asked about logistical problems affecting the supply of relief materials to a disaster–stricken country, an international lawyer may well focus on the legal constraints imposed by customs regulations. Yet, the same problem might be seen by a logistics expert as a matter of cargo capacity, trucking and warehouse facilities. In other words, what an organization perceives it can achieve is determined to a large extent by the specialists whom it employs.

Paradoxically, an organization is prone to employ the specialists that it requires based on a criterion of need determined by specialists within the organization. Hence, to some extent, specialists not only determine the perspective of an organization, but also reinforce that perspective through employment practices. The particular perspective of an organization is constantly reinforced by its employees, or, if not, the employee may need to seek a position elsewhere. However, it is relatively rare for an organizational deviant to remain within the organization, for, by definition, the employee has committed him or herself to an organization because the rewards justify the adoption of an organization's perspective, or because the individual really does subscribe from the outset to the organization's values.

Uncertainty Control. It would be impossible for an organization to produce 'its product' if it could not control the variables that affect its end-result. Controlling the effect of unwanted or random variables is, therefore, a major preoccupation of all organizations; all organizations seek to avoid uncertainty. Both the day-to-day operations, as well as the future planning of organizations are geared towards eliminating or isolating factors that would disrupt the normal flow of problem-solving and production. This applies to organizations that are service-orientated as well as to those involved in manufacturing.

The devices that ensure the elimination of unwanted interferences also determine the organization's perspective. Screening mechanisms and standard operating procedures are but two means by which factors, assumed to be irrelevant to the organization's objectives, are removed. The mechanisms of uncertainty control, however, will be discussed later on, but here it is worth dwelling for a moment on the general implications of the organization's efforts to eliminate uncertainty.

An organization cannot operate in a realm of ambiguity, and it deals with ambiguity by focusing on those issues that it can extract as definable and tangible issues from ambiguous situations. Definition and tangibility are ultimately determined by what the organization recognizes as a problem, and recognition *per se* is a result of what the organization is able to handle. What the organization is able to handle are essentially those matters to which its experts are attuned. When executives talk about getting to grips with the 'immediate problem', more often that not they are talking about the organizational propensity to deal with problems that are most readily definable and unambiguous. This is not to suggest that such problems are synonymous with simplicity, but rather to stress that what one author has referred to as 'lower task management' reflects the tendency to tackle as a matter of priority those issues that are institutionally most definable.[4]

The propensity to eliminate uncertainty also explains in part why, in so many organizations, planning departments are regarded as institutional backwaters.[5] Effective long-range planning runs in the face of uncertainty control. Where the tendency of an organization is to eliminate uncertainty by focusing on issues that it is able to handle, the tendency of an effective planner is to engender simultaneously contrasting options from a sea of ambiguity.

Complexity. By definition, an organization is designed to deal with complex problems on a continuous basis. It achieves this function by 'factoring', or decomposing complexity into manageable component parts, each component part to be handled by specialists. Specialists define and respond to a problem based on their expertise and, in theory, their individual solutions are coordinated by a supervisory rung higher up the organizational ladder. However, for components within the organization as a whole, it would be impossible to treat each problem introduced into the organization as 'brand new' or one that would have to be reassessed at each organizational stage. Hence, the solution to dealing with complexity on a continuous basis necessitates standard operating procedures which provide types of responses and answers to various types of problems. These standard operating procedures (SOPs) allow for even the most complex problems to be dealt with on a 'normal' and continuous basis and provide supervisors with the relative assurance that, while they cannot monitor every aspect of a response, SOPs at least provide a consistent performance level. These four factors profoundly influence the ways in which organizations respond to problems. This may become clearer by tracing the institutional complexities posed by disasters for a relief organization and the ways in which such an organization determines its response to such problems.

Tracing Organizational Responses to Disasters

There would seem to be six broad categories that mark the process by which organizations respond to disasters. Of prime importance is how information about a disaster enters and flows through an organization. These two points will be discussed under the headings: (1) 'entry points' and (2) 'screening'. How such information will be handled at a preliminary stage will be considered in terms of (3) 'factoring' and (4) 'communication flows'. Finally, the response itself will be looked at in terms of (5) 'structuring solutions' and (6) 'standard operating procedures, repertoires and programmes.'

Entry Points. Information about disasters enters into the relief network in a variety of ways, ways frequently unpredictable and inconsistent. The randomness with which disaster information enters into the relief network does not in and of itself explain why relief operations often appear to be slow off the mark or inadequate. There are instances where unconventional entry points into the network have proved to be a distinct advantage. When, for example, Rosalyn Carter, the wife of American President Jimmy Carter, decided to make the crisis of the Kampuchean refugees her personal *cause célèbre*, the relief machinery of the United States government was rapidly set in motion and adequate relief appropriation was rarely a problem.[6] In all too many instances the fates of afflicted peoples have had to depend on the vagaries that brought their plight to the attention of others.

For the organization, the unpredictable and inconsistent ways in which disaster information is brought into its purview present three problems: miscueing, misdirection and prejudgement. 'Miscueing' stems from the fact that information about a disaster may emanate from a wide array of sources and be passed through channels that tend to load on information not relevant to the disaster *per se*. In 1979, the Minister of Health from a Central African nation approached a United Nations agency official at an international conference 'to mention' his concern that his country was facing a serious cholera epidemic. The minister emphasized that the matter of international assistance would have to be broached gingerly since his Cabinet colleagues were sharply divided over the need for foreign relief. The United Nations official, in trying to reflect both the urgency and the sensitivity of the epidemic, inadvertently loaded his report by focusing on the issue's sensitive nature. He in no sense disguised the seriousness of the epidemic, but as the information 'entered' the organization, it was already miscued. The reporting official was a senior person in the agency, not normally directly involved in disaster relief issues, and those receiving the information within the agency interpreted the official's report as emphasizing the priority of awaiting cabinet agreement before taking action.[7]

Equally as relevant as miscueing is the hazard of 'misdirection'. In discussions with a British High Commission staff member in 1977, an Indian official recalled that requests were made during those discussions for building materials needed for shelters after a devastating cyclone in Andhra Pradesh. The British representative included these requests for relief assistance in a general report on his discussions with the Overseas Development Administration. Yet, these emergency requirements went through ODA channels concerned with longterm development and only arrived at the appropriate department, i.e. the ODA's Disaster Unit, after a circuitous route through normal development channels.[8]

A third problem that arises as information approaches an organization is that of 'prejudged information'. Disaster information is passed on at a variety of levels through a variety of people, often with differing levels of expertise. One official described the problem created when a politician on a formal state visit might be made aware by his or her host that a disaster has occurred. The visitor might feel compelled to make some gesture towards the nation which he or she is visiting, and put in train relief assistance that is not appropriate. Nevertheless, the initial commitment is locked into the process once the gesture has been made. And, while more accurate assessment of need may be made further down the line, part of the process has been predetermined for reasons that are not based on a clear understanding of the specific problems faced by the disaster victims.

The ways in which information enters the network should not lead one to the conclusion that miscueing, misdirection and prejudged information need always lead to failed or ineffective responses. However, here, neither accuracy nor expertise is the main issue. Far more important at this stage is the consequence of unpredictability and inconsistency of informational entry points upon the organization attempting to define a problem.

Screening. Every organization screens information. In other words, organizations are designed to recognize matters either relevant or irrelevant to achieving their prescribed tasks. Such screening is performed by specialists who, from their own perspectives, view the input into their organizations in terms of what they feel are appropriate considerations. Therefore, where and how information comes into the organization becomes a paramount consideration in determining the process by which organizations define problems. The very fact that disaster information has so many unpredictable and inconsistent entry points means that information may be screened in different ways, or indeed even screened out, depending on how and where the information enters into the organization.

The penetration of information into an organization so often depends on the degree to which that information is tangible, specific, manageable and relevant. Organizations, as suggested earlier, cannot deal with ambiguity as a constant; they cope with ambiguity by extracting from ambiguous situations those aspects that are recognizable, or those aspects that organizations have the capacity to define as problems. For example, despite research on famine indicators which provides 'tell-tale' signs of famine onsets (e.g. local market price fluctuations, population drifts), the observer can explain these away in a variety of ways. Population drift might be explained as a pattern of migrant labour; price fluctuations as normal market adjustments, and so on. No matter how important the steps taken to provide guidelines for famine onsets, from an organizational perspective the inherent ambiguity of these indicators lacks problem-defining tangibility.

From the perspective of organizational behaviour, not only does organizational screening depend on the relative tangibility of the input, it also depends on the input's degree of specificity. Disaster information that penetrates the organization's screening process must either be sufficiently specific to enter the appropriate niche or—if not—lack of specificity will mean that information may be 'screened out' (e.g. fall between two stools) or defined by internal referents (e.g.

what experts think the problem is). Both the International Committee of the Red Cross and the League of Red Cross Societies were acutely aware that, by July 1984, large numbers of famine victims were fleeing to the town of Makele in the war-torn Ethiopian province of Tigray. If these displaced peoples had fled their homes principally because they were victims of civil war, then they were ostensibly the responsibility of the ICRC. However, if the principal reason for their flight was impending starvation owing to famine, then they would fall under the protection of the LORCS. Yet, in a complex situation in which civil war and famine are intertwined, organizational specificity is difficult to determine, and specificity is the key to determining how a problem is defined and who does what.[9]

One is all but too familiar with the complaint that there is still no agreed standardization of relief that can be applied to the different types of disasters that occur. Since there exists no uniform or recognized standard of appropriate relief measures, specificity is very often determined by standards derived from the organization's own perspective. This perspective, in turn, depends on what the organization deems to be manageable.

Zia Rizvi, who had been involved in well over a decade of refugee emergencies for UNHCR, suggested that 'what appears to guide an organization is success measured in terms of "if we go ahead, can we pull this off".'[10] The more likely the incoming information appears to match the capabilities of an organization to deal with the problem, the more likely is that information to receive attention. There are many factors that determine whether or not incoming information is organizationally manageable. One factor of particular note is that of finance. If a particular operation is 'doable' because resources are available or would attract additional resources, informational input gains a higher manageability rating than information that will not attract resources. Hence, as Rizvi and others have bemoaned, the priority needs of refugees are more often than not determined by the amount of funding any particular relief operation can attract and not by an objective criterion of which refugee group might be most in need.[22]

Perceived relevance is another determinant of whether or not information penetrates an organization. According to one USAID official, one reason why information about the 1984 famine in Ethiopia was so incomplete was that no one in the United States Embassy in Addis Ababa had forwarded material presented by the Ethiopian Relief and Rehabilitation Commission. Since dramatic cuts in American Embassy staff, beginning in 1977, the Embassy's mission did not include any USAID representatives, and when finally one USAID official was on temporary assignment to Ethiopia in mid-1983, he found 'stuffed in the back of a file in the embassy' a 1982 report from the RRC, indicating that thirteen provinces were threatened by severe food shortages. 'Nobody had focussed on it.'[12] It was not perceived as relevant.

Factoring. Organizations 'recognize' problems based on the expertise of specialists. The first stage of problem recognition occurs when specialists screen information which they deem relevant to their organizational tasks. Yet, most problems that penetrate an organization are 'complex', complex to the extent that they entail the involvement of more than one type of expertise. Hence, a basic principle of organizational behaviour is to deal with complexity by breaking problems down into manageable parts, or, factoring. Factoring suggests not only how organizations handle a problem, but also how the problem itself is actually defined. The highly focused attention that factored components receive ultimately shapes and defines the problem.

While, from the perspective of organizational behaviour, factoring is both logical and essential, factoring as part of the problem-defining process is not without its hazards. Specialist attention may lead to problems falling outside the net of any particular specialist. Up through 1984, the European Community viewed disaster relief as a three-staged process: the immediate emergency phase, the post-catastrophe stage and the rehabilitation phase. The immediate emergency phase falls into the orbit of the EC's Emergency Services Section and 'in the third phase we can do what we like provided the [rehabilitation] project is limited to rural areas or in other areas where the allotted sum remains within 5 to 6% of the allotted budget under article 930.'[13]

However, it is in the second phase, the post-catastrophe stage, when there is a high propensity for the problem to slip through the net, for the needs of disaster victims in this intermediate stage is not within the orbit of any single specialist within the Commission. Assistance might be provided from the EC's Food Aid Committee if the situation of the victims can match the criterion of the overall country programme established between the Commission and the afflicted country. Yet, while since 1982, the Commission had greater flexibility in moving assistance from one country programme to another, the Food Aid Committee, for example, is limited in its flexibility by both the overall ceiling on food aid and by individual regional desks that are reluctant to have their own particular food programmes diverted.[14]

Without acknowledged specialist focus on the rehabilitation phase of disaster relief, the problem itself begins to lose definition, its relevance and urgency either dissipated or enmeshed in irrelevant criteria of other specialists. Similarly, factoring of complex problems can affect the priority given to problems. The responsibilities of the Emergency Relief and Humanitarian Assistance Unit include emergency aid to refugees. There are increasing instances, however, when the very scale of such emergencies goes beyond the immediate resources of the unit to deal with them. Despite the fact that these emergencies may involve 'life threatening situations', scale and resources on occasion mean that the problem has to be passed on to the Ministry's section that deals with longer-term refugee assistance. 'My concern', stated a senior official from the Emergency Unit, 'is that when I cannot take care of it [the refugee emergency], it will pass to the [refugee] unit next door. But the problem then is that with the issue going next door, the more structural the problem becomes, the less it has priority.'[15]

For the 'unit next door', refugee problems are defined as longer-term rehabilitation. Its focus is principally determined by the ways in which, for example, refugees can be more effectively integrated into the societies of their host countries. The Emergency Unit views a particular problem differently from a unit with its own specialist perspective.

Communication Flows. For the organization, communications should be the glue that binds various factored definitions of any single problem into a coherent whole. It is the flow of communications throughout the organization that alerts specialists to the need for highly focused attention, and it is the flow of communications again that determines how the organization should make an overall response. Yet, the path that such communications follow is in and of itself a major determinant of how the problem requiring an organizational response will eventually be defined.

The most evident communications problem involved in emergency operations is that of overload. Despite the dramatic images that surround any single disaster, specialists within an organization may be dealing in one way or another with a variety of matters deemed to be urgent. One observer described the daily pressures on a UNICEF desk officer like this:

Today the UNICEF desk officer might have received 54 telexes about various emergencies. He is reading telex No.11 under a certain amount of pressure since he shortly will be having a meeting about telex No.3. Glancing at telex No. 11, he spots the need for a particular type of serum, but misses the portion requesting adequate supplies of syringes.[16]

These daily pressures and the mistakes that can arise from them are inevitable in all realms of human activity. However, the accumulative effect of such pressures throughout an organization can have significant consequences. Throughout 1984 the Ethiopian Red Cross was inundated with requests for assistance, particularly from the more obviously drought-affected provinces in the north. At the same time, there were various contradictory reports coming in from the southern region of Wolayta about the possibility of drought emerging there too. Officials in Addis Ababa who could have checked out the discrepant reports were, however, focusing their attention on the north. The overall consequence was that the Wolayta reports were never passed through channels as a serious problem. 'We just had to assume', said one LORCS representative at the time, 'that the problem was just not as bad as some of the reports were suggesting.'[17]

While accumulative overload can actually suppress a problem from the normal flow of communications, even ostensibly effective communication procedures do not guarantee that problems may gain appropriate definition. Martin Howell, a former director of the United States Office of Foreign Disaster Assistance, once remarked that communications in organizing a relief operation was analogous to steering a ship. 'By the time the signal and decision are given and the ship is beginning to turn, the problem itself has already changed.'[18]

To ensure effective communications and coordination in times of major disasters, USAID normally takes the lead in forming an 'inter-agency coordinating committee', comprising various types of specialists from relevant government departments. Even in such highly focused settings, though, fundamental aspects of problems may be overlooked. When John Kelly took on the chairmanship of the Inter-agency Task Force on Ethiopia and the Sudan, food to the famine victims was regarded as the fundamental issue. Yet, as he was to admit in 1985, it was not until October of the previous year—nine months after the first indications of famine were becoming fully appreciated—that the need for transport as a priority was seriously considered.[19]

Structuring the Solution. A former East Pakistan Relief Commissioner, A.M. AnisuzZaman, described his initial response to the devastating cyclone disaster of 1970 in this way: 'We never recognised the magnitude of the disaster. We tried to do something in a routine and ritual way. I watered down my concern because I was looking to the boss; I didn't dare embarrass him, because to respond more effectively I would have to carry along the support of the organisation.'[20]

The Relief Commissioner was initially uncertain about the true extent of the cyclone's destruction. Given this uncertainty, he felt that the routines already established by the East Pakistan relief section would prove to be an adequate response that was consistent with his organization's style and one which would meet an acceptable performance criterion. In terms of cost calculations, the preprogrammed response by the Relief Commissioner seemed appropriate.

Organizational style, acceptable performance criteria and cost calculations all circumscribe the behaviour of organizations and tend to standardize the ways in which organizations structure solutions. The organizational style of the East Pakistan Relief Commission—strapped for manpower and resources and faced constantly with a variety of disasters—was never to allow any single disaster to become 'exaggerated'. The Relief Commission could not be seen as an unwarranted strain on the already stretched finances of East Pakistan's provincial authorities unless one could be certain that an event justified an unusual response.[21]

'Prudence', suggested a former senior official in the Office of the High Commissioner for Refugees, reflects the organizational style of many institutions in the international relief network. 'Prudence is not as much a question of individual courage as it is a matter of an organisation's perspective reflecting the reluctance of pushing the organisation's response beyond what those within it feel will be accepted.'[22] The organizational style of USAID's Office of Program and Policy Coordination was described as one of 'professional scepticism'. 'Our responsibility is to be sceptical. The fact is that we have to deal with the budget [for relief and development programmes], and we are designed to doubt and question from the outset. This is our initial approach to everything.'[23]

Acceptable performance criteria reflect the balance between formal organizational goals and organizational health. AnnisuzZaman was extremely conscious of the dangers of overreacting to the cyclone disaster, for it was of vital importance to ensure the Relief Commissioner's credibility. To seek extraordinary measures or to request that his minister do so when uncertainty about the cyclone's impact remained so high might—if the reports were to prove exaggerated—undermine the Relief Commissioner's authority.

In considering how to respond to reports of the cyclone disaster, AnnisuzZaman was confronted with a wide range of cost calculations. He was uncertain about the true nature of the disaster, but the cost of delaying his decision in order to gain further information was just too high. He did not want to appear irresponsible by not responding, but, alternatively, he did not want to do so in a way that would embarrass him in front of his superior. Also, he was a man under considerable pressure. Relief work was just part of his personal portfolio. While acting as Relief Commissioner, he also served as Secretary to the Revenue and Land Administration and was Custodian of Enemy Property. The cost in terms of time, personal status and competing priorities initially made it impossible for him to structure the relief response in any other way than one that met institutionally acceptable criteria.

In structuring solutions to problems, cost calculations are a constant preoccupation. As Chadian drought victims began to stream across the western border of Sudan's Darfour province, one world Food Programme officer had to admit that the influx could have been anticipated well in advance. 'However, we all live in encapsulated little worlds, and neither of us [namely, WFP's representatives in Chad and in the Sudan] ever got down to exchanging information.' The cost of initiating communications and eventually having to respond in an appropriate way to the implications of such information were just too high. Despite the fact that, earlier in the year, both had agreed in a regional meeting in Nairobi to exchange information, the pressures of time and effort meant that they did not.[24]

Cost calculations are also made by individuals about the consequence of their actions on their own positions. Not dissimilar to the situation in which Annis-zuZaman found himself in 1970, various officials in Ethiopia recalled the personal cost calculations they had to make when famine conditions began to appear in 1972. Once again, there was a significant lack of clear information about the extent of the unfolding disaster. To recommend that resources 'from a very small cake' be diverted to a relief operation meant 'that some bureaucrat would have to put his head in the noose.'[25]

Standard Operating Procedures, Programmes and Repertoires. Organizations provide solutions to problems through routine performance. Routine performance is controlled by standard operating procedures (SOPs), programmes and repertoires. Procedures to deal with problems are 'standardized' to ensure that the organization is able to manage complex problems on a continuous and often simultaneous basis. SOPs are designed to eliminate uncertainty, provide criteria of acceptable performance and reflect the overall style of the organization.

Once specialists have focused on their particular component of a problem, the organization needs to group the various SOP responses into an overall organizational solution. This grouping or coordinating process results in a 'programme'. A programme, too, becomes standardized, reflecting the overall organizational approach to any particular problem. Given that an organization continually confronts problems—some perceived as similar and others as different—the organization has an arsenal of programmes that it can apply to a variety of matters that fell within its purview. This accumulation of programmes is the organization's repertoire, and it is from this repertoire of pre-programmed responses that the organization normally picks and chooses what it deems the best solution to any particular response.

'We all have our own cosmologies; we all approach problems from different angles', reflects a well-established expert at USAID.[26] This perhaps only too obvious fact emphasizes not only the relative rigidity of organizational response mechanisms, but also the difficulty of reconciling the differing procedures of organizations with each other. In Mozambique, in 1983, the German Red Cross and the European Community Emergency Services Unit launched a joint effort to relieve victims of famine and civil war. The EC insisted that the Community's logo be placed on all vehicles involved in the operation, despite the fact that it was warned that the crescent-shaped E would probably be unfamiliar to insurgents within the area of the relief operation. The German Red Cross had maintained that only the red cross symbol was universally recognized as a symbol of neutrality. Community procedures, however, dictated that the EC logo be used where EC assistance was provided. The net result, according to one observer, was that the EC logo was indeed not recognized, costing the life of one driver and injuring another.[27]

'The problem with the FAO's March 1984 assessment of Ethiopia's needs', according to the UNDP's Resident Representative in Addis in 1984, 'was that the FAO relied upon a deficit year as their basis of comparison.'[28] The reason why the FAO relied on a deficit year as a comparative basis can best be understood by what FAO officials call their 'methodology'. The FAO does not analyse country needs in terms of:

nutritional levels that should be required, but rather in terms of past patterns of consumption. To all of this one has to add food aid estimates against what a country might be able to buy commercially. The analysis begins by assuming that a country will be able to buy the same quantities that it has bought in the past. If we are erring on any side, we are erring on the lower side.[29]

'The methodology', or the standard operating procedures for assessing Ethiopia's needs were consistent with the FAO's general assessment procedures. The fact that Ethiopia's consumption levels had steadily and significantly fallen between 1981 and 1983 was not taken into account. Nor was the fact that the Ethiopian government's purchasing power was rapidly declining taken into account. Measured against the previous year, the discrepancy between what the Ethiopian government was claiming it required and what the FAO assessment indicated was considerable. However, based on the procedures that led to the FAO's conclusions, the source of the discrepancy was nevertheless understandable.[30]

A frequent observer of disaster responses once remarked that:

each agency goes out doing what each wants to do. Your agency man gets out into the field and the fact is that he is faced with the difficulty of determining what are the priorities. Few agencies have objectives in real terms, that is they don't really choose to recognise the long-term effects of their actions.[31]

This observation points to a fundamental dilemma faced by organizations in seeking to structure solutions. While on the one hand the need for standard procedures is quite obvious, on the other, the solutions proffered by the process can be inappropriate or irrelevant to the problem.

Standard operating procedures are based on assumptions about an organization's capability to respond to certain types of situations. Means, in other words, determine the ends; the ends become blurred by the means that the organization has at its disposal. As mentioned earlier, among the contributions that the World Food Programme has made to the hundreds of thousands of refugees assembled in Somalia are consignments of dried, skimmed milk and beans. While it is well recognized that these refugees find both unacceptable, the WFP keeps forwarding them.[32] These consignments, though costly, are available to the WFP. It is the WFP's responsibility to meet relief requirements, and DSM and beans are commodities available for disposal. The nutritional requirements of the refugees—the ends—are in fact determined by the availability of the means, appropriate or not.

The very function of standard operating procedures, programmes and repertoires is to provide coherent guidelines for responding to information and problems that enter in the organization. It is for those within the organization to determine which guidelines are most relevant to deal with a particular set of inputs. 'Matching', therefore, becomes an essential organizational concern, namely, determining which pre-programmed response best suits the matter in hand. However, not every input will fit exactly into an organization's established procedures. Hence, solutions that approximate or come as close to an effective response as a pre-established programme will allow the dominant procedure for problem solving.

In the wake of droughts and floods stemming from El Nino in Bolivia in 1983, a series of donors meetings organized by the United Nations led to specific proposals to assist both disaster relief and development. Much to the consternation of donors and certain United Nations officials, 'somebody from the 38th floor (the office of the Secretary-General) all of a sudden decided to make this a regional problem. Ecuador and Peru, also affected by El Nino, were all merged into the same solution.'[33] What had been a programme specifically designed for Bolivia was now being used as appropriate solutions for the problems of its two neighbours.

The pressure to adhere to established organizational routines and procedures also tends to focus the attention of those within organizations upon what has been described as 'lower tasks', e.g. preparing budgets, producing reports.[34] A focus on lower tasks does not imply that those within organizations have no sense of the organization's overall goals. It does suggest, however, that organizational goals become enmeshed in a process that can obscure such goals. 'Accountability' is a relevant example. Most relief organizations insist in one way or another that funds and materials used for relief operations be 'accounted for'. Not only is this important for obvious administrative reasons, but it is also regarded as good public relations.

And yet accountability is just the kind of lower-level task—indeed a tangible task—that diverts attention away from what should be regarded as more abiding objectives. One WFP representative maintained that a serious disaster in the Sudan was ignored because WFP's Emergency Officer was unhappy with the way that accountability had been handled in a Sudanese emergency six months earlier.[35] A representative from UNHCR complained that he was under constant pressure to spend allocated funds for an emergency operation even though the needs for those funds were no longer warranted.[36]

Organizations are constantly faced with issues that trigger off incompatible procedures. Conflicts between these incompatible choices are frequently avoided by handling each procedure sequentially. Hence, when famine struck Wolayta in mid-1984, relief agencies were quick to set up relief camps on the main roads that were easily accessible to delivery trucks. This procedure, as many had surmised, would draw already hungry families away from their homes to camps that were miles away from the villages. It was only when the failings of this procedure were demonstrated that the agencies sought to find a feeding solution that would not require the affected population to move from their villages and farms.[37]

Dealing with incompatible procedures in a sequential manner also explains UNDRO's reactions to donor requests in 1984 that UNDRO should monitor Ethiopian transport. Because of persistent criticism of the organization, UNDRO's instinctive response to donor requests is to comply. At the same time, an equally persistent theme is UNDRO's insistence that it lacks the resources to fulfil its role adequately. 'Some people at UNDRO wanted to do it [undertake transport monitoring]. It has accepted a responsibility which it cannot fulfil. It has accepted the responsibility for monitoring 200 trucks at 15 different locations with only one man in the entire country!'[38] Having accepted the first choice, which was essentially incompatible with the second—namely, that donors must be made aware of UNDRO's limited resources—UNDRO only afterwards raised the issue that its office in Addis Ababa was under-manned and under-financed.

Often, when confronted with incompatible choices, organizations will avoid hard decisions and opt to 'fudge' the issue. For example, by 1983 the United Nations Development Programme had undertaken to coordinate the United Nations system in times of serious emergencies. 'The initial proposals for a UNDP coordinating role entailed [New York] headquarters coordination of policies and operational procedures and we [Resident Representatives] in the field would coordinate based upon these procedures.' However, when it became clear to UNDP headquarters that other United Nations agencies 'saw this move as a violation of their territory . . . the onus of coordination was placed at the field level.'[39] Rather than deal with the inherent conflict in its original decision, headquarters passed the problem down the rungs of the organizational ladder. However, without clear guidelines from New York about the meaning of 'coordination', in the light of other agencies' resistance, the Resident Representatives had no authority to act. The issue was fudged, and UNDP's initiative remained vague and ineffectual.

Even when those in organizations may attempt initiatives that depart from organizational procedures, they often find themselves constrained by administrative technicalities. When the Disaster Unit of Britain's Overseas Development Administration wanted to send out immediate assistance to Italian earthquake victims, it was blocked by a particular rule requiring authorization on:

matters dealing with Italy by the diplomatic wing, the Foreign and Commonwealth Office and [the Foreign Minister] Lord Carrington. It was a Friday, and the goods could have been delivered to the disaster area the following day. [However] Carrington was in Brussels at the time, and it was not until Wednesday that the Minister received the authorisation request. He signed it immediately, but the fact is that goods had to wait for at least six extra days because of a three-second authorisation procedure.[40]

Similarly, the office of the European Community in Addis Ababa wanted to provide seed to Ethiopia in 1984 so that farmers could begin to prepare for the next growing season. According to EC regulations, such purchases would have to be made on the open or 'free market'. Since the socialist regime of Ethiopia was not a 'free market', the Ethiopian government would have to buy the seed or the seed would have to be purchased outside the country. The EC representative in Addis 'complained bitterly to Brussels that strange seeds that were not tried and tested would just not do and that the Ethiopian government did not have the funds available to purchase the quantity of seeds that were required even locally.'[41]

Despite these protestations from the EC's representative, the issue dragged on from April through September 1984. Local EC officials were compelled to follow procedures they knew were of little relevance. Estimates of stocks in the hands of private suppliers had to be made, 'although it was well known that no private supplier had in hand the amount which was being sought.' The officials were required to ascertain the availability of seed outside the country, but, once again, as is already well-known, this seed was not deemed appropriate for local farming conditions. Finally, after months of complying with administrative tasks required by the European Commission, officials in Brussels relented. Local seed was allowed to be purchased with EC funds, but by the time the decision was made, 'it was too late for the next planting season'.[42]

Inevitable procedural conflicts can lead to what might be described as 'quasi-conflict resolution'. Real priorities and solutions are lost in compromises that in turn result in below-optimizing strategies, designed to satisfy the participants in the conflict rather than deal with the consequences of the problem. Using the European Community as an example, one can see the difficulties facing a 'manager' in resolving conflicts arising out of requests for emergency food aid. A desk officer may press the Food Aid Department dealing with non-ACP countries for immediate assistance to a needy country. However, those involved with accounting for such assistance may maintain that there are no available allocations from the Frame Regulations, a problem compounded by the fact that other desks are unwilling to allow diversions from their own allocations.

Hence, the manager or those more senior officials responsible for resolving contending issues must find a solution. The solution or, in this case, the resolution of possible conflicts has to be considered in the context of three considerations—that only indirectly have anything to do with the request for assistance. In the first place, the manager must keep an eye on the procedures that best approximate the preferred options of the organization, namely, those that are the least disruptive. Secondly, he or she must ensure that the solution will not undermine the morale or effectiveness of the particular department involved in the matter. Thirdly, the manager must be seen to have resolved the dispute equitably in order to ensure that his or her performance is deemed to be acceptable.[43]

All these kinds of organizational factors are certainly understandable. While, in too many instances they may distort the true nature of effective responses to disaster victims, they are nevertheless the natural outcome of structures designed to cope with complex problems that both threaten and sustain institutional survival. It is in this context that one may appreciate matters affecting relations between organizations involved in the relief process.

Inter-organizational Relations

'Coordination is a commonly discussed subject confused by the various assumptions about its meaning. To some it implies the sharing of information; to others coordination implies centralised decision-making. The implication is that a common understanding must exist between the parties involved.'[44] Along with over-bureaucratized behaviour, lack of coordination ranks high on the list of standard criticisms of international intervention in relief. However, as the above quote suggests, the term, coordination, is indeed 'confused by the various assumptions about its meaning'. Not only is the term itself difficult to define, but the reality of disaster relief can only lead one to the conclusion that what might be appropriate coordination for one situation might well not be appropriate for another.

One might begin, for a definition of coordination at the sub-optimal level, or, the minimum that one should expect from organizations engaged in a seemingly common endeavour to provide assistance, namely, with a willingness to share information. Yet, even at this level, coordination is replete with difficulties. An agency might be reluctant to pass on information to others because its campaign to gain much-needed funds for a particular relief effort may depend upon getting to the donor market first. Alternatively, an agency might not wish to have its involvement in particular kinds of relief activities known for fear of either undermining its donor base or alienating its host government. There are also instances where an agency just does not have sufficiently accurate information to disseminate to its counterparts, despite the clear pictures of despair it is presenting to donors.

If a realistic definition of coordination even at this minimalist level poses difficulties, then more ambitious definitions are indeed fraught with complexities. Some view coordination as the positive acquiescence by agencies to a single operational authority, where that single authority would determine what and who would deliver particular types of relief assistance. This kind of coordination is only rarely evidenced, for relief actors maintain with varying degrees of justification that their independence is critically important to ensure against accusations of corruption and political bias.

Coordination might stem from relief participants' self-regulation. Here, one might regard coordination in terms of a process by which relief actors agree among themselves as to the types of functions and assistance each will provide. In practice, this interpretation, too, can fall prey to difficulties. In many instances, the imperative to intervene is not left to what might be regarded as rational choice. Pressures from donors, organizational constraints and the uncertainty of what resources and experts might be available may mean that such self-regulation is an unlikely outcome.

Sharing available resources to effect a relief operation is by no means unknown. It occurs on occasion both at field and at headquarters level.[45] Overall, however, the incidents are relatively rare. If each of these aspects of coordination pose difficulties, then, broadly speaking, what are the factors that influence inter-organizational relations? Or, put in another way, what are the conditions that hamper effective working relations and under what circumstances can such conditions be avoided?

The answer to both aspects of this question arises from an amalgam of considerations covered earlier in this book. The perceived nature of disasters—the view that such events are aberrant and isolated phenomena—in part explains the chaos that complicates cooperative efforts. So, too, do the diverse motives that underpin what we have called the priority formulation process account for the inter-organizational disharmony that frequently accompanies major relief efforts. Similarly, perceptual variables and organizational behaviour muddle the prospects for effective inter-organizational cooperation and coordination. Hence, in trying to understand the conditions that either hamper or enhance inter-organizational relations, it is worth returning to some of these factors.

The Disaster Context

The vast proportion of disasters are marked by uncertainty, contradictory information and ambiguity. That is to say that, no matter how large the event itself, no matter how grim the media's reporting of it, critical unknowns—affected populations, damage assessment, needs—are prone to serious distortions and contradictory evidence.

Part of the reason for this is that the pre-planning and preventative considerations paid to disasters are normally given a very low priority. The poorer the disaster-prone country, the more this is the case. Therefore, even basic tools for assessment such as pre-disaster population censuses are often not available. Yet, even with these basic tools, the reality of a disaster is that, in so many instances, one of the first 'victims' is the communications system. Telephone lines, road and rail links may be the first casualties—if they even exist in the disaster-stricken area. Communication about the event may filter through in a belated or haphazard way. This, alone, may trigger off a pattern of disaster assessment, which we shall consider below, namely, 'the information loading cycle.'

In the light of such uncertainty and ambiguity, one must also bear in mind that rarely do disasters fundamentally impact upon a nation as a whole. Life goes on as normal; governmental and institutional priorities may well remain unaffected until the clarity of the incident begins to penetrate the priority formulation process. And even when it does, relief institutions, domestic and international, must contend with a whole range of issues that merely add to the complexities of disaster relief. Who has appropriate equipment to cut through re-inforced concrete to rescue victims in the aftermath of Mexico City's 1985 earthquake disaster? What manpower is available to dig people out of the sludge deposited by the reactivated Colombian volcano, Nevada del Ruiz? Is there river transport available to deliver relief supplies after all normal means have been washed away by the 1985 cyclone in Bangladesh? All these kinds of basic issues are complicated even more for outside relief agencies by other problems. Will the Sudanese government issue visas to those foreigners seeking to assist? How long will it take to get relief materials cleared by Indian customs officials? What are the procedures to follow to get travel permits in Ethiopia.?

These realities are the constants in the world of disaster relief. In one way or another, their effects frequently turn the plight of disaster victims into a competitive scramble to assist. No matter how well-intentioned, the need to corner available transport, to get goods cleared by customs, to demonstrate the appropriateness of one's techniques and expertise, to get visas and travel permits, creates tensions that affect relations among relief participants. And all these operational prerequisites are pursued under the perceived pressures of time and urgency.

When ambiguity and uncertainty collide with the pressures of operational prerequisites, the result leads to what might be called an 'information loading cycle' that, in turn, impinges on relations among relief actors. The information loading cycle is a term that reflects the consequences of the way in which institutions process information and return that information back into the environment in which it is operating. The more incomplete and ambiguous the initial information input, the more that input is moulded by the receiving institution's own internal referents. This loaded information is, in turn, thrown back into the environment where it has to contend with information similarly loaded by other actors. The result is informational inconsistency. Instead of 'clarity' in the objective sense, one has clarity that reflects individual institutional perspectives of a diverse set of participants.

The loading cycle does not end with this initial formulation of perspectives; rather, it feeds on itself in a process of re-inforcement. Once committed to a particular interpretation of information, the actor seeks to justify that interpretation and tends to shut out interpretations that fundamentally diverge from his own. These informational re-inforcements mean that because relief assessments, for example, become enmeshed in the institutional perspectives of individual actors, so an 'objective reality' becomes mired in other competing and contending realities.

A case in point arose in the early stages of the relief operation in Ethiopia in 1984. Despite the world's awakening to the famine, the unfolding relief efforts were riddled with uncertainties. From the perspective of various non-governmental organizations, there were at least three competing views of what priority relief they should be providing: medical assistance, supplementary feeding or mass ration assistance. The choice mattered, since, given the inadequate handling facilities at the major ports and often hazardous roads, the issue of priority was indeed often a matter of life or death.

The NGOs were by no means unaware of the need to determine priorities, but in a relief operation in which so many unknowns were at play (including their own individual relief capabilities), the critical question was clearly which of the three areas should be the principal focus of attention. To a great extent, individual agencies based their assessments of needs on what they had the capacity to do. Hence, those agencies with medical capabilities, or which specialized in mother-and-child health care or supplementary feeding each pushed for their own view of needs, based on their individual perceptions. Those contending perceptions influenced the relief environment in at least three ways. It meant, in the first place, that Ethiopian officials in Addis Ababa were uncertain about what their 'operating partners' regarded as priorities. Even in the coordinating forums of the Christian Relief and Development Association, there was little agreement about priority needs, either about what needs the agencies should be meeting or where such needs should be most urgently met.[46]

Secondly, because there was little agreement about types or destinations of resources, there was a general competition by the agencies at the port of Assab and elsewhere for available transport, off-loading and storage facilities to get their own relief materials to the relief sites where they were working. This competition reflected a hardening of attitudes towards interpretations, and significantly re-inforced the inconsistencies and uncertainties about relief priorities. Finally, the inconsistent interpretations flowing from the afflicted country to NGOs' headquarters justified the latters' efforts to seek resources consistent with their own institutional perceptions of needs, again re-inforcing the initial confusion about priorities.[47]

This case is an interesting demonstration of the information loading cycle, and seems to sustain three important points:

(i)   the greater the ambiguity, the more preconceived notions prevail to counter uncertainty;

(ii)   the greater the ambiguity, the more do institutional referents replace objective assessments;

(iii)   the greater the ambiguity, the greater is the possibility of competition among institutions with contending views, and the greater is the prospect for objective assessment to be delayed or never achieved.

Contending Priorities. Network-wide, one must inevitably acknowledge the fundamental unpredictability of the responses of relief actors. The time at which each can or will intervene in a disaster is dependent upon factors both within and outside the control of the components of the relief network. If one looks briefly at the variety of reasons that leads individual institutions to undertake assistance, one can see why the myriad of motives that compel them to intervene may intensify the likelihood of coordination failures and generate inter-organizational competition.

Lack of predictability is a fundamental feature of institutional responses to disasters. Although West Germany, for example, might be more predictably inclined to come to the aid of Turkey, or the United States might look more favourably upon relief requests made by 'friendly' countries, the way in which these demonstrations of goodwill are made may have unpredictable consequences for the relief effort as a whole.

To demonstrate and to be seen to be demonstrating its goodwill, a government may wish to have its contributions recognized in particular kinds of ways. A government seeking to have its aid recognized may only be willing to give to high-profile relief projects. Hence, in the aftermath of many disasters, governmental donors provide funds to build temporary hospitals when, in all too many instances, such projects are neither wanted nor needed.[48] Donors' desires for publicity and a high profile to satisfy domestic constituencies may also lead them to make time-consuming demands upon senior officials of afflicted states.

It is not, however, the misspent funds or the time-consuming demands of donors that are at issue here. Far more important is the consequence of a host of actors at any one time expecting similar kinds of recognition. As each representative seeks to gain maximum publicity for his or her agency's assistance, the prospect for disjointed activities and for competition to be recognized increases. The motives and the reasoning behind the search for such recognition may be very understandable, but the net result does not lead to greater harmony.

There is also what might be called a sense of 'priority rights' that affects the behaviour of organizations in times of relief operations. For organizations that have developed links with a particular country or region, the influx of outside relief agencies may lead old hands to look with dismay or disdain upon those less well-established organizations seeking to assist in times of disasters. At the emotional level, there is a concern that the bonds established between local peoples and the old hands will be undermined by the influx. On a more practical level, there arise concerns about the capabilities and confusion caused by an invasion of groups and institutions unfamilar with the country. Even in times of disaster, the perceived 'interloper' can affect the atmosphere in which a relief operation is conducted.[49]

Whether an organization is well-established or not, each one comes with a perspective about its interests and expertise which also affects the climate of cooperation and coordination. Some relief actors are prompted to intervene because of particular kinds of commitment or linkage. A religious-based organization may feel obliged to work in an area where it has pastoral obligations or with organizations with which it has established relations, for example a local church. Some more evangelical donors may even feel compelled to mix the spiritual with the practical.[50] Some may become involved because the disaster opens the door to longer-term development projects, or because of institutional fears about negative publicity if they do not become involved. These disparate motives are all understandable, but they nevertheless reflect particular kinds of interests that may estrange one agency from another.

Earlier, it was suggested that differing expertise can be a factor in promoting what we called the 'information loading cycle'. Expertise can also affect the relations between and among organizations. Contrasting expertise, if faced with limited time and resources, may result in clashes over approaches and priorities. The utility and costs of mass inoculation programmes may be regarded by some as a waste, by others as a necessity. The right level of rations, or the ways in which rations are to be distributed, or even the question of whether rations should be continued or terminated may prove to be a source of great friction. The motivations of all those who feel compelled to apply their particular expertise may be well-intentioned, but these well-intentioned demonstrations of concern can fuel discord that leads to communication breakdowns, competition and a disinclination to cooperate.

These kinds of problems occur even when organizations feel secure in their particular roles. They are compounded, however, when institutional mandates are either uncertain or too restricted. In Chapter 3, we addressed the particular problems that uncertain mandates caused for inter-governmental organizations. Yet, the issue of uncertain or restricted mandates also has a more universal relevance. The difficulty of determining mandated responsibilities to deal with particular kinds of disasters is clearly reflected in the often uneasy relations between the League of Red Cross Societies and the International Committee for the Red Cross.[51] More subtle and unpredictable perhaps, is the variety of restrictions imposed on individual actors by specific constitutional provisions, formal limitations imposed by support bases or informal constraints resulting from sensitivities to the attitudes of such support bases.

Constitutionally, an organization may be restricted to the ways in which it can channel relief. Even if these channels prove inadequate (for example a government department with little expertise or interest in disaster relief), there is little that that organization can do but bear the opprobrium for poor judgement and watch other less restricted organizations gain the kudos. Organizations may be limited in their flexibility by formal constraints arising from particular situations. Fixed ration levels and relief assistance that does not have any developmental component are the kinds of restrictions that a support base may impose upon relief provided to certain types of countries or in certain types of situations. Organizations may also feel themselves to be limited by informal constraints emerging from the sensitivities of their own support bases. Hence, for many organizations working in Ethiopia in 1985 and 1986, the prospect of working on resettlement projects, where serious food and medical shortages seemed to exist, created a considerable degree of role tension. Some organizations felt it impossible to support a project that would be greeted with hostility by Western donors; others risked it, despite its potential unpopularity and questionable outcome.[52]

The uncertainties and gaps that such formal and informal restrictions cause can in the most practical sense make it difficult for organizations to cooperate. The fact that such uncertain mandates may open up opportunities for some while closing them for others may leave some looking incompetent, may raise the profile of one while obscuring the effort of another—all kindle the possibility of disharmony. In additon, one must also add certain closely inter-related institutional pressures that are frequently at play.

Institutional Pressures. 'It is here in Geneva where they have a policy oriented approach that the rivalry becomes an issue', commented a member of the League of Red Cross Societies about responses of both IGOs and NGOs. 'They want their organisation to be first. Here there is a lot of monkey business going on—trying to send their own people out quickly, giving them more money and so on.'[53] Despite this assessment, it would be wrong to view headquarters as the single source of competition between agencies during relief operations. One's inclination might be to differentiate between policy-makers massaging narrowly-defined institutional interests from comfortable offices and those in the field concerned solely with the functional aspects of relieving suffering. Yet, this seemingly sensible delineation misses both the interactive process between headquarters and field levels and the kinds of factors—discussed earlier—that prompt competition at every level. Indeed, headquarters might well be anxious to secure a foothold in a particular relief operation because that was what it should be seen to be doing, since involvement would satisfy donors' demands, and resources would be available for just such an initiative. No less intense, however, is the field-level concern at ensuring that its own workers will have a site and resources to provide relief, that its own efforts are recognized and that it can satisfy the demands of headquarters, for example for publicity, in order that continuing support be maintained.

Of course, as with all generalizations, there are exceptions. In some instances, those at field level have complained with no small degree of bitterness that their headquarters only seemed concerned with gory pictures for promotional material.[54] There have been assurances that, had it not been for some irrelevant motive of an organization in New York, field operations among agencies in Thailand, for example, would have been far more harmonious.[55] Equally often, however, headquarters blame the field for breakdowns in cooperation. According to a former senior official at UNDRO, in most instances:

> where agency representatives might have discretion in country X, there may be conflicting views amongst those in the field about which ways they should respond, or they just may not be on good terms; but this doesn't mean that this spills over to headquarters level. Disputes can be resolved at the headquarters level, and I don't recall any disputes like this reaching my level.[56]

The source of potential rivalry, in other words, cannot necessarily be laid at the doorstep of any single level within an organization. It is the organization as a whole that is the appropriate focal point for understanding the strains and stresses that affect inter-organizational relations. These strains and stresses, in turn, are generally influenced by the expectations of those who support the organization, the organization's own view of its role and what we shall call 'the size of the cake'.

In the above section on 'contending priorities', we considered the array of motives that leads organizations to undertake relief operations. Besides the commitment to assist the disaster-afflicted, we suggested various issues that stimulate or constrain the behaviour of individual relief actors as they each enter the relief fray. The influence of these factors does not necessarily end once relief actors become embroiled in the operation. To the contrary, the factors that might have led them to their involvement in the first instance may well continue throughout the operation. Yet, besides these diverse motivations, a set of common concerns is imposed by those who support relief institutions.

Every type of organization that becomes involved in a relief operation seeks to justify the effectiveness of its role to those who support it. The organization is 'consumer-driven', and the consumer is the donor, or support base, that enables the organization to operate . . . and not the disaster victim. High visibility in a relief operation is generally of critical concern for governments, NGOs and IGOs alike, for it is through visibility that the organization justifies itself to those who support it.

The propensity for individual organizations to wave their particular institutional flags over a disaster site is the natural consequence of organizations seeking to prove their worth to their donors. Publicity, high profiles and promotion are all inter-related. But before one condemns the crassness of these marketing techniques, one should remember that the international relief network, as presently structured, still depends upon competition for resources in order to perform its function. This sad fact by no means applies solely to non-governmental organizations. It is a standard, though in some instances more subtly demonstrated, principle affecting most relief actors most of the time.

Donors, however, may not be satisfied merely with the high profiles of those organizations that they support. They may well demand particular kinds of accounting methods. Hence, as discussed in Chapter 3, inter-governmental organizations spend an increasing amount of time dealing with donors' earmarked funds. Donors may also only want their support to be used to assist certain types of victims in certain types of ways. One sees, therefore, instances in which organizations are lumbered with certain types of relief projects, e.g. mother-and-child care, when in fact they know that their resources would be better spent on sanitation.

The consumer-driven orientation of relief actors is in all too many ways imposed upon them by governmental bodies, as well as by the public at large—either lacking an appreciation of the complexities of relief or choosing to ignore them. Yet, on the other hand, relief actors are not innocent victims of the process. They are in a sense co-conspirators. High visibility, perceived effectiveness, and so on, in a relief operation is not irrelevant to more abiding institutional concerns. Be it UNICEF or Médecins Sans Frontières, UNHCR or German Agro Action, banner-waving can lead to the kind of publicity that may ensure greater institutional security. A successful relief operation may be weighed in terms of the numbers of lives saved, but it can also be calculated in terms of resources brought in to ensure institutional stability. Institutional stability may span a range of institutional needs. One direct spin-off from an effective relief operation could be extra money to devote to development projects. It might also entail less tangible benefits, such as donor approval that is eventually translated into larger appropriations in coming years which, in turn, could ensure particular jobs or expanded organizational activities.

None of these motives are in and of themselves solely self-serving, but they do suggest why it would be wrong to view relief actors as innocent victims of donors' dictates. For this very reason, the size of the resource cake put on any individual relief table becomes a critical variable in the responses of relief organizations. The resource cake represents the potential value—in terms of available funds and material—that any one disaster can generate. Where a disaster might generate considerable resources, the cake generally stimulates a high level of institional appetites. Where the cake is small, so, too, do institutional appetites appear commensurately reduced.

The formula, however, is not as rational as it might appear. The factors that determine the size of cake all too often have little to do with the severity of disasters *per se*. The ingredients are frequently dependent upon motivations that encompass the kinds of interests discussed in the preceding section on 'contending priorities'. Relief actors find it difficult to ignore the opportunities presented by well-funded operations since these operations may present not only long and short-term institutional advantages, but they also reflect standards of what their support bases regard as acceptable levels of performance.

The consequence of these pressures is ultimately seen in scrambles for what is called 'turf', and for portions of the cake. Where a disaster relief operation is potentially large—in a consumer-driven sense—relief actors tend to compete for operational space, or turf. This space may be a physical area at the disaster site, or it may be a major role in determining the general direction of the overall relief operation, or it may be both. Where a relief response affords opportunities not only to provide assistance but also to enhance institutional interests, turf becomes an important issue.

Yet, the more actors who recognize the benefits arising out of a disaster, the greater is the demand for turf, be it of geography or influence. The greater the demand, the greater is the propensity to compete for available space. And, naturally, the greater the competition, the more strains are placed on relations between organizations seeking involvement in the disaster relief operation. The battle for turf may be reflected in the unwillingness of one organization to share information with another. It may be'seen in the reluctance of organizations to share transport, to make joint assessments or to divide functional responsibilities. There are many ways in which such strains are reflected, but in the final analysis what ultimately suffers is the coordination of effort that serves the interest of the victim.

Similarly, the cake is an integral part of the rush for opportunities. Inter-governmental organizations compete with each other for monies that governments make available, and so too do non-governmental organizations bid for funds made available through governmental and inter-governmental sources. Once again, the search for ever larger pieces of the cake becomes part of the dynamics of the relief process, and fuels competition on a variety of levels among the relief actors.

Despite the disruptive effects of competition for turf and resources, competition does not occur in all relief operations. However, there would appear to be three inter-related considerations that bring competition more readily to the fore. The first is the size of the disaster. The larger the disaster—in terms of perceived numbers of victims—the more probable it is that a greater number of relief actors will attempt to intervene. This, of course, will depend upon the perceived ability of the intervening actors to raise sufficient resources. Hence, the second consideration that determines the degree of competition in any disaster response depends upon the structure of funding.

Jackson once referred to the stabilizing effect upon relief efforts produced by what he called 'the power of the purse'.[57] The more that any single authority has control over funds, the more that authority will be able to ensure that participants will have necessary resources to perform their functions. Rarely, though, in any relief operation has such an authority emerged.[58] Operations in which resources have not triggered unnecessary competition have normally been those in which the size of the operation has cohered with readily available emergency reserve funds, with only a modest need to supplement such reserves with additional resources. Here, again, one sees the relationship between the size of a disaster and the funding structure.

Thirdly, where indigenous structures are relatively efficient and demonstrate an ability to control, there has been less inclination to compete for turf. The reality is, however, that few disaster-prone countries have developed truly effective disaster relief structures. Indigenous relief cells have to survive bureaucratic battles within their own governments and have to have demonstrable governmental authority to be able to guide and constrain outside relief actors. Without this indigenous authority, the propensity of relief agencies is to establish their operations where they individually feel that they might best serve. And, even when these indigenous relief cells do exist, the tendency of agencies is so often to seek ways to evade their authority. Agencies' protection of their mandates, their mixed motives and concerns for visibility, their perceived obligations to their own support bases make it difficult for an indigenous relief cell, even when it has the backing of its own government, to impose order.

The International Relief Process in Review

No single factor reviewed in these last two chapters is the prime determinant of the ways in which the international disaster relief network intervenes in a disaster. The four factors—priority formulation, perceptions, organizational and inter-organizational dynamics—are all integral parts of the relief process. One should be aware that not all disaster relief operations succumb to the worst aspects of these factors. There are indeed instances where their more negative effects are limited. Nor should one conclude that the structural and what might appear as almost predeterministic considerations deny the genuine concern of so many for the plight of disaster victims.

The international relief network is composed of well-intentioned and concerned individuals in abundance. They, however, like so many people in their personal and professional lives, rarely have the luxury of easy choices. Options always have costs; individual perceptions tend to cloud what under different circumstances would be common interests; all are affected by institutional perspectives; and all are ultimately forced to balance immediate and defined objectives against the indeterminate consequences of pursuing long-range goals. And yet, from this analysis of the international relief process, must one conclude that the constraints on more systematic approaches to relief are so immutable that improvement is really not possible? It is in Chapter 6 that the answer to this question is considered.

Notes

1. The quotes, in order of sequence, come from the following sources: Wain, B., *The Refused: The Agony of the IndoChina Refugees*, New York, Simon & Schuster, 1981; Sheets, H. & Morris, R., *Disaster in The Desert: Failures of International Relief in the West African Drought*, Washington, DC, Carnegie Endownment for International Peace, 1974, p.62; Green, S., *International Disaster Relief: Toward a Responsive System*, New York, McGraw-Hill Book Co., 1977, p.31; Davis, M., *Civil Wars and The Politics of International Relief*, New York, Praeger, 1976, p.86.
2. Duncan, W., *Organizational Behaviour*, Boston, Houghton Mifflin Co., 1978, p.4.
3. The Office of The United Nations Disaster Relief Coordinator is a good example of an organization about which its founders did not wish to be too precise. Faruk Berkol, UNDRO's first coordinator, commented to this writer in an interview on 21 March 1984 in Geneva that 'UNDRO would not be an operational body, but rather a sort of 'chef d'orchestre' to coordinate aid between donor sources and the UN system. This had led to many susceptibilities which, unless there was going to be some 'flexibility' in its wording, the initial resolution to create UNDRO would not have been passed during the 26th session of the General Assembly.'
4. Allison, G., *Essence of Decision: Explaining the Cuban Missile Crisis*, Boston, Little, Brown & Co., 1971, p.83.
5. For the consequences of information that cannot mesh with organizational procedures, see, for example, Steinbrunner, J., *The Cybernetic Theory of Decision*, Princeton, Princeton University Press, 1974.
6. Interviews with Sir Robert Jackson, New York, 26 September 1983; and with Victor Palmieri, New York, 23 September 1983.
7. Interview with a former official from UNDRO, Geneva, 21 March 1984.
8. Interview with an official from the Ministry of Supply and Rehabilitation, New Delhi, 16 March 1983.
9. These issues were discussed in an interview with Leon de Riedmatten, Head of Delegation, International Committee of the Red Cross, Addis Ababa, 3 October 1984.
10. Interview with Zia Rizvi, Independent Commission on International Humanitarian Issues and former assistant to the UN High Commissioner for Regugees, Geneva, 23 March 1984.
11. Ibid; also, Sir Robert Jackson, B. Harrell-Bond.

12. Interview with Hunter Farnham, USAID, Washington, DC, 15 September 1983. David Korn, the Chargé d'Affaires at the United States Embassy in Addis Ababa at the time, accepted that perhaps no one in the embassy had focused as much as they should have on the report, but since the Ethiopian government had restricted the amount of staff the United States Embassy could have, and also did not allow American officials to go outside Addis Ababa, there was little that could be done with the RRC's report. (Interview with David Korn, London, 22 January 1986.)

13. Interview with David Lee, DG-VIII (Financial and Technical Assistance to non-ACP countries), Commission of the European Community, Brussels, 23 May 1984. For an interesting discussion on EEC procedures to be followed by NGOs to obtain EEC emergency food aid, see: Search, H., 'Emergency Food Aid in the European Community', *Disasters: The International Journal of Disaster Studies and Practice*, **10**, No.4, 1986, pp.247-9.

14. Interview with Louis Huby, DG-VIII (EC Food Aid), Commission of the European Community, Brussels, 23 May 1984. See 'Frame Regulation on Food Aid' (No. 3331/82 du Conseil, December 1982, Official Journal No. L352/1, 14 December 1982).

15. Interview with J.F.L. Blankenberg, Department of Development Cooperation, Dutch Ministry of Foreign Affairs, The Hague, 29 May 1984.

16. Interview with Frances D'Souza, Director, International Disaster Institute, London, 25 November 1981.

17. Interview with C.-G. Landergren, League Chief Delegate, League of Red Cross Societies, Addis Ababa, 5 October 1984.

18. Interview with Dr Martin Howell, Director, Office of US Foreign Disaster Assistance, Washington, DC, 13 September 1983.

19. Interview with John Kelly, US Agency for International Development, Washington, DC, April 1985.

20. Interview with A.M. AnnisuzZaman, Secretary, Ministry of Agriculture, Government of Bangladesh and former Relief Commissioner to the Provincial Government of East Pakistan, 1970, Dacca, 24 November 1982.

21. Ibid.

22. See note 100.

23. Interview with Len Rogers, Office of Program and Policy Coordination, USAID, Washington DC, 14 September 1983.

24. Interview with Douglas Freeman, World Food Programme, Khartoum, 1 November 1984.

25. Interview with Julius Holt, London School of Hygiene and Tropical Medicine, London, 6 September 1983.

26. Interview with Larry Crandall, USAID, Washington, DC, 15 September 1983.

27 Interview with Jurgen Kronenberger, Director for International Disaster Relief and Development Programme, German Red Cross, Bonn, 24 May 1984.

28. Interview with Kenneth King, UNDP Resident Representative, Addis Ababa, 12 October 1984.

29. Interview with B.P. Dutia, Food and Agriculture Organization, Rome, 4 July 1984.

30. Interviews with H. Dall, FAO Representative, Addis Ababa. 12 October 1984 and Kenneth King, UNDP Resident Representative, Addis Ababa, 12 October 1984.

31. See note 16.

32. Interview with Stafford Clarry, ELU/CARE, Mogadishu, 18 October 1984.

33. Interview with Margaret Anstee, United Nations Assistant Secretary-General, Department of Technical Cooperation for Development, New York, 23 September 1983.

34. Producing reports is obviously a necessary organizational function, particularly in a large bureaucracy that ostensibly places a high value on information. However, as Warwick implies in *A Theory of Public Bureaucracy: Politics, Personality and Organization in the State Department* (Cambridge, Harvard University Press, 1975, pp.115

ff.), officials become preoccupied with report writing—'the word count . . . often inflated by the traditional emphasis of the Foreign Service on faultless prose and the well-turned phrase'.

35. The veracity of this statement was never checked by this writer. The official from the World Food Programme from whom this information derived stated that WFP's Emergeny Office

> refused to declare an emergency [in November 1984] because of the experience which WFP had earlier in the year when a twenty-five day emergency was declared. That emergency operation was a disaster. The misuse of aid was horrendous. Relief supplies were found in the market; 47,000 tons of supplies were lost in some warehouse. And the consequence was that the emergency officer was not willing to go through that again given the donor hostility that the incident generated.

36. Interview with an official from UNHCR, Geneva, 20 March 1984.
37. Interview with an official from the Christian Relief and Development Association, Addis Ababa, 2 October 1984.
38. Interview with Jorgen Lissner, Assistant Resident Representative, UNDP, Addis Ababa, 3 October 1984.
39. See note 28.
40. Interview with an official from the Disaster Unit, British Overseas Development Administration, London, 7 July 1981.
41. Interview with an official from the office of the European Community in Addis Ababa, 10 October 1984.
42. Interview with A. Devolt, UNDRO representative, Addis Ababa, 5 October 1984.
43. Interview with an official from the Commission of the European Community, Brussels, 23 May 1984. Non-ACP countries are developing countries not included in the Lomé convention between the European Economic Community and those African, Caribbean and Pacific states (ACP) with special relations with EEC states.
44. Office of the United Nations Disaster Relief Coordinator, *Disaster Prevention and Mitigation: A Compendium of Current Knowledge*, Vol. 12, *Social and Sociological Aspects*, Geneva, United Nations, 1986, p.27.
45. In Britain, large-scale international disaster appeals have frequently been coordinated through an NGO consortium called the Disaster Emergency Committee. However, one step further was really taken by the British agencies Oxfam and Save the Children Fund, when they undertook not only a joint appeal but also integrated relief measures to assist famine victims in Mozambique.
46. See note 37. In September 1984, when the famine in Ethiopia began to receive wide international publicity, Save the Children Fund's John Seaman hinted at his problem before his NGO colleagues at a Christian Relief and Development Association meeting in Addis Ababa:

> As the present food situation in Ethiopia is receiving wide publicity outside the country, it is possible that new agencies may wish to establish programmes in the country. As the technical competence of agencies varies considerably and as agencies sometimes congregate in the same area, it is important that the RRC and the NGOs agree on the programmes to be undertaken by the agencies. [J. Seaman, Christian Relief and Development Association, 24 September 1984.]

47. When a CRDA official was asked why Seaman's warning could not be acted upon by the CRDA, he replied, 'You can't force anyone to do anything. The CRDA would collapse if you did. Take a project that's ridiculous. You can't say, "This is stupid". ' See Note 37.
48. During the 1970 East Pakistan cyclone disaster, the Pakistan authorities explicitly informed the government of Belgium that a mobile hospital unit was not required. Nevertheless, the Belgian government set up a mobile hospital. Similarly, it was only after considerable effort that United States Ambassador Joseph Farland was able to persuade the American government not to send a full American Army hospital:

> One afternoon a message comes in from Washington [stated Farland]. Some US Senators

wanted to send a complete US army hospital. That means one helluva logistics problem. I sweated blood that night, but I decided that it would only clutter up the works. That was a rough decision to make, but I wasn't going to clutter up the whole situation, and they [the East Pakistanis] had to eat! [Interview with Joseph Farland, Washington DC, 18 September 1983.]

49. See note 46. H. Olaffson of Norwegian Church Aid maintained that available resources in Ethiopia were so scarce that the only solution would be for the agencies to adhere 'to strict coordination'. He suggested that the agencies with experience in the country might accept this, but he doubted that those new agencies that were likely to become involved in the emergency would do so. The result would be an increase in tension within the non-governmental sector in Ethiopia, he maintained. (Interview with H. Olaffson, Addis Ababa, 5 October 1984.)

50. In many interviews which this writer had with members of the NGO community, the conceptual divide, if not distrust, between religious and secular agencies was a frequently mentioned theme. The line between providing relief and saving souls might be perceived as thin, at least according to Peter Searle of World Vision in an interview in Northampton on 2 October 1986.

51. One of the 'old hands' of the Red Cross movement accepted that the 'grey areas' between the responsibilities of the League of Red Cross Societies and the International Committee of the Red Cross are increasing.

In the first place [he said] there are few old hands left in Geneva. The new people [at the LORCS and ICRC] want to show their competence. The League should have held back their decision on becoming involved in the Tamil problem in Sri Lanka, but they didn't. Secondly, governments are increasingly [self] protective; they prefer working with the League because they feel that they have some control over national societies. The grey areas are increasing, and the more I think about it, the role of the ICRC is something that we must protect. [Interview with an official from the Norwegian Red Cross, Oslo, 4 June 1984.]

52. Interview with Fr Jack Finucane, Irish Concern, Addis Ababa, 13 November 1986. Concern was working in the resettlement areas, and felt its mission to be worthwhile. However, some people were extremely critical about the implications of such work, for example Ruth Anne Fellows, Office for Emergency Operations in Ethiopia, in an interview in Addis Ababa, 17 November 1986. The level of emotion and discord that the resettlement issue can generate is evidenced in Clay, J. & Holcomb, B., *Politics and The Ethiopian Famine 1984-1985*, Cambridge, Mass., Cultural Survival Inc., December 1985.

53. Interview with Sven Lampall, League of Red Cross Societies, Geneva, 21 March 1984.

54. Interview with Julian Francis, Field Director, Oxfam, New Delhi, 15 March 1983.

55. See note 53.

56. Interview with Faruk Berkol, former Coordinator, UNDRO, Geneva, 21 March 1984.

57. Interview with Sir Robert Jackson, United Nations, New York, 21 November 1980.

58. Perhaps one of the best examples of such authority emerging is the United Nations Relief Operations in Bangladesh, as described by Oliver, T., *The United Nations in Bangladesh*, Princeton, Princeton University Press, 1978.

6 Towards a Responsive System

> The relief operation was pluralism run riot. These sorts of situations have a considerable degree of efficiency losses. You've got to measure this in terms of marginal systems. Not as many died as might have; perhaps this is the key.[1]

The above quotation reflects a very important appraisal of the international relief network. For all the energy and resources expended assisting disaster victims, is the only conclusion to be that 'not as many died as might have'? In a world increasingly disaster-prone, must one accept persistent efficiency losses, inappropriate and unpredictable responses, and lack of coordination and cooperation of such 'marginal systems'?

These same questions led Stephen Green in 1977 to suggest means of reorganizing relief in order to move the international community 'toward a responsive system'.[2] Green felt that there were three changes 'likely to occur' in what he referred to as the 'international disaster relief system':

(i) Coordination. 'The United Nations system . . . will gradually begin to predominate in the coordination of major relief operations . . . [and] as national relief organisations are formed and begin to function in more and more developing countries, they will increasingly assume direct responsibility for the local operational matters.'

(ii) Technology.'Modern technology can make relief operations more efficient and systematised. What is perhaps less obvious is that its application can also provide early warning that can substantially reduce the physical, psychological and political costs of disasters.'

(iii) Preparedness. 'Early activity and progress in this field seem very likely, partly because so many least-developed, "Fourth World" countries have had a devastating disaster within the last four years. More often that not, their national governments have been tried and convicted in the international press of backwardness, callousness, inefficiency and worse.'[3]

Based on these predictions, Green proposed that an international convention on the human rights of disaster victims be agreed, and that, towards this end, practical interim measures be taken that would define the duties of those deemed responsible for relief intervention. Hence, in cooperation with local relief agencies, UNDP would oversee preparedness measures and coordinate the United Nations system in times of disaster, UNDRO would play an operations managerial role and the International Committee of the Red Cross would act as a disaster monitor.

As goals, Green's proposals were sound, and they remain so ten years on. However, his beliefs that the United Nations would play a greater international coordinating role and that national relief organizations would become increasingly accepted focal points have not really evolved as Green and many others would have hoped. Nor for that matter have preparedness measures grabbed the attention of governments in disaster-prone countries or throughout the international community with the alacrity and urgency that he foresaw.[4] And technology, while rapidly advancing, has too frequently led to what Hewitt has called 'technological fixes' rather than appropriate solutions.[5]

Arguably, a ten-year perspective may be insufficient to judge Green's fore-casts. If one looks at the evolution of what has been described as the 'interna-tional relief network' in Chapter 2, one is struck both by the degree of continuity as well as by change in the world of international disaster assistance. Changes have been several. There has been a considerable proliferation of relief actors over the past century, and certainly since 1945. Of course, one must add to these changing perceptions about the frequency of disasters and even the sources of such phenomena. To some extent, the responsibility of the international com-munity towards disaster-afflicted nations has also changed significantly. Where pre-1945 approaches to relief saw international actors fulfilling their 'obligations' by donations, the post-World War II world witnessed a surprising degree of active intervention at all levels of afflicted societies, from the disaster site itself to senior levels of government.

These changes reflected new developments on a wider global scene. Newly independent states that intermittently found themselves objects of bipolar competition often lacked the experience, resources and structures to enable them to prosper in the general economic upsurge of the 1960s and onwards. In their struggle to find appropriate development models, developing states all too frequently undermined their own societies and drained them of resources. They were duly abetted in their struggles by developed societies which, for an amalgam of reasons—ranging from altruism, geo-politics and commercial inte-rests—sought to impose development solutions that were all too often inapprop-riate or impossible for recipients to sustain. Intervention, in other words, driven by an admix of motives, had become a habit.

Yet, despite, or even because of the changes—the increase in actors, the habit of intervention—there were certain features of the relief process that seemed not to alter fundamentally. These features centred around the all-too-persistent, unpredictable, inappropriate and disjointed responses of relief actors to disasters. There were a variety of attempts to address these failings, but for all the emerging awareness of the failings, few attempts effectively changed the charac-ter of the relief process.

Certain factors in international disaster relief remain constant, particularly the very conception of disasters. Throughout this work stress has been laid on both the expedience of viewing disasters as aberrant phenomena and the many conceptual problems to which this traditional view has given rise.

By divorcing disasters from daily life, we ignore the root problems that cause disasters. We can take refuge in the statistically comforting notion that disasters are relatively infrequent occurrences.

If, on the other hand, one accepts the proposition that disasters are generally reflections of far more basic social, economic and political vulnerabilities, then statistical shelters offer far less assurance. Humanity is becoming increasingly vulnerable, its exposure to a growing number of disaster agents far greater, as evidenced in the first instance by the greater number of states that have become disaster-prone in the developing world. It is not, however, the isolated volcanic eruption or the devastating cyclone that is our only concern. Rather, it is the growing complexity of disasters. A single disaster may increase the vulnerability of a society as a whole. A natural disaster may lead to a man-made disaster, or vice versa, and the consequences of one or both may spill over into other societies.

By dealing with disasters as isolated phenomena, we lose a sense of the real causes of vulnerability. Conceptually, it is a way of avoiding the full implications of the causes of and solutions to disasters. One need not address the global inter-relationships between international trade, currency fluctuations, geo-political and commercial interests and a flooded delta in Bangladesh. In practical terms, by isolating disaster phenomena, one can demonstrate goodwill and test one's technological solutions without being 'mousetrapped' into more long-term commitments.

Similarly, the conceptual and practical convenience of isolating the pheno-mena also explains much about the ways in which the international relief network proffers assistance. Disaster victims are treated as if they were detached from their societies, as if they had regressed to a helpless sub-species of humanity. Yet, 'victims are rarely a "huddled mass of dazed humanity" ', notes Schmitz. 'They normally are calm and start their own rehabilitation before any outside help arrives.'[6]

This essential fact is so often missed or ignored in the wake of international responses to disasters. One of the cornerstones of effective relief must be a commitment to work with those affected by a disaster. The propensity to impose solutions, 'to know what's best' for seemingly hapless communities, only too often undermines the confidence and destroys the initiative of those very people whom the relief network seeks to assist.

In practical terms, the failure to communicate and to work with disaster victims is also a convenience as well as being evidence of neglect. It is a convenience in at least three respects. Working with people can be a time-consuming and frustrating activity. 'Victims' may actually disagree with one's assumptions and challenge one's own conception of needs. Imposing assistance circumvents these discomforts. Secondly, relief workers on the ground may have little control over the assistance they are able to provide. The amount and type of relief aid is frequently determined by factors that often have little to do with the needs of victims. Awkward requests by the afflicted might well demonstrate the inadequacies of relief actors. Finally, it is more convenient to dictate solutions when relief actors, all too often with little knowledge of the traditions and cultures of affected communities, have to contend with pressures to be seen to be responding to 'victims'.

The imposition of assistance also suggests a fundamental neglect in the relief process. Mankind certainly has the social scientific and scientific ability to predict and prepare for many of the worst kinds of disasters that may occur. In the criteria of relief that were considered in Chapter 1, the potential for prediction and preparedness was seen as one of the breakthroughs that could significantly alter the haphazard responses of the international relief network. So, too, has the potential for more effective assessment procedures developed, and certainly lessons about appropriate and timely intervention as well as enhanced coordination—at least in theory—have not been lost on the network of actors that provide disaster relief assistance.

Throughout this book, we have asked why, if such potential exists, disaster relief still remains so often unpredictable and inappropriate. Of course, a good deal of the answer stems from the way in which one views disasters themselves. Yet, this is only part of the answer. If one looks at the strengths and weaknesses of those elements that comprise what we have called the international relief network, then clearly relief efforts stumble on a shambles of contending goals, interests and procedures that at the best of times resembles a kind of constrained anarchy. There are no actors, as we have seen in Chapter 3, who are free from contending pressures that influence their willingness or ability to respond. There is, in other words, a variety of factors which have nothing to do with the requirements of afflicted peoples and which ultimately determine how, when and where each type of relief actor will intervene.

Geo-politics, we are often told, is one reason for the unpredictability of humanitarian intervention. Of course, politics at any level of human activity is a crucial factor, and it certainly is in the case of disaster relief. Yet, as we have tried to argue in Chapters 4 and 5 in our attempt to analyse the relief process, to point to the pursuit of geo-political interests as the prime determinant of the relief process misses important nuances. Clearly, those governments that have vested interests in particular disaster-stricken countries normally respond with greater alacrity. Their responses, however, are by no means guarantees of effective relief. These demonstrations of concern can prove to be disruptive and inappropriate—indeed, a considerable handicap to a rational and coherent relief operation. Equally important, however, is the priority formulation process that goes on within governments that often denies the assumption of geo-political calculations. Contending interests within government agencies and across departments, conflicts between roles, norms and allocative priorities all suggest that geo-politics is but one factor—and not always the most important one—in the political process that determines a relief response.

While one might challenge the predominance of rational geo-political calculations as a determinant in relief responses, one nevertheless has to ask whether the imbroglio arising from the priority formulation process offers any greater prospects for more predictable and appropriate responses to disaster victims. The answer is 'no'. Although the gulf between humanitarian and state values may frequently not be as unbridgeable as Haksar maintained, the priority formulation process offers little comfort that predictable and appropriate international aid will be the result.

Perceptual variables obviously influence the priority formulation process, and, for that matter, all aspects of the relief process. The very persistence of the ways in which relief actors view disasters and disaster victims is but a demonstration of the importance of perceptions in the relief process. Below that abiding conceptual level, however, are the more practical, day-to-day considerations that determine the ways in which one reacts to information.

Given the ambiguities and uncertainties associated with disasters, information and communications often depend upon the predispositions, schemas and belief systems of those who receive information. What makes information and communications believable—whether they are concerned with the occurrence of a disaster or with damage and need assessments—will depend upon considerations that may have to do with the persuasiveness of the communicator, the attributions the recipient makes and the dissonance that discordant information creates for the recipient.

Perceptual variables are an integral part of what we have described as the information loading cycle. They point to the all-too-apparent fact that ambiguous, uncertain or contradictory information often means that clarity is determined by the internal referents of individuals and organizations for whom they work. The propensity for organizations to screen, accept or reject incoming information is consistent with other seemingly mechanistic responses to disaster relief. Organizational responses frequently reflect what organizations are good at doing, whether or not they are appropriate for a particular disaster situation. This is to a very significant extent an understandable result, given the nature of organizations. Experts see their roles in ways that cohere with the general interests and objectives of the organization, and that therefore reinforce the proclivity to provide standard, pre-programmed responses to situations in which they become involved.

To view these responses are merely mechanistic would be to ignore very real and human dilemmas posed by organizational characteristics. Organizational survival is a basic motivating factor for organizations as a whole and for those who work in them. 'Health'—in terms of available resources, acceptable performance and growth—is a principal determinant in the way organizations view their responsibilities. Generally speaking, where responsibilities and health conflict, it is normally the former that is sacrificed. It is perhaps the natural reaction of any entity that can justify or rationalize its decisions in terms of existing in order to fight another day.

Responsibilities and survival become intertwined when organizations find themselves seeking to satisfy both in the same arena. The more ill-defined or overlapping their responsibilities, the greater is the propensity to react to a perceived clash of interests. Such reactions are exacerbated when the stakes are high—stakes defined as gaining considerable resources and visibility.

It is in the context of such realities that one must view recommendations to improve the international relief network. Green, for example, suggests an international convention that links the rights of disaster victims to the most basic of human rights—the right to life. However, as Young has made only too clear, 'regime'-based proposals such as these depend for their effectiveness on an acceptance that 'all' are potentially threatened and that all are potential beneficiaries.[7] Without a clear perception of mutual interests, grandiose schemes fall prey to the vagaries of contending interpretations and to claims of exceptional circumstances that remove the necessity for compliance. To give principal relief responsibilities to an isolated set of organizations, for example UNDP, UNDRO, ICRC, as Green also recommends, would never survive the machinations of the barons of the United Nations system. There are occasions when the concept of a 'lead agency' has proved successful, but, as discussed in Chapter 3, such successes as there have been have depended upon particular contexts; and these contexts are too case-specific to form the basis of a general arrangement. As Schmitz points out, even during one of the largest and ostensibly most controlled relief efforts in recent history, namely, the Ethiopian relief operation in 1984–6, United Nations agencies continued to clash over responsibilities and institutional interests.[8]

If this was the case when government donors were actively demanding greater coordination, what hope might there be for constraining the barons when donors' attentions are less focused? Were the issue merely one of constraining the 'United Nations family', the prospect for assigning principal relief responsibilities might nevertheless be brighter. However, the United Nations *per se* is but one component of a far larger network—and problem. There is little that the international relief network can do as a whole to pace, constrain, control or guide those who comprise its loosely defined membership.

Given the constituents of the network and the dynamics of the relief process, there is an interactive dynamic that fuels anarchy rather than controls it. Nowhere is such anarchy felt more acutely than in the nations whom the international relief network seeks to assist. As research for this work began to draw to an end, one conclusion seemed to stand out above all: the ultimate responsibility for dealing with international intervention had to be placed at the doorstep of responsible indigenous institutions of afflicted countries. It is a proposition that should remain high on any list of priorities.

Developing indigenous relief authorities, or cells, is by no means an original idea. One of the principal tasks of UNDRO at its inception was to promote such cells, and together with them, appropriate preventative and planning measures. Yet, as one surveys activities in these areas, it becomes apparent that there are only a few isolated examples of progress. The fault lies with disaster-prone countries as much as it does with the international community at large.[9]

The same attitude to disasters that imbues the international community is mirrored in the attitudes of disaster-prone countries. Disasters are aberrant phenomena; there are other priorities to be addressed. These other priorities all too often isolate disaster prevention and relief measures from regular government channels and resources. International intervention has also wittingly or unwittingly reinforced this isolation. Pre-established links, distrust of indigenous capabilities, concern about accountability and the desire for high visibility are but four reasons that lead all too many components of the relief network to bypass indigenous authorities.

Thus, given the dynamics of the relief process, one is constantly confronted with a range of constraints that limit the types of changes which would make the relief process more effective. There is indeed a need for an internationally agreed charter on the rights of disaster victims. However, such a charter would be subject to the same vagaries of interpretation as the Universal Declaration on Human Rights. Certainly one must chide and push those intergovernmental organizations with relief responsibilities towards greater cooperation and coordination, but in so doing, one must be aware that grandiose schemes ultimately will be defined in terms of institutional interests.

Yet, IGOs are not alone in this admix of responsibilities and interests. Nongovernmental organizations, despite their rhetoric, have all too often failed to set an example to the relief network at large. They, too, calculate their involvements in terms of what might be regarded as acceptable behaviour—defined in terms both of perceived responsibilities and institutional health. Thus, from all of this must one draw the conclusion that the relief dynamics that we have sought to explore in this book are to all intents and purposes not open to significant improvements. Must one accept that the very nature of those elements that hamper effective relief responses is so inherent that those stricken by disasters will depend for the foreseeable future on the vagaries of 'marginal systems'?

In one sense, the answer must be 'yes'. There is little indication that the international community has been willing to redefine its concept of 'a disaster'. Whether for conceptual reasons or for reasons of convenience, disasters will continue to be treated as isolated and aberrant phenomena. Disaster relief will continue to be at the mercy of a priority formulation process that is underscored by diffuse power and interests. Perceptual variables—in the absence of any objective assessment and monitoring mechanisms—will also tend to increase undesirable 'noise' in the process. Institutional procedures and interests will inevitably define responses, and clashes arising out of such conflicting institutional procedures and interests will leave all too many disasters as memorials to yet more inter-organizational struggles.

As presented here, the factors that influence the dynamics of the international relief network seem to be intractable. The solutions that might significantly improve the process appear to demand the kinds of moral commitment and institutional adjustment for which there appears to be little apparent enthusiasm. Grandiose schemes, the rhetoric of human rights, the persistent critiques of past relief interventions all disappear before the complex factors that determine the ways in which the international relief network is mobilized. And yet, for those concerned to see improvements in the relief process, there are approaches that in a realistic sense should certainly be tried, and should succeed. They are incremental adjustments; they are small measures that, if successful, should directly improve the responsive capability of the relief network and should ultimately lead to other measures that might continue the slow move towards a more responsive system. They are not brave and direct assaults on those inherent factors that continue to determine the activities of relief actors; rather, they are undramatic small steps that gnaw at the periphery of the problem.

Gnawing at the Periphery

If one looks at the present state of international disaster intervention, then inadequate information and low levels of expertise, while remaining two of the most persistent problems, are at the same time the most readily resolvable. Improvements in both these areas will not directly eliminate the political process calculations and the institutional vagaries that hamper the effectiveness of relief. However, to the extent that enhanced information and expertise will eliminate a degree of the ambiguity that so often permeates and distorts the relief process, they represent important—though perhaps mundane—starting-points. In the broadest of terms, international relief intervention could be improved in six ways, which together address these two major questions.

Mapping

If one accepts that disasters merely expose the existing vulnerabilities of potential victims, then it would seem to follow that one can at least foresee which groups are most likely to be threatened by disasters. For this reason, it would not seem impossible in so many instances to 'map' those groups that might be exposed to the impact of a disaster agent. Vulnerable groups in particularly disaster-prone states could be catalogued well before a disaster struck. Vulnerability, here, would not be restricted to those groups prone to natural disaster agents. Vulnerable groups would also be defined as those groups and communities who, in terms described elsewhere in this book, form mass migratory movements. This kind of mapping would not only include an assessment of vulnerability, but also an evaluation of the general kinds of needs (e.g. types of acceptable food) that such groups might have when an emergency does strike. Technologically, there exists the ability to garner and store as well as update such information, and the responsibility for this task should be allotted to a single international authority, such as the Office of the United Nations Disaster Relief Coordinator. UNDRO would undertake this task in conjunction with 'international regional monitors' (see below), and would be responsible for an annual compilation of such material in what will be described later as the UNDRO 'State of the World Survey'.

For an organization such as UNDRO to undertake this kind of compilation task, its role and responsibilities would at last have to be clarified. UNDRO's sole task should be that of information gathering. All pretences at 'mobilizing, directing and controlling' should be dropped for the far more important and clearly defined responsibility of global monitoring and information gathering.

Those who might regret the loss of UNDRO's advisory role in disaster preparedness and prevention should bear in mind that the compilation of information will in and of itself point to vulnerabilities that ought to be addressed, and these will have to be born in mind in what is later discussed as the 'disaster-development nexus', a concern that will have to be carried by other institutions.

UNDRO's informational role should encompass five basic tasks. The first would be to map and update the state of global vulnerabilities—principally those in disaster-prone areas. The second would be to provide relief guidelines on suitable provisions for particular types of disaster in particular types of area. The third would be to compile rosters of experts able to deal with particular relief needs both within the afflicted country and outside it. The fourth would be to continue to monitor relief inputs from the international community into a relief operation. Finally, UNDRO would be responsible for in-depth post-evaluation reports. These reports would be objective assessments of all disaster operations in which the international community played a role.

The structure of UNDRO would have a more regional orientation. Rather than random visits from headquarters, permanent UNDRO officials would be assigned to particular regions to ensure that its monitoring and compilation work was continuously updated. In that way, UNDRO would liaise with appropriate authorities within that region, certainly including relevant governmental and non-governmental organizations within disaster-prone countries. This kind of permanence would permit UNDRO to double check on the ground inputs into relief operations without infringing upon the coordinating role of the UNDP Resident Representative.

Regional Monitors

UNDRO's regional role would generally enhance its overall ability to compile, monitor and update. However, one must not be under any illusion that such a redefinition of roles would unleash torrents of consistent and timely information from governmental, inter-governmental and non-governmental bodies. The flow of information might be improved, but still remain all too imperfect. To some extent, additional sources of information—directly linked to UNDRO regional offices—should be provided by 'regional monitors'. Regional monitors would be those officials selected by regionally-based non-governmental organizations, both indigenous and international, who would supplement information gathered by UNDRO. The appointment of a monitor would be for no longer than a period of three years, and would not be renewable.

Regional monitors would have four responsibilities. They would be required to liaise with UNDRO regional officials on mapping activities; they would act as liaison between NGO, IGO and governmental authorities; they would be responsible for compiling their own regional surveys, which would be incorporated into the UNDRO 'State of the World Survey'; and they would be focal points for NGO post-evaluation assessments.

Anyone who has been involved in disaster relief operations knows full well that NGOs are not always the most willing dispensers of information, nor are they always conveniently situated to provide the kind of information that would be required for mapping, compilation or monitoring activities. There is also the problem that indigenous governmental authorities might regard such regional monitors as yet another layer of 'surveillance' imposed by a supposedly caring international community.

As with all prescriptions, one cannot speak of perfect solutions. What one can suggest, however, is that regional monitors would at least prove to be an additional step towards getting a better flow of information than at present obtains. Ultimately, however, the effectiveness of regional monitors leads directly to the issue of experts.

Experts

How does one define an expert? Even after three decades of experience, the international community, according to so many who have been involved in disaster relief operations, appears to be bereft of sufficient people with the knowledge and skills required to be operationally effective. Yet, adequate operational skills and knowledge are only part of the kind of expertise that is needed. Experts have to be communicators; they have to have an understanding of local conditions, of the psychological, political and sociological consequences of relief. It is no use having an expert who can drill for water if that expert at the same time has little sensitivity to the consequences of his or her activities upon the community at large.

Therefore, there has to be a greater concentration upon training of experts, not only in areas of technical skills but also in how to deal with local conditions. Here, one needs a pre-trained pool of experts for each region.

Perhaps in looking at experts in terms of societal sensitivity as well as operational skills, one might well begin to look at the manpower resources available in disaster-prone countries. Regional monitors as well as UNDRO regional officials should also be trained with this in mind. In the world of disaster relief, the individual attuned to local conditions as well as to the complexities of relief is, from an overall operational point of view, every bit as important as the medical or nutritional expert. Compiling a regionally-based roster of experts would be the responsibility of UNDRO. A suitable training criterion or standard—let alone who would provide the subvention for such training proposals —must at this stage remain for others to decide.

State of the World Survey

One of the key reasons for separating out an informational role from an operational one is that the combination of the two frequently becomes encumbered with political and institutional constraints. Of course, it would be unrealistic to suppose that even information-collecting activities are not burdened with similar constraints, but to attempt to work in both worlds takes an even greater toll on the quality of information. The main responsibility of UNDRO, therefore, would be that of information, and one of its main annual targets would be to issue a compendium at the level of the United Nations General Assembly in which the following were fully described:

- regional reports on vulnerable populations;
- regional updates on preparedness measures;
- rosters of available emergency experts on a region-by-region basis;
- in-depth, case-by-case analyses of relief operations in which international intervention has been required.

This detailed 'document' would have to be noted by the General Assembly, and in so doing would bear the hallmark of international recognition.

Disaster-Development Nexus

It is increasingly being recognized that the solution to so many relief operations lies in the need to promote durable solutions, or the kinds of development that would eliminate the vulnerabilities of people. While this reflects a growing sensitivity to the nature of disaster phenomena, the goals of development at the best of times are for the most part long-term. Many millions of people will become disaster victims before—if ever—the achievements of development can eliminate vulnerabilities. Nevertheless, in the development process, one might increasingly look at the way in which development projects themselves can be structured in order to incorporate disaster preparedness or preventative measures. Thus, for example, in devising irrigation systems in Bangladesh, the problems of dealing with river flooding should be addressed at the same time.

Both the United Nations Development Programme, the World Bank and its subsidiary agencies should be required to incorporate disaster prevention and preparedness measures into the projects they support. At present, there are many areas in which UNDRO and UNDP do seek to promote disaster preparedness. This facet of their work should, however, be a standard feature of all programmes and projects supported by inter-governmental agencies involved in development.

Local Capabilities

In several instances this book has emphasized the need to enhance the capabilities of governmental and non-governmental organizations in disaster-prone countries. We have also mentioned the all-too-frequent occasions when such institutions have been—intentionally or unintentionally—undermined by international intervention.

Nevertheless, it remains a vital as well as a realistic objective to continue to press for more effective indigenous relief capabilities. Here, the international voluntary sector can play a useful role in providing training as well as small-scale preventative and preparedness measures. Similarly, inter-governmental organizations, particularly in disaster-prone regions, can take active steps to establish 'pre-disaster' contacts and plans with relevant local authorities. UNDP Resident Representatives should as a matter of course determine with the government to whom they are accredited the focal points that should be used in times of emergency and these arrangements should form part of the compendium that is annually updated by UNDRO.

Resident Representatives, as part of their official responsibilities, should determine with relevant customs and excise authorities clearance procedures in cases of emergencies. Through UNDRO, Resident Representatives would have determined with governments seaport and airport offloading and discharging capacities. Through regional monitors and UNDRO regional officers, UNDP Resident Representatives should also have established some clear idea of NGO emergency capabilities and local networks. All such information should form part of a consultative process with designated officials within appropriate government authorities.

Added to the disaster role of the UNDP Resident Representative should be the obligation to meet formally or informally with potential donor governments to determine whether there were any kinds of activities that they might be willing to undertake in times of disaster. The substance of this kind of information should be relayed to the local government, and should be incorporated into that country's general disaster plan.

Towards What End?

We are all too aware that the chaos, uncertainties and ambiguities that surround most emergencies belie the rather clinical neatness in these six suggestions. We are also aware that inevitably contending perceptions and institutional perspectives, political priorities and organizational rivalries are not readily addressed by these proposals.

Perhaps our own analysis of the dynamics of the international relief network has left us too reluctant to press for radical reforms. Realism seems to dictate that at this stage the only practical route towards enhancing the relief process is by incremental steps, modestly adjusting the focus of individual relief participants and the international relief network. In conclusion, it is hoped that by raising the level of available information, expertise, degree of pre-planning and indigenous capabilities, relief efforts might gradually advance towards a more sensitive and systematic response to disasters.

In a sense, this is a sad and inadequate conclusion. For those who can recall the rows of corpses that lined the shores of the Bay of Bengal in 1970, the stench of Salt Lake refugee camp outside Calcutta in 1971, the bowed head of the woman who lost her third child that week in a camp called Korem, the Eritrean who sought help across the Sudanese border late in 1984, is it acceptable?

Notes

1. Interview with Victor Palmieri, formerly US Assistant Secretary of State, Bureau for Refugee Programs, New York, 23 September 1983.
2. Green, S., *International Disaster Relief: Toward a responsive system*, New York, McGraw-Hill, 1977, pp.44ff.
3. Ibid.
4. See 'Table 2: Disaster Preparedness and Prevention in Developing Countries' and subsequent discussion in Kent, R.C., 'The Disaster Monitor' in *Third World Affairs 1987*, London, Third World Foundation for Social and Economic Studies, 1987, pp.266–74.
5. Hewitt, K. (ed.), *Interpretations of Calamity*, Boston, Allen & Unwin, 1983, p.8.
6. Schmitz, C., *Disaster! The United Nations and international relief management*, New York, Council on Foreign Relations, 1987, p.12.
7. Young, O., 'Coping with Nuclear Accidents: Toward an International Regime', a paper presented for the forum on 'Global Disasters and International Information Flows', organized by the Annenberg Schools of Communication, Washington, 8–10 October 1986.
8. Schmitz, op.cit., pp. 40–1.
9. 'Official indifference [of governments in disaster-prone countries towards preparedness and prevention] is difficult to predict', remarked UNDRO's John Tomblin. 'The issue is not one of indifference, but generally lack of attention'. Interview with John Tomblin, Special Office for Preparedness, UNDRO, Geneva, 21 March 1984.

Appendix 1: Categories of Donors

Distribution of Aid Units Table

Explanation

Table 1 is an attempt to extract suggestive features from the admittedly unsystematic and incomplete data available on international disaster aid. Samples of fifty disasters were taken from those in the United States Government series of Aid Reports (OFDA, etc.), the samples covering the three periods *1971–4, 1974–80* and *1981–4*. *Any reported* aid provided by a given nation for a disaster was counted as an *Aid Unit* from the aiding nation to the afflicted nation.

The nations were listed and assigned to the following economic categories:

Category 1: USA;
Category 2: Highly developed nations (e.g. nations of the EEC, Japan, Scandinavian countries);
Category 3: Eastern bloc, centralized economies (e.g. USSR, Poland);
Category 4: People's Republic of China;
Category 5: Oil-based economy nations (e.g. Saudi Arabia);
Category 6: Newly Industrializing nations (e.g. South Korea);
Category 7: Developing nations (e.g. Zimbabwe, India).

Nations that had not been included in the original list appeared in connection with later disasters as the work progressed, and were temporarily assigned to Category 0. These included, for example, Hungary, Czechoslovakia, Tunisia, and some small African and Asian nations.

Table 1 shows the number of aid units provided by the nations in each category to afflicted nations in each category, for the three separate fifty-disaster samples (early 1970s, late 1970s and early 1980s) and totalled for all 150 disasters.

Discussion

The grand totals at bottom right show that aid activity, measured in aid units per fifty disasters, rose during the 1970s and fell away badly in the 1980s.

The totals at far right show that the United States gave aid to over 90 per cent of the disasters sampled, but this is hardly surprising since the information surveyed was collected and reported by the United States government. The dominating contributor of aid units is Category 2, but the twenty or so rich countries in this category provided only five times as many aid units as the United States.

The totals at the foot show that reported disasters are predominantly found in the poorer countries. There were none reported in the United States or the People's Republic of China.

Table A. Distribution of Aid units by economic categories of aiding and receiving nations, three periods and totals

Aid units from category	To category 0	1	2	3	4	5	6	7	Totals
0	0	0	0	0	0	1	0	1	2
	0	0	0	0	0	0	4	7	11
	2	0	0	0	0	0	3	1	6
	2	0	0	0	0	1	7	9	19
1	0	0	2	0	0	2	18	26	48
	0	0	0	1	0	0	7	37	45
	6	0	4	0	0	0	11	29	50
	6	0	6	1	0	2	36	92	143
2	0	0	9	0	0	7	88	109	213
	0	0	0	15	0	0	30	259	304
	35	0	4	0	0	0	41	135	215
	35	0	13	15	0	7	159	503	732
3	0	0	2	0	0	3	14	17	36
	0	0	0	5	0	0	6	46	57
	3	0	0	0	0	0	2	14	19
	3	0	2	5	0	3	22	77	112
4	0	0	1	0	0	1	4	5	11
	0	0	0	1	0	0	1	7	9
	2	0	0	0	0	0	2	6	10
	2	0	1	1	0	1	7	18	30
5	0	0	0	0	0	2	11	14	27
	0	0	0	1	0	0	6	24	31
	4	0	0	0	0	0	4	16	24
	4	0	0	1	0	2	21	54	82
6	0	0	0	0	0	1	20	23	44
	0	0	0	3	0	0	7	23	33
	2	0	0	0	0	0	4	5	11
	2	0	0	3	0	1	31	51	88
7	0	0	0	0	0	1	7	21	29
	0	0	0	3	0	0	5	33	41
	13	0	0	0	0	0	1	11	25
	13	0	0	3	0	1	13	65	95
Total	0	0	14	0	0	18	162	216	410
	0	0	0	29	0	0	66	436	531
	67	0	8	0	0	0	68	217	360
	67	0	22	29	0	18	296	869	1301

Author's Note: I would like to express my thanks to Mr. R.H. Tucker who, with assistance from the Nuffield Foundation, found time to compile and tabulate this material.

Table B. Major donor governments in order of 1985 contributions reported to UNDRO

United States
Italy
Federal Republic of Germany
Saudi Arabia
United Kingdom
Canada
Netherlands
Australia
Switzerland
Norway
Sweden
Denmark
Belgium
Japan
Bulgaria
USSR

Source: Report of the Secretary-General of the United Nations; Office of the United Nations Disaster Relief Coordinator, 1 May 1986

Appendix 2: United Nations Agencies Involved in Disaster Relief and Related Activities

Food and Agriculture Organization—through the Office for Special Relief Operations.

International Atomic Energy Agency—Since the Chernobyl nuclear disaster in April 1986 in the Soviet Union, the role of the IAEA as a disaster-monitoring and advisory body has been increased.

International Bank for Reconstruction and Development—The World Bank group, including the International Development Association and the International Finance Corporation, provides financial assistance to countries requesting rehabilitation and construction assistance.

International Labour Organization—The ILO has the mandate to devise employment programmes and training measures following disaster incidents.

International Telecommunications Union—The ITU offers advice on the use of international communications during and following disasters.

Office of The United Nations Disaster Relief Coordinator—Initially designed to mobilize and coordinate disaster relief and to promote disaster preparedness and prevention measures.

United Nations Development Programme—UNDP Resident Representatives act as coordinating focal points for the United Nations in countries to which they are accredited.

United Nations Educational, Scientific and Cultural Organization—Supports scientific studies relating to natural disasters.

United Nations Environment Programme—Produces population studies relevant to vulnerability research and, together with the World Meteorological Organization, has established a Global Environmental Monitoring System.

United Nations High Commissioner for Refugees—UNHCR is the focal point for assistance to refugees, including emergency assistance.

United Nations Industrial Development Organization—Seeks to ensure that disaster preparedness measures are implemented in all industrial development projects in which it is involved.

World Food Programme—The Emergency Unit assists disaster-stricken nations in assessing emergency requirements and coordinating bilateral and multilateral food aid.

World Health Organization—WHO provides technical assistance and advice concerning medical requirements of disaster victims.

World Meteorological Organization—WMO focuses on warning systems and monitoring of weather-related disasters.

Select Bibliography

Administrative Management Service, 'Report on the Function, Strategy and Organisation of the Office of the UN Disaster Relief Coordinator', Report No. 6-81, 1981.

Allison, G., *Essence of Decision: Explaining the Cuban missile crisis*, Boston, Little, Brown & Co., 1971.

Bauer, R. & Gergen, K. (eds), *The Study of Policy Formation*, New York, Free Press, 1968.

Barnet, R.J., *The Lean Years: Politics in the age of scarcity*, London, Abacus, 1981.

Braybrooke, D. & Lindblom, C., *A Strategy of Decision: Policy evaluation as a social process*, New York, Free Press, 1970.

Brown, B., *Disaster Preparedness and the United Nations: Advance planning for disaster relief*, New York, Pergamon Press 1979.

Cipolla, C., *The Economic History of the World Population*, Harmondsworth, Penguin, 1981.

Cathie, J., *The Political Economy of Food Aid*, Aldershot, Gower, 1982.

Chen, L. (ed.), *Disaster in Bangladesh: Health crises in a developing nation*, New York, Oxford University Press, 1973.

Churchman, C., *The Systems Approach*, New York, Dell Publishing Co., 1968.

Ciraola, G., *L'Union Internazionale di Soccorso*, Rome, 1934.

Clay, J. & Holcomb, B., *Politics and the Ethiopian Famine, 1984-1985*, Cambridge, Cultural Survival Inc., December 1985.

Cohen, R., *Threat Perception in International Crisis*, Madison, University of Wisconsin Press, 1979.

Collins, B. & Guetzkow, H., *A Social Psychology of Group Processes for Decision-Making*, New York, J. Wiley & Sons, 1964.

Cornell, J., *The Great International Disaster Book*, New York, Scribner, 1976.

Cox, R. & Jacobson, H., *The Anatomy of Influence: Decision-making in international organizations*, New Haven, Yale University Press, 1974.

Cuny, F., *Disasters and Development*, New York, Oxford University Press, 1983.

Davis, I. (ed.), *Disasters and the Small Dwelling*, Oxford, Pergamon Press, 1981.

Davis, M., 'Some Political Dimensions of International Relief: Two Cases', *International Organisation*, Vol. 28, 1974, p.127.

Davis, M. (ed.), *Civil Wars and the Politics of International Relief*, New York, Praeger, 1975.

Davis, M. & Seitz, S., 'Disasters and Governments', *Journal of Conflict Resolution*, Vol. 26, 1982, p.547.

De Castro, J., *The Geopolitics of Hunger*, New York, Monthly Review Press, 1977.

Deutsch, K., *The Nerves of Government: Models of political communication and control*, New York, Free Press, 1966.

Disasters: The International Journal of Disaster Studies And Practice, Bradworthy, Foxcombe Publications, **4–10**, 1980–86.

Duncan, W.J., *Organizational Behavior*, Boston, Houghton Mifflin Co., 1978.

Easton D., *A Systems Analysis of Political Life*, New York, Wiley, 1965.

Economist Development Report, London, *The Economist*, January 1984 to March 1986.

Evans, W., *Organization Theory: Structures, systems and environments*, New York, J. Wiley & Sons, 1976.

Faaland, J. (ed.), *Aid and Influence: The case of Bangladesh*, London, Macmillan, 1981.

Ferrara, G. (ed.), *The Disaster File: The 1970s*, London, Macmillan, 1980.

Garcia, R., *Drought and Man, Vol. 1: Nature Pleads Not Guilty*, Oxford, Pergamon, 1981.

Gill, P., *A Year in the Death of Africa: Politics, bureaucracy and the famine*, London, Paladin, 1986.

Glantz, M. (ed.), *The Politics of Natural Disasters: The Sahel Drought*, New York, Praeger, 1976.

Goodwin-Gill, G., *The Refugee in International Law*, Oxford, Clarendon Press, 1983.

Gorge, C., *The International Relief Union*, Geneva, IRU, 1938.

Green, S., *International Disaster Relief: Towards a responsive system*, New York, McGraw Hill, 1977.

Haendel, D., *The Process of Priority Formulation*, Boulder, Westview Press, 1977.

Halperin, M., *Bureaucratic Politics and Foreign Policy*, Washington, DC, The Brookings Institution, 1974.

Hanf, K. & Scharpf, F. (eds), *Interorganizational Policy Making: Limits to coordination and central control*, Beverly Hills, Sage Publications, 1978.

Harrell-Bond, B., *Imposing Aid: Emergency assistance to refugees*, Oxford, Oxford University Press, 1986.

Harris, M., *Ethiopia: Before and after*, Document No. 7, Geneva, International Council of Voluntary Agencies, May 1985.

Harrison, P., *The Third World Tomorrow*, Harmondsworth, Penguin, 1981.

Hayter, T. & Watson, C., *Aid: Rhetoric and Reality*, London, Pluto Press, 1985.

Heirs, B. & Pehrson, G., *The Mind of the Organization*, New York, Harper & Row, 1977.

Henkin, L., *How Nations Behave*, New York, Columbia University Press, 1979.

Hewitt, K. (ed.), *Interpretations of Calamity*, Boston, Allen & Unwin, 1983.

Hill, M., *Towards Greater Order, Coherence and Coordination in The United Nations System*, Research Report No. 20, New York, UNITAR Research Reports, n.d.

House of Commons, Second Report from the Foreign Affairs Committee, *Famine in Africa*, Session 1984–1985, London, HMSO, 24 April 1985.

Inbar, M., *Routine Decision-Making: The future of bureaucracy*, Beverly Hills, Sage Publications, 1979.

Independent Commission on International Humanitarian Issues, *Famine: A man-made disaster?*, London, Pan Books, 1985.

Independent Commission on International Humanitarian Issues, *Refugees: Dynamics of displacement*, London, Zed Books, 1986.

Jackson, T. & Eade, D., *Against the Grain*, Oxford, Oxfam, 1982.

Jacobson, H.K., *Networks of Interdependence: International organizations and the global political system*, New York, Alfred A. Knopf, 1979.

Janis, I., *Victims of Groupthink*, Boston, Houghton Mifflin, 1972.

Janis, I. & Mann, L., *Decision-Making: A psychological analysis of conflict, choice and commitment*, New York, Free Press, 1977.

Jervis, R., *Perceptions and Misperceptions in International Politics*, Princeton, Princeton University Press, 1976.

Junod, M., *Warrior Without Weapons*, Geneva, International Committee of the Red Cross, 1982.

Karadawi, A., 'Constraints on assistance to refugees: some observations from the Sudan', *World Development*, **11**, No. 6, p.537.

Kaufmann, J., *United Nations Decision Making*, Rockville, Sijthoff & Noordhoff, 1980.

Korany, B., *Social Change, Charisma and International Behaviour: Toward a theory of foreign policy-making in the Third World*, Leiden, A.W. Sitjhoff, 1976.

Korn, D., *Ethiopia, The United States and the Soviet Union*, Carbondale, Southern Illinois University Press, 1986.

Larsen, D., *Origins of Containment: A psychological explanation*, Princeton, Princeton University Press, 1985.

Lindzey, G. & Aronson, E., *Handbook of Social Psychology*, Vol. 2, 1985.

Linear, M., *Zapping The Third World: The disaster of development aid*, London, Pluto Press, 1985.

Lissner, J., *The Politics of Altruism: A study of the political behaviour of development agencies*, Geneva, Lutheran World Federation, 1977.

Lofchie, M. (ed.), *The State of The Nations: Constraints on development in independent Africa*, Berkeley, University of California Press, 1971.

Luard, E., *International Agencies: The framework of interdependence*, London, Macmillan, 1977.

Macalister-Smith, P., *International Humanitarian Assistance: Disaster Relief Actors in International Law and Organization*, Dordrecht, Martinus Nijhoff, 1985.

Mason, L. & Brown, R., *Rice, Rivalry and Politics: Managing Cambodian relief*, Notre Dame, University of Notre Dame Press, 1983.

Morgenthau, H.J., *Politics Among Nations*, 5th edn, New York, Alfred A. Knopf, 1973.

Morris, R. & Sheets, H., *Disaster in the Desert*, Washington, DC, Carnegie Endowment for International Peace, 1975.

Morss, E., 'Greater Coordination of NGOs in Refugee Work', paper written for the Independent Commission on International Humanitarian Issues, December 1985.

National Research Council, *Assessing International Disaster Needs*, Washington, DC, National Academy of Sciences, 1979.

National Research Council, *The Rule of Technology in International Disaster Assistance*, Washington, DC, National Academy of Sciences, 1978.

National Research Council, *The US Government Foreign Disaster Assistance Program*, Washington, DC, National Academy of Sciences, 1978.

Newland, K., *Refugees: The new international politics of displacement*, Worldwatch Paper No. 43, Washington, DC, Worldwatch Institute, March 1981.

Oliver, T., *The United Nations in Bangladesh*, Princeton, Princeton University Press, 1978.

Prigogine, I. & Stengers, I., *Order Out of Chaos: Man's new dialogue with nature*, London, Flamingo, 1984.

Pugh, D. (ed.), *Organization Theory*, Harmondsworth, Penguin, 1977.

Quarantelli, E. (ed.), *Disasters, Theory and Research*, Beverly Hills, Sage, 1978.

Schmitz, C., *Disaster!: The United Nations and international relief management*, New York, Council on Foreign Relations, 1987.

Sen, A., *Poverty and Famines: An essay on entitlement and deprivation*, Oxford, Clarendon Press, 1981.

Shawcross, W., *The Quality of Mercy: Cambodia, holocaust and modern conscience*, London, André Deutsch Ltd., 1984.

Shepherd, J., *The Politics of Starvation*, Washington, DC, Carnegie Endowment for International Peace, 1975.

Simon, H., *Administrative Behavior: A study of decision-making processes in administrative organizations*, New York, Free Press, 1965.

Spero, J., *The Politics of International Economic Relations*, London, Allen & Unwin, 1980.

Stein, J. & Tanter, R., *Rational Decision-Making: Israel's security choices*, 1967, Columbus, Ohio State University Press, 1980.

Steinbruner, J., *The Cybernetic Theory of Decision: New dimensions of political analysis*, Princeton, Princeton University Press, 1974.

Stephens, L. & Green, S., *Disaster Assistance: Appraisal, reform and new approaches*, New York, New York University Press, 1979.

Stephens, T., *The United Nations Disaster Relief Office: The politics and administration of international relief assistance*, Washington, DC, University Press of America, 1978.

Stevens, C., *Food Aid and the Developing World: Four African case studies*, London, Croom Helm, 1979.

Swedish Red Cross, *Prevention Better Than Cure*, Stockholm, SRC, 1984.

Taylor, P. & Groom, A.J.R. (eds), *International Organisation: A conceptual approach*, London, Frances Pinter Publishers, 1978.

Tendler, J., *Turning Private Voluntary Organizations into Development Agencies: Questions for evaluation*, Paper No. 12, Washington, DC, US Agency for International Development, April 1982.

Thompson, J., *Morality and Foreign Policy*, Baton Rouge, Louisiana State University Press, 1980.

Turner, B., *Man-Made Disasters*, London, Wykeham, 1978.

United Nations Association of the United States, *Acts of Nature, Acts of Man: The global response to natural disasters*, New York, UNA-US, 1977.

United Nations Children's Fund, *Assisting in Emergencies: A resource handbook for UNICEF field staff*, New York, UNICEF, 1986.

United Nations Disaster Relief Office, *Disaster Prevention and Mitigation: A compendium of current knowledge*, Vols 1–12, New York & Geneva, United Nations, 1976–1986.

United Nations General Assembly, *Report of the Group of High Level Intergovernmental Experts to Review the Efficiency of the Administrative and Financial Functioning of the United Nations*, New York, GA 49(A/41/49), 1986.

United Nations High Commissioner for Refugees, *Handbook for Emergencies*, Geneva, UNHCR, 1982.

United Nations Joint Inspection Unit, *Evaluation of the Office of the United Nations Disaster Relief Coordinator*, Geneva, October 1980.

United Nations Joint Inspection Unit, *Some Reflections on Reform of the United Nations*, Geneva, 1985.

United Nations Office for Emergency Operations in Africa, *Africa Emergency Report*, Nos 1-9, New York, April/May 1985 to August/September 1986.

United States Comptroller General, *Need for an International Disaster Relief Agency*, Washington, DC, GAO, 1976.

United States House of Representatives, *Relief Problems in East Pakistan and India*, Vols I-III, Washington, DC, US Government Printing Office, 1971.

————, *Relief Problems in Bangladesh*, Washington, DC, US Government Printing Office, 1972.

————, *The Tragedy in Indochina Continues: War, refugees and famine*, Washington, DC, US Government Printing Office, 1980.

————, *Africa: Observations on the impact of American foreign policy and development programs in six African countries*, Washington, DC, US Government Printing Office, 1982.

————, *Reports on Refugee Aid*, Washington, DC, US Government Printing Office, 1981.

United States Senate, *World Hunger, Health and Refugee Problems*, Part 1: *Crisis in West Africa*, Washington, DC, US Government Printing Office, 1973.

————, *World Hunger, Health and Refugee Problems*, Part 4: *Famine in Africa*, Washington, DC, US Government Printing Office, 1974.

————, *World Hunger, Health and Refugee Problems*, Part 6: *Study Mission to Africa, Asia & Middle East*, Washington, DC, US Government Printing Office, 1975.

————, *World Hunger, Health and Refugee Problems*, Part 7: *International Health and Guatemala Earthquake*, Washington, DC, US Government Printing Office, 1976.

United States Office of Foreign Disaster Assistance, *Annual Reports*, Washington, DC, US Agency for International Development.

Vasquez, J., *The Power of Power Politics: A critique*, London, Frances Pinter Publishers, 1983.

Wain, B., *The Refused*, New York, Simon & Schuster, 1981.

Warwick, D., *A Theory of Public Bureaucracy: Politics, personality and organization in the state department*, Cambridge, Harvard University Press, 1975.

Weiss, T.G., *International Bureaucracy: An analysis of functional and global international secretariats*, Lexington, Lexington Books, 1975.

Westgate, K.N. & O'Keefe, P. *Some Definitions of Disaster*, Occasional Paper No. 4, Bradford, Disaster Research Unit, University of Bradford, 1976.

Whitaker, B., *A Bridge of People: A personal view of Oxfam's first forty years*, London, Heinemann, 1983.

White, G. (ed.), *Natural Hazards: Local, national, global*, Oxford, Oxford University Press, 1974.

Whittow, J., *Disaster: The anatomy of environmental hazards*, Harmondsworth, Penguin, 1980.

Wijkman, A. & Timberlake, L., *Natural Disasters: Acts of God or acts of man*, Washington, DC, Earthscan, 1984.

Willetts, P. (ed.), *Pressure Groups in The Global System*, London, Frances Pinter Publishers, 1982.

Wiseberg, L.S., 'Humanitarian Intervention: Lessons from the Nigerian Civil War', *Revue Des Droits De L'Homme*, Vol. 7, 1974, p.61.

Index